BOTANICAL
PRINTS IN LINOCUT

AN ARTIST'S GUIDE

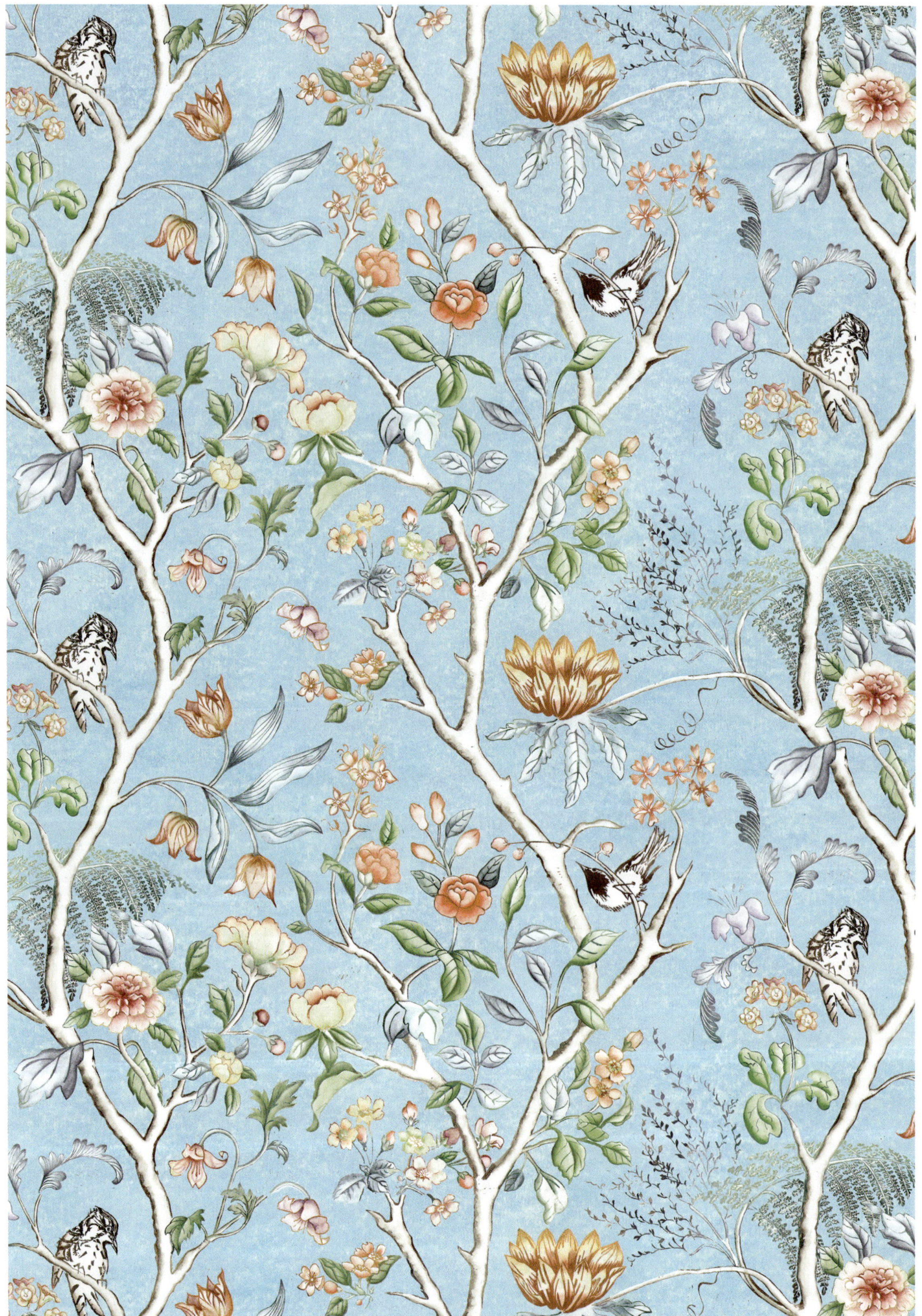

Laura Sowerby

BOTANICAL
PRINTS IN LINOCUT

AN ARTIST'S GUIDE

THE CROWOOD PRESS

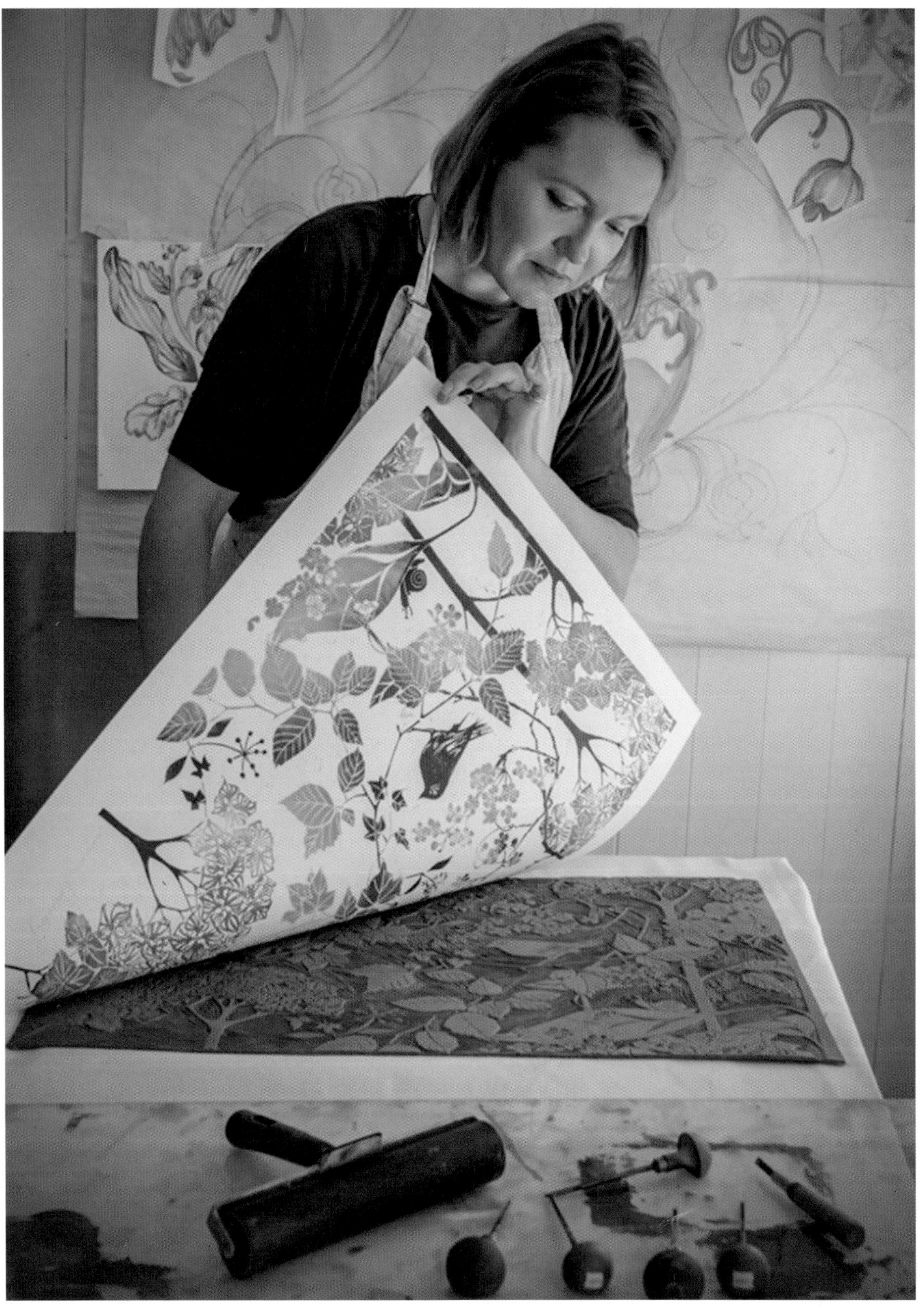

CONTENTS

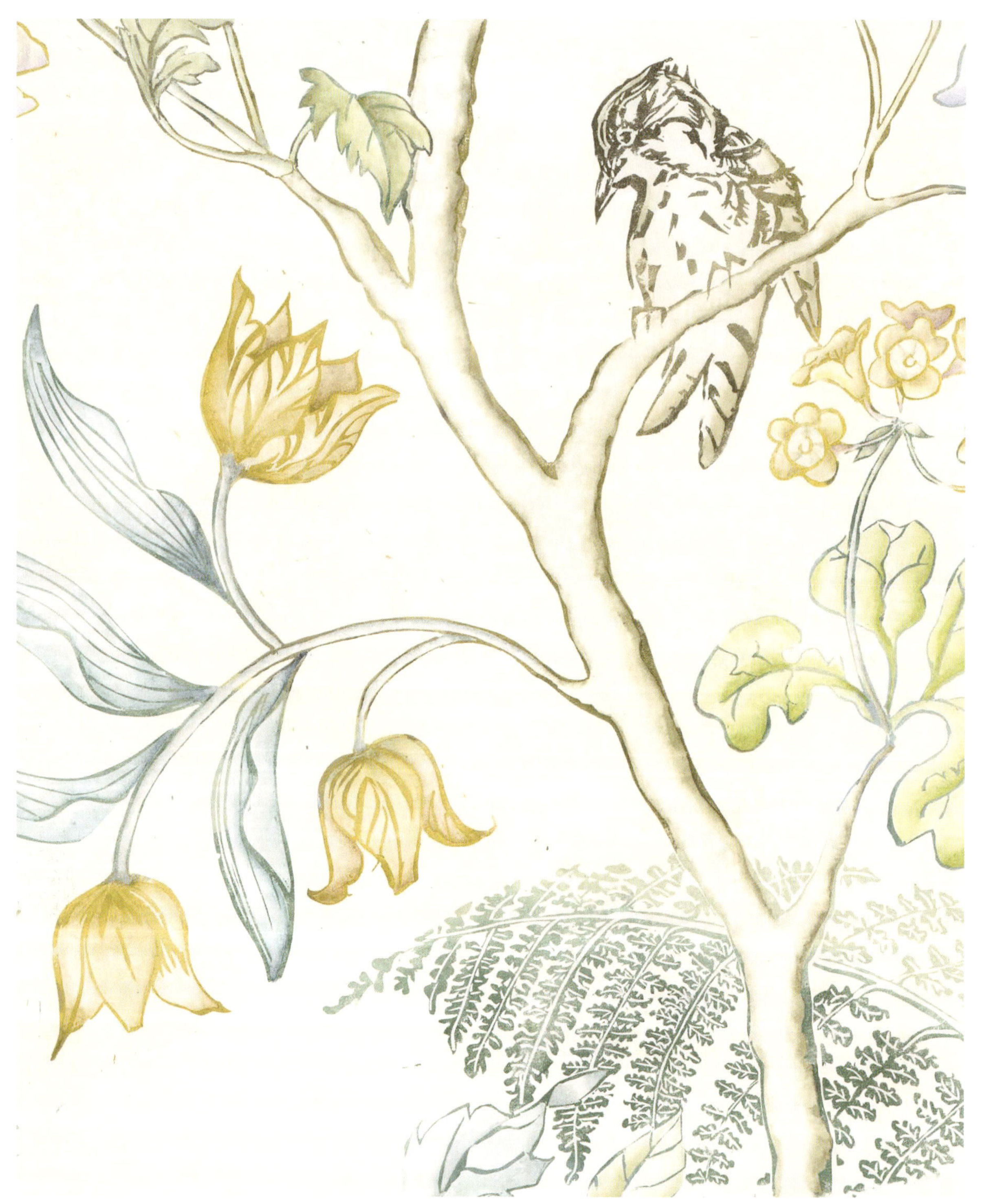

INTRODUCTION

Making prints from lino is a very accessible medium and the process of making a linocut is relatively simple. This book covers all the basics in detail, with an emphasis on both good design and using colour throughout. If you are a beginner, you have chosen the perfect starting point; if you are already a printmaker or artist, there will be plenty here to satisfy. Once familiar with the building blocks, the printmaker can develop in all sorts of directions. My hope with this book is to give you a sense of the great scope for invention, which is inherent in the medium.

If you are new to printmaking, I suggest you tackle the projects in a methodical way. Start small with a print made from a single block – you may never wish or need to go bigger or more complex than that. There's nothing inherently better about a bigger print made from two blocks rather than one. It is worth bearing in mind that there are quite a few steps to making even the simplest print. Once you are familiar with the basics, it can be satisfying to see how far you can stretch them. Move on to making prints from two blocks then to larger prints or patterns, if that appeals.

Picking the best approach depends on what you're trying to achieve. Even though I now have a large etching press for making wallpaper, I often choose to print by hand instead, especially when printing onto large sheets of thin, lightweight Japanese paper (the kind I recommend in this book). These papers buckle and crease easily in a press. Large blocks take a long time to cut, but this doesn't have to be done all in one sitting – cutting lino can feel therapeutic if you take your time over it. The real work comes when it is time to print using a wooden spoon (more on which later).

Exploring pattern is yet another direction that lino printing can take you in, which we dive into in the final chapter. Never quite knowing the result until a design is repeated, the intrepid will discover a magical world which reveals itself fully only after all the work is done.

Responding to plants and flowers in print feels rewarding. The subjects themselves are endlessly generous. I tend to have certain favourites such as dahlias to which I return again and again, each time getting more intimate with their colour and structure; each time finding something new. I hope some of this enthusiasm comes through in this book and gives you some new tools to develop your own passions further.

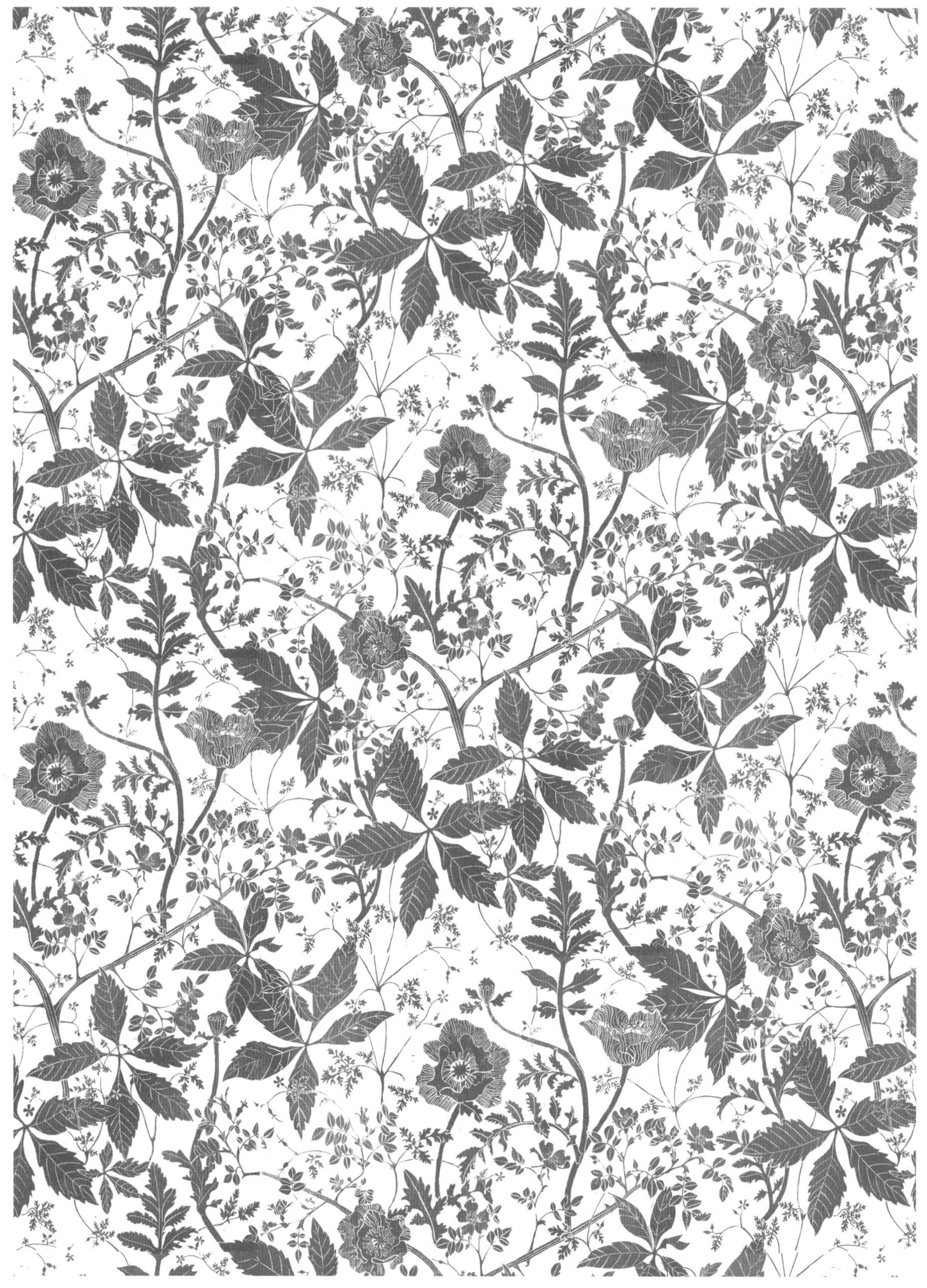

CHAPTER 1

OVERVIEW AND EQUIPMENT

Linocuts are a form of relief printing – the part of the design that is 'in relief' creates the print. This chapter gives an overview of the process of making a print from a single block, applying all the colour in one go. We will also look in detail at the equipment necessary to achieve this. By the end, you will be ready to start designing your first print.

The first and most essential point to get to grips with is this: the surface area of the lino block receives the ink. Handheld rollers are used to apply ink to the surface. The lower gouged-away part may look interesting in terms of texture, but it will have no bearing on the final image – those gouged-out areas will be blank.

Demonstration: *Foxgloves* – Making a Print

This demonstration gives you an overview of the general process of printmaking. It is a good idea to familiarise yourself with this before you embark on your first creation. The subsequent chapters will set out all the information you need in greater detail.

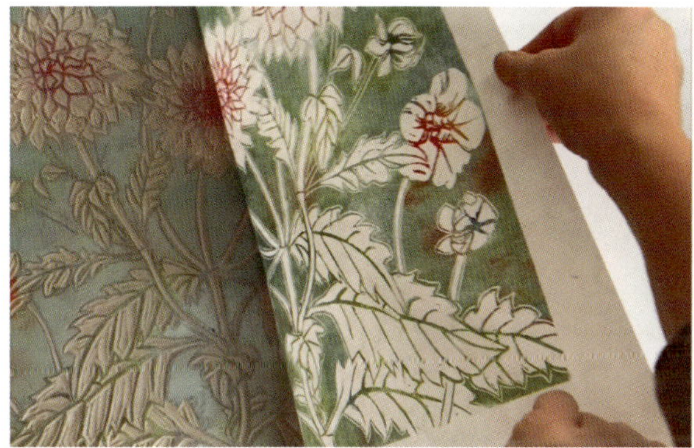

Linocuts are a form of relief printmaking – the surface takes the ink.

The Ideal Size

The block for *Honeysuckle* also features cow parsley and fern; three subjects from my sketchbook that I've put together into one composition. It measures approximately 15 × 20cm (6 × 8in) and fits comfortably when centred onto an A4 sheet of paper. An A5 piece of lino is a good size to begin with – any smaller is fiddly to cut and ink; any bigger is too laborious. If you prefer something bigger, choose a size between A5 and A4.

Poppies wallpaper.

You Will Need

- Drawing paper
- Pencil
- Block of lino
- Graphite or carbon paper
- Tracing paper
- Masking tape
- Cutting tools: one fine V-shaped tool, one medium U-shaped gouge and one wide, shallow background remover
- Ink rollers: one for each colour
- Set of six inks: red, yellow, blue, black, white and extender
- Palette knives (or substitute)
- Palette
- Baby wipes and/or rags
- A wooden spoon or specialist baren
- Printing paper
- White spirit
- Thin nitrile gloves and heavy-duty protective gloves
- Old newspaper to protect surfaces

Notes on the Tools and Equipment

Lino

Lino is sold by Essdee (*see* Suppliers). Buy your lino pre-cut, as larger pieces or even as a roll to cut to size as desired (score the top in a straight line from edge to edge, fold back and cut the hessian). Buy only as much as you will use within two years; the lino becomes difficult to cut after that.

Cutting Tools

For artist-quality tools, I use the Swiss brand, Pfeil (*see* Chapter 3 for more details). You will need a fine no. 12 V-shaped tool for cutting around your shapes, a 5mm U-shaped tool for your second 'go round' (I prefer the slightly more expensive Japanese tool: a Komasuki, 4.5mm) and a large, shallow no. 7 U-shaped tool to remove the background at right angles to your shape.

Alternatively, to get you started without much expense, purchase Japanese economy cutters, available from Intaglio (you will need to add to the

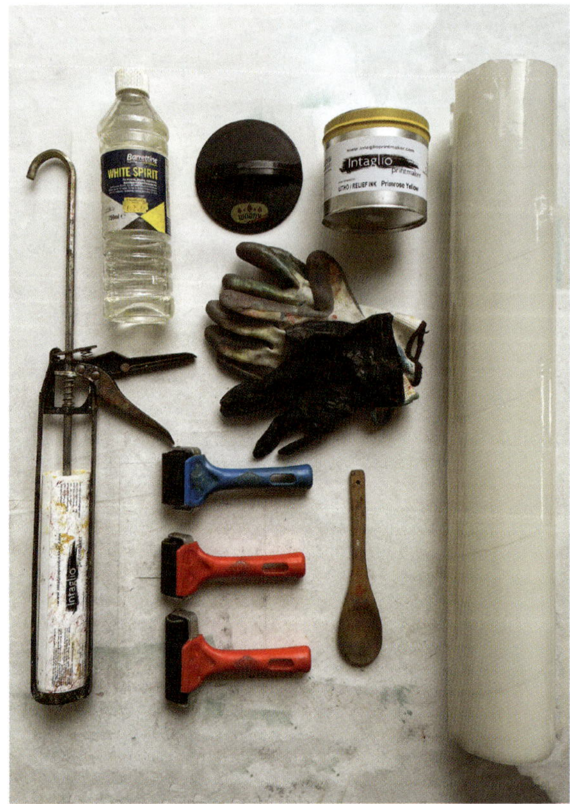

Printmaking kit, including: ink in 500g (18oz) tin, rollers, wooden spoon, Japanese baren, ink cartridge, extruder, white spirits, and sticky-backed plastic to use as an improvised palette.

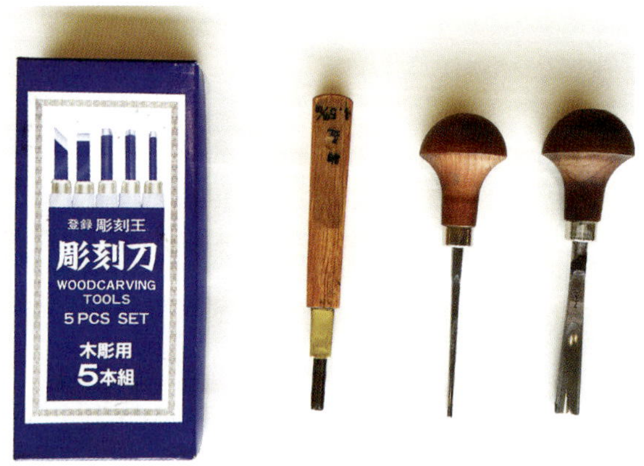

Artist-quality tools are an investment, but you only really need three. Economy Japanese woodcutting tools are an inexpensive alternative to get you started.

box with a fine V-shaped tool sold separately) and Lawrence (this is a complete set).

Ink
All the prints created in this book are made using oil-based ink from both

Intaglio Printmaker (litho relief ink) and Lawrence Art Supplies (original linseed oil relief ink – *see* Suppliers).

I would advise using primary colours as a starter, unless you are already familiar with colour mixing. Don't forget to buy extender (colourless binder), white and black as well as your three primary colours (red, yellow and blue). For more information on colour selection, *see* Chapter 4.

Other options are from Hawthorn Printmakers. Look for 'stay open' and linseed relief inks. For those who prefer not to use white spirit to clean up, Cranfields Caligo Safe Wash is worth a try as this washes with soap and cold water.

A builder's extruder is needed to extract ink from cartridges. These are more inconvenient to use, but ink in 300ml (10fl oz) cartridges is reasonably priced compared to small 150ml (5fl oz) tubes. When buying in bulk but not needing as much as a 500g (18oz) or 1kg (35oz) tin, 300ml (10fl oz) cartridges are a cost-effective choice – double the amount of ink for only a third more money. Prices vary slightly according to cost of pigments.

Palette
Possible improvised palettes include a piece of Perspex, mirror or toughened glass. A roll of self-adhesive sheet plastic works well stuck directly to any smooth tabletop as an alternative to a conventional palette and can be disposed of, rather than cleaned at the end of a session.

Rollers
Use Essdee rollers, 5cm (2in) wide. At least five rollers are needed; one for each colour. The

blue-handled rollers are marginally better than the red-handled ones, though either type are perfectly good. Rollers with a large gap between the handle and roller are easier to clean but harder to come by.

Gloves
Heavy-duty gloves are essential when using white spirit for the final clean up. For the printing process itself, use thinner nitrile powder-free gloves. Thin gloves would disintegrate when used with white spirit, but do provide the greater sensitivity needed for the creative ink-laying process.

Spoon or Specialist Baren
Choose a wooden spoon for the printing stage that is small and flat, usually available from craft websites. The circular, flat, black Japanese-style baren is another piece of equipment to try, though I prefer a wooden spoon as I can target certain areas, such as edges or details, more effectively. Alternatively, you could use a combination.

Paper
Use 90–120gsm cartridge paper or inexpensive, machine-made Japanese papers. The Awagami brand produces paper called Masa, Hosho, Inbe or Silk – all will work well as they are thin yet strong, but do not chose a paper that is lighter than 90gsm. These papers take watercolour beautifully (*see* Chapter 6). Always print on the smooth side rather than the textured side.

Equipment for Trimming Lino to Size
To cut a piece of lino from a larger block or roll, first measure and mark the front surface of the block in pencil. Score the front surface using a Stanley knife and a straight edge – there is no need to make a deep cut. Fold the lino back on itself – it will do this easily. Finally, cut the hessian by running your blade along the fold.

1. Draw your design onto a sheet of cartridge or tracing paper, the same size as your lino block. A line drawing in pencil is all that is required; extra details such as shading are superfluous.

2. Place the graphite transfer (or carbon) paper, inky side down, sandwiched between your line drawing and the lino. Attach the line drawing to the block with masking tape so it stays in place while you trace over it. Use a pen to go over the pencil lines and make sure you have all the information you need before detaching the drawing.

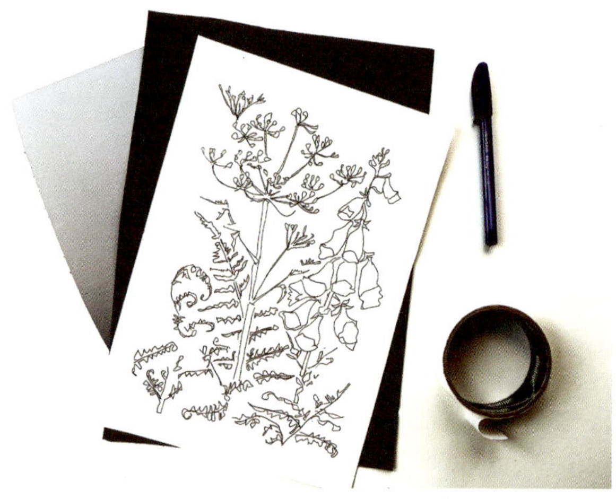

Take your drawing and transfer it onto your block using the graphite transfer (or carbon) paper.

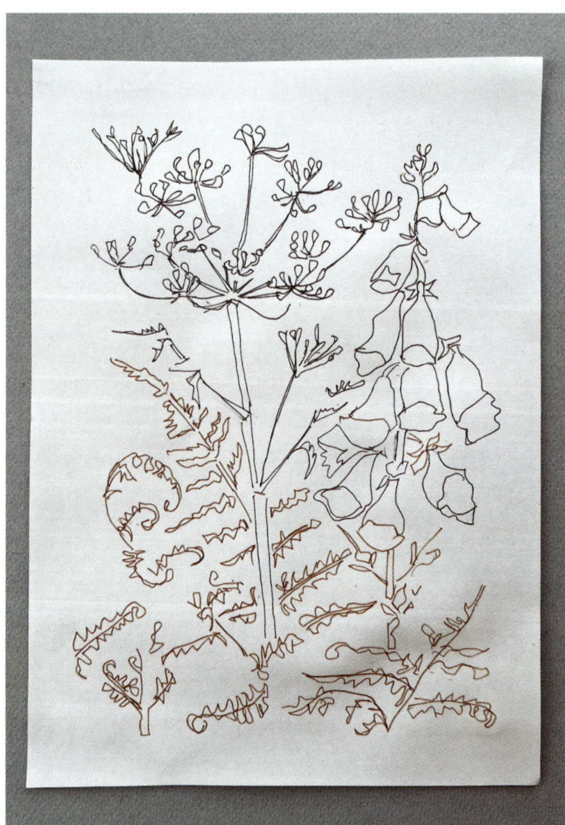

Start small and plan your design.

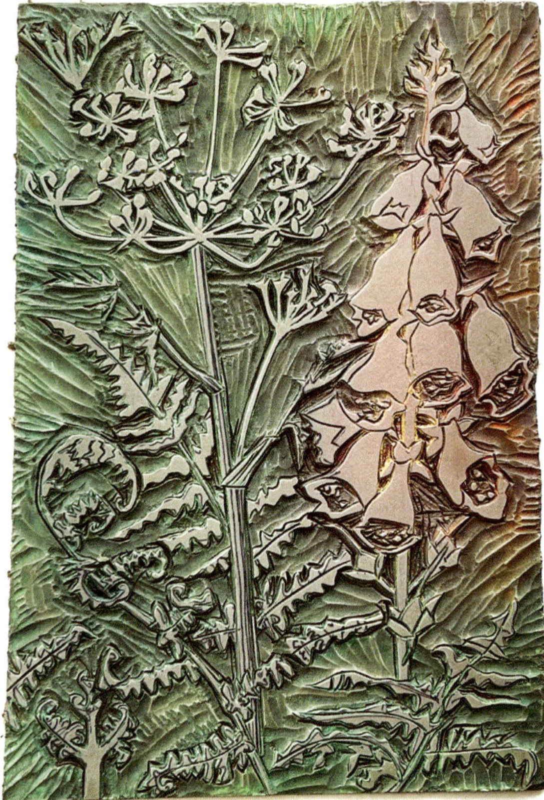

The block of linocut, trimmed and ready to print.

When choosing the size of your printing paper, leave at least 5cm (2in) all around the image. How much space you leave depends on how you decide to display your work, with or without a mount.

At the beginning of a session, when your block is clean and free of ink, prepare a printing base. Take a sheet of paper the same size as the paper on which you have chosen to print. Centre the block accurately on it and draw around it with a pen.

The aim is to ensure that your print is perfectly centred on your printing paper every time you make a print. In this way, you can place your inked block within this marked area, knowing that as long as you align your printing paper to the outer edges of this base you will have a perfectly centred print every time.

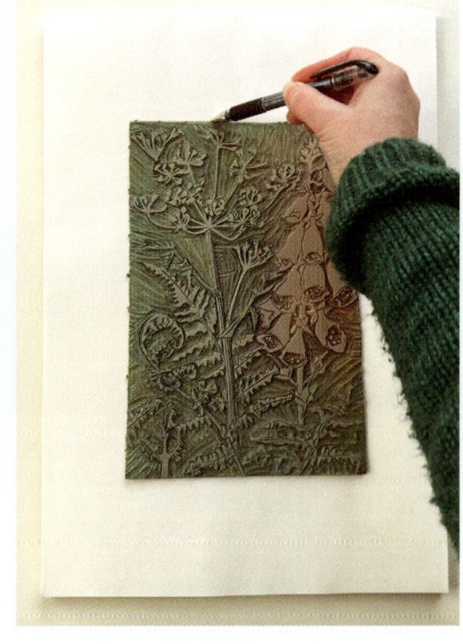

Draw around the block on a base the same size as the printing paper.

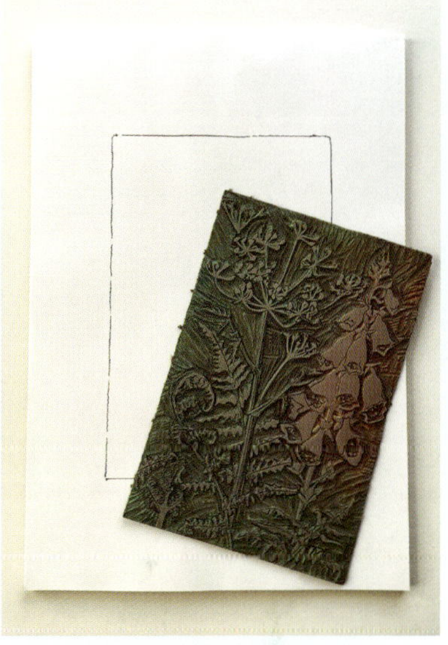

The print 'bed' for the block. Keep this area clean and have your printing paper cut ready to use alongside it.

3. Use the three tools to cut the block (*see* Chapter 3 for a full explanation).

4. Put on gloves. In a separate area, mix all the inks you intend to use on your palette.

5. Use the rollers to apply ink, ensuring there is an even layer over the entire block.

6. Remove your gloves and make sure your hands are clean. To centre the print, place the inked block within the lines of your prepared printing bed to perfectly align your printing paper. To avoid unwanted ink spoiling the clean paper, hold the paper vertically and place the bottom-left corner of the paper down using your left hand until you are satisfied that the corners and bottom edge align exactly with the base. Lower your paper carefully onto the inky block and smooth it over with your right hand.

7. Using the fleshy part of the base of your thumb, which fits comfortably into the bowl of the spoon, apply pressure to the paper with back of the spoon. Apply pressure to the top surface area

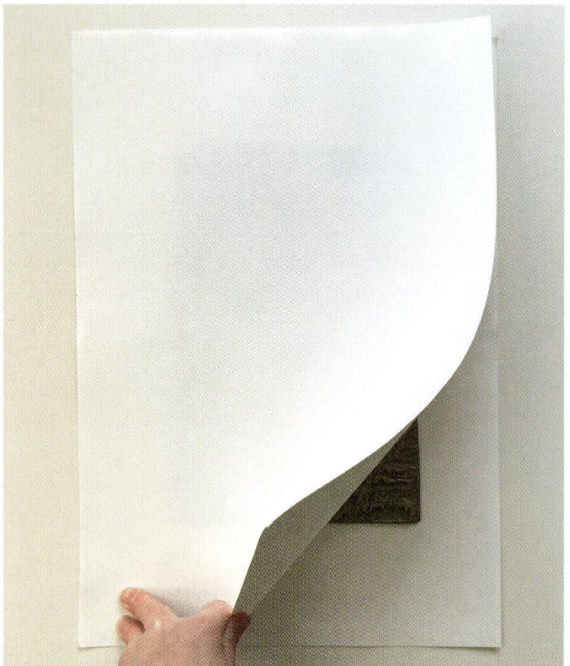

Linocuts are a form of relief printmaking – the surface takes the ink. If necessary, as a check before printing, wrap a baby wipe around your index finger to remove any unwanted, excess ink from background areas.

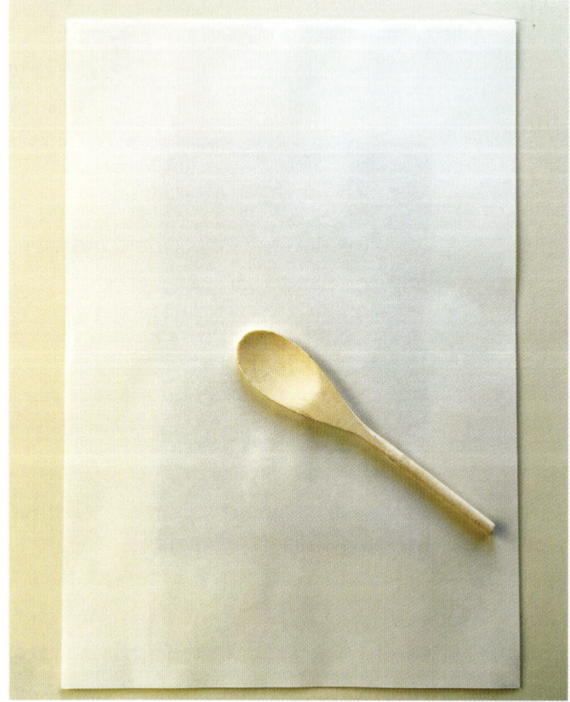

Use any type of wooden spoon or baren – the flatter the better.

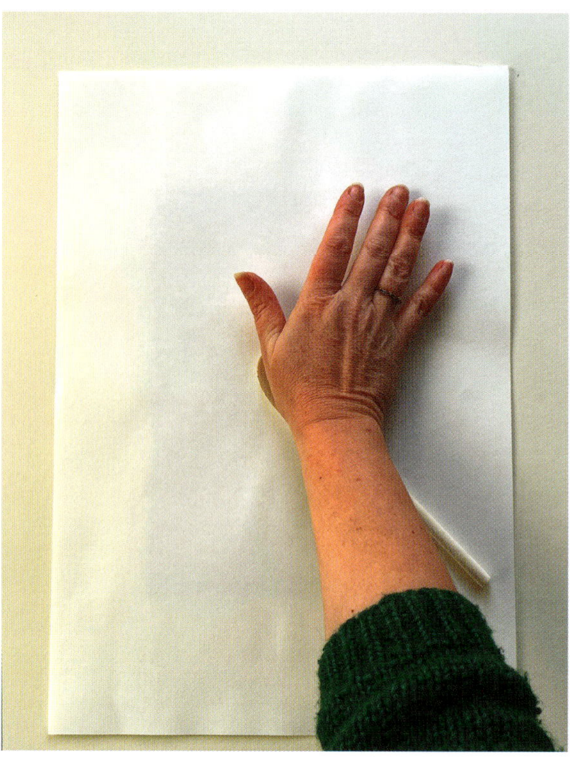

Rub the wooden spoon or baren all over the back of the paper to make the print.

FIRST CHECK THE PAPER

Just before laying on the paper, I have developed a habit of checking the smooth side is face down by rubbing the top corner of the paper between my thumb and forefinger.

only, avoiding concentrating any pressure where it is not required, i.e., avoid the background that you have gouged out. The aim is for these areas to remain clean and ink-free. Avoiding these blank areas is easy, as your image will start to be visible through the back of the paper, plus you will be familiar by now with your design, having spent time cutting it.

Swap to using your index and middle finger, raising the spoon to a shallow angle to concentrate pressure on any straight edges and corners, as these need extra attention to print well.

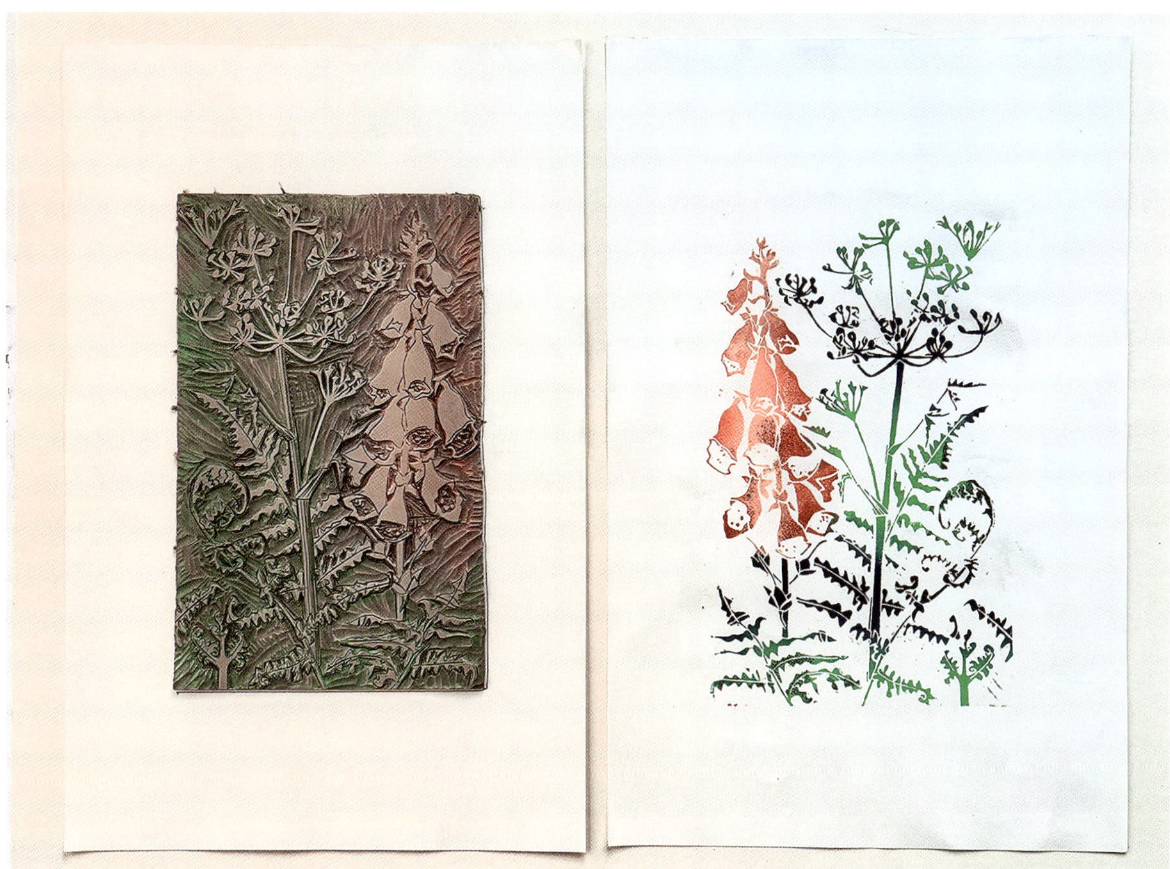

The lino block with the finished print alongside.

8. Carefully peel back the paper to reveal the finished print. Notice how the print is a mirror image of the block.

Ink, Print, Repeat
To create more prints, begin from step 5, without the need to clean the block in between. Colours can be adjusted and varied, as will be explored in Chapter 4.

Drying
If space allows, leave your prints on a flat surface to dry. If you have a lot of prints to dry, consider hanging them with bulldog clips from a string.

TRANSFERRING YOUR DRAWING

If you want your print to be the same orientation as your drawing, you will need to reverse it. The easiest way is this is to have your drawing on tracing paper and simply turn it over. Proceed to transfer the drawing to the block by tracing on the reverse.

Cleaning Up
When you are finished with your printing session, clean up using white spirit, heavy-duty protective gloves, baby wipes and rags in a well-ventilated area.

Now that you have a good general overview of how to make a print and the equipment that you will need, you are ready to move on to the exciting design stage.

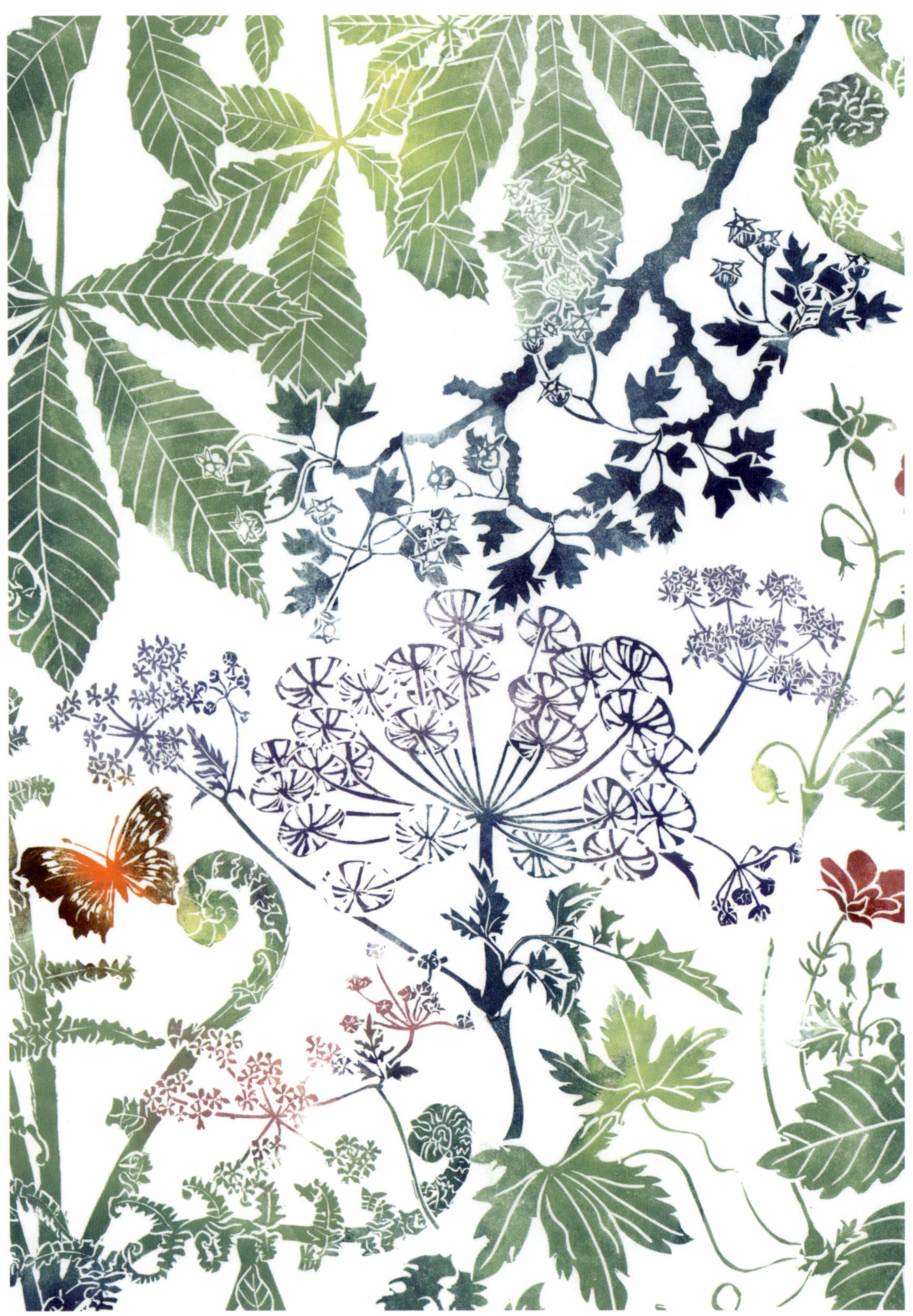

CHAPTER 2

DESIGNING AND PLANNING A PRINT

In this chapter we will explore some of the features that go into making a successful print. We will pay particular attention to how to combine different elements together effectively, thinking about form, balance, contrast and harmony. We will consider scale and how this relates to the medium of lino. The overarching theme will be to encourage you to use the design stage as an opportunity to play. The merits of drawing versus tracing will be discussed as well as uses of technology. There will be plenty of inspiring imagery and encouragement to develop your artistic practice more generally. We will also touch on an alternative method for making prints; an inversion of the norm.

It pays to have a good plan. It is important to have a basic understanding of what goes into making a print, as shown in Chapter 1, so that you are ready to begin designing your first print by carefully choosing a subject.

Every artistic medium has its limitations. To design for success you need a sense of what these are and what you can achieve with this medium, to know how to compensate, play to your strengths and avoid disappointment. The medium of print is different to a drawing, painting or other type of rendering. You will not be able to replicate an image exactly. An understanding of how to translate an image into print will help you to make good choices at the outset; a skill that gets easier with practice.

COMPOSING YOUR DRAWING

Colour

The first thing not to lose sight of is that the more surface area of the block you leave intact, the greater opportunity you will have for rolling it up with ink – that means colour. You'll want to exploit this, so make sure that your chosen subject has at least some larger areas of exciting colour. For example, the Foxgloves print demonstrated in Chapter 1 includes a lot spindly, intricate ferns as well as fussy stems of cow parsley. The chunky foxglove – in tones ranging from pink to purple – comes as a welcome relief of colour and form.

Horse Chestnut print.

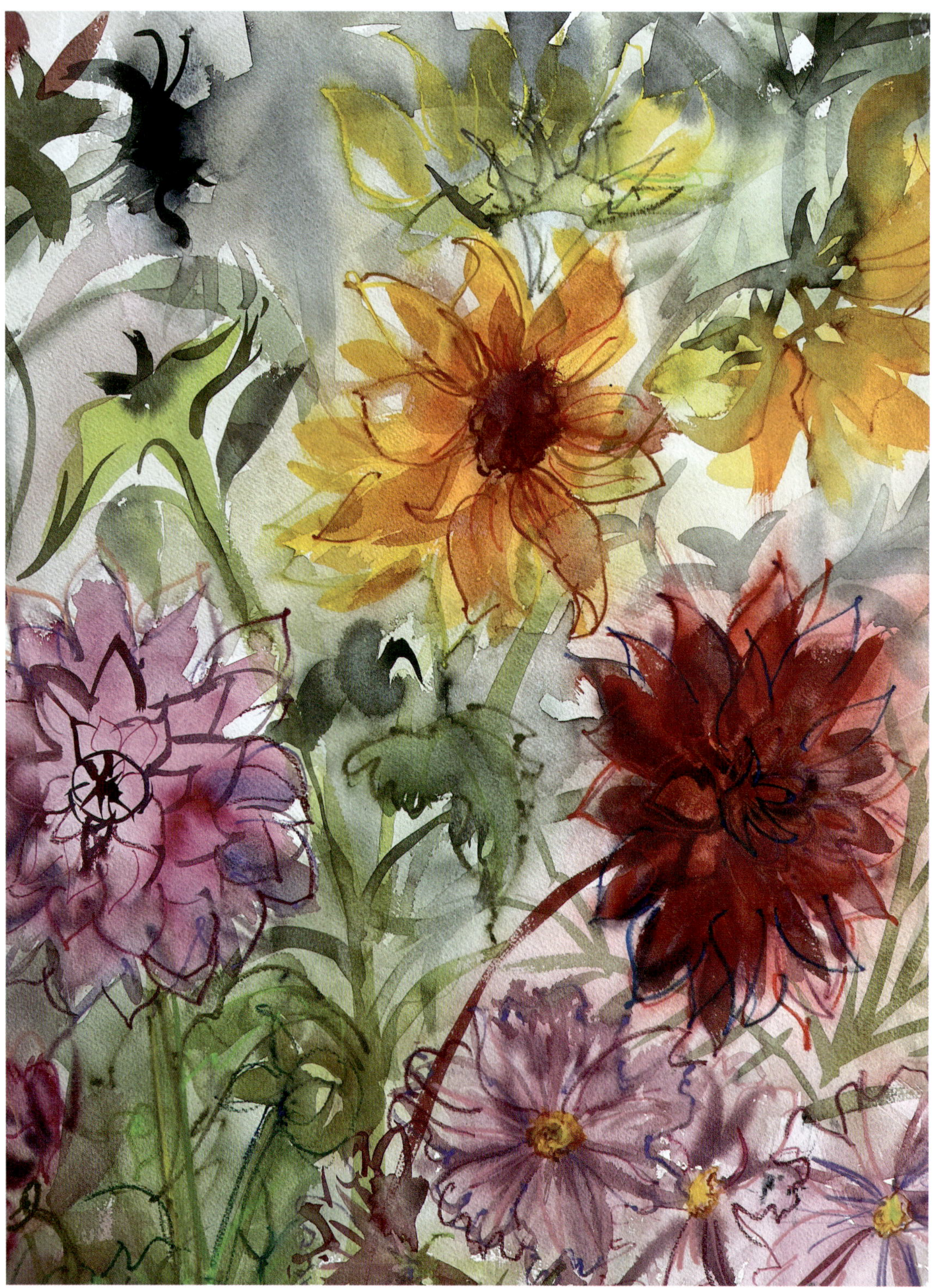

Enjoy your subjects and bring some spontaneity to your work by trying watercolours. Including line work helps make it possible to translate your artwork into potential source material for a print.

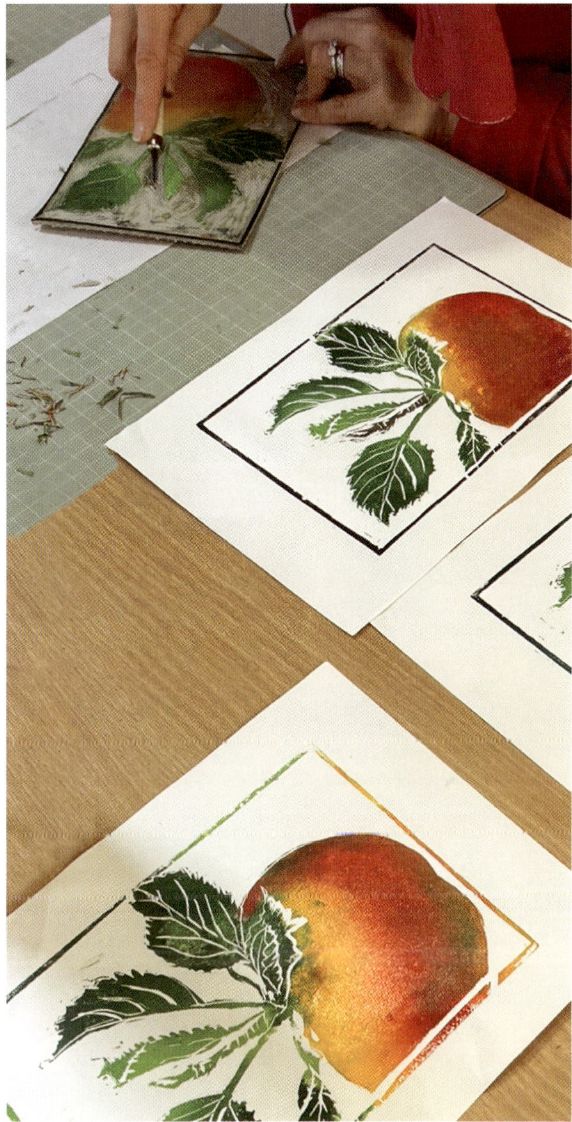

At a day workshop, this printmaker has used the opportunity to successfully exploit colour on a small, A5-sized area. In addition to their use of colour, the arrangement of the leaves contributes to a sense of depth. The delicate stems contrast with the other more solid forms. A border has been added to frame the design so that it is not lost and floating. To maximise impact, the printmaker has increased the scale of their original drawing and placed the fruit to one side of the composition.

Size

Think in terms of an A5 (or maximum A4) print to start with. Compose your drawing on a sheet of paper of the same dimensions, but bear in mind that you will print this onto a larger sheet size so your image fits comfortably. Remembering this at the design stage means you will pay attention to the full final effect of your design.

Three-Dimensionality

Design an image that will give a sense of three dimensions. A print is, after all, a flat, two-dimensional work on paper, so designing to give the impression of three dimensions is essential. There are two ways to achieve this:

1. The arrangement of your botanical subjects.
2. The use of colour.

Another way to increase the sense of three-dimensionality is by using colour to provide a sense of depth. Tones from light to dark give form to otherwise flat shapes. Two contrasting tones blended on the same roller give this effect, as will be shown in more detail in Chapter 4. Make sure the composition has at least one area large enough to ink effectively it in this way.

Contrasting Forms

Choose contrasting forms to add interest. Printing from a single block requires emphasising bold silhouettes and contrasting shapes. These contrasts come not only from shape but also from size. Combining small, intricate details with large, flat bold shapes and outlines can create a pleasing contrast.

Take the print, *Horse Chestnut*, that opens this chapter; the horse chestnut leaves that feature provide a solid a mass of colour, anchoring the design and contrasting well with the diminutive hawthorn leaves. Aim for bold silhouettes against the blank white paper. Later chapters will give you further design considerations for making prints from multiple blocks.

Time to Play

At this stage in the process, give yourself the freedom to play and experiment until you come up with the most pleasing arrangement of shapes and

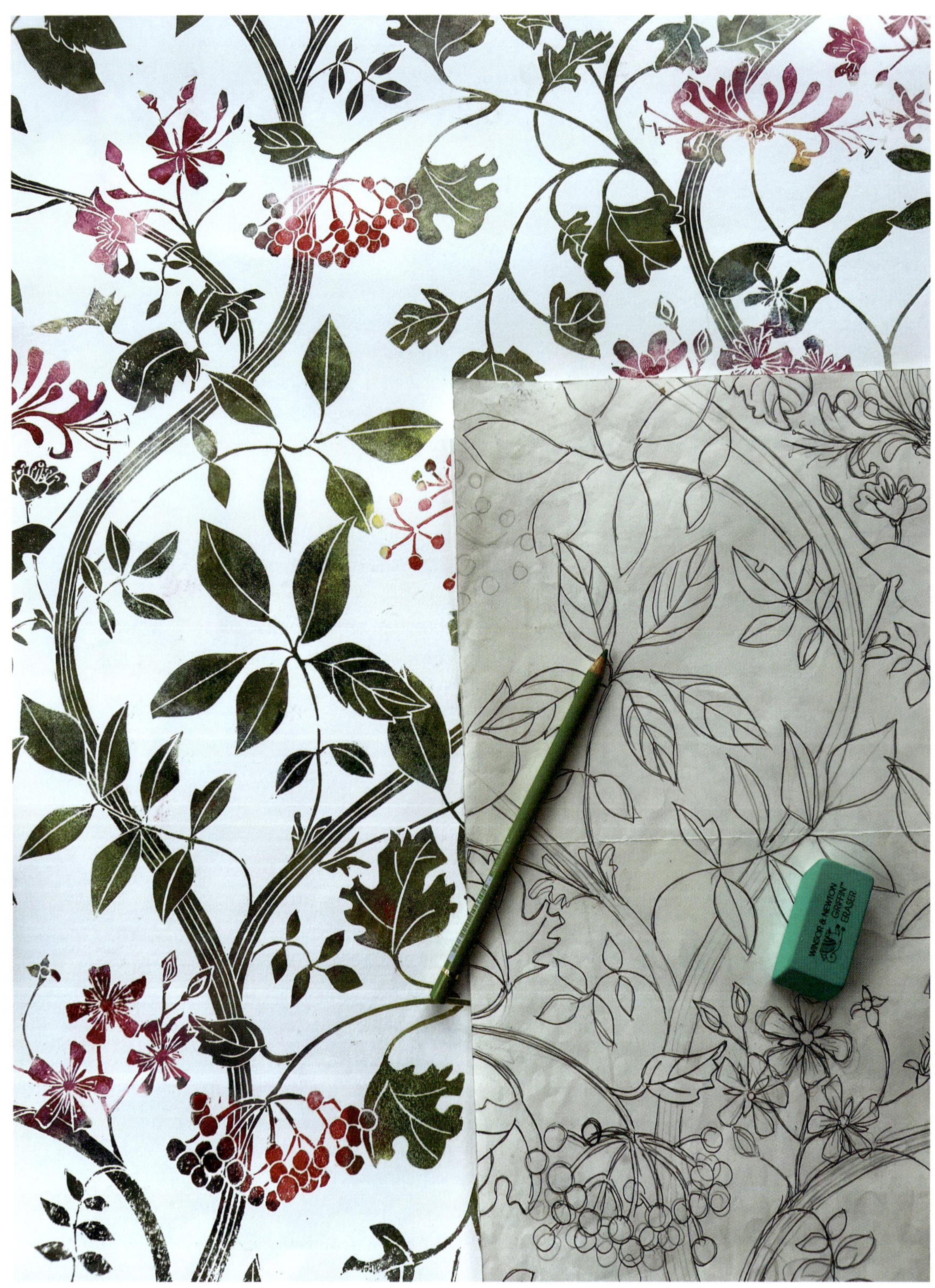

Hedgerow Tangle pattern for wallpaper - the line drawing together with the finished print.

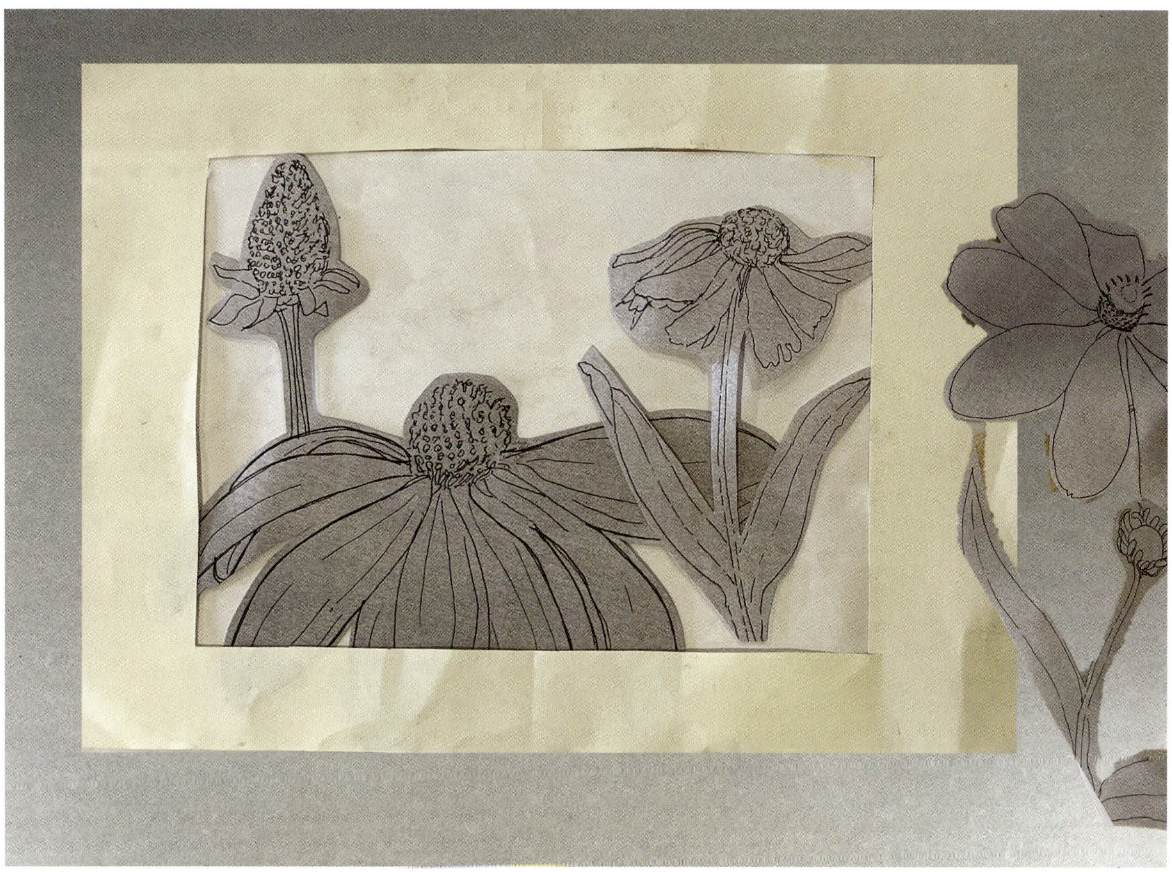

Working things out in rough means you can play around until you are happy. One way to compose an image is to cut closely around the different elements. Try them out in different positions within a paper frame until you find a pleasing composition.

forms before you set out. This is where you make the design decisions that determine the success of your print. Try to make critical assessments of what needs improvement. Ask yourself: does that leaf shape look limp and weak – even though it's a faithful representation of my photograph, does it need altering? Is it a bold enough silhouette or does it need clarifying? Do you need to find something extra to fill a gap?

Be ready to discard an element in favour of another that will work more successfully. Designs with multiple elements may require some extra attention at the design stage. Use plenty of scraps of paper so that you can rough out your design. Give yourself choice, perhaps composing at least a couple of options to work out the best one.

Compositions can take various forms – centred, like a traditional botanical print, or offset and asymmetric in a Japanese or Arts and Crafts style. You might prefer a dynamic arrangement that 'dances' across the composition, or you could explore subjects that fill the entire space, interacting with one another by overhanging, overlapping, twinning around and curling.

THE DRAWING STAGE

All you need in terms of drawn information for a lino block print is a simple line drawing, such as in the example. Spending extra time shading or drawing superfluous contour lines is surplus to

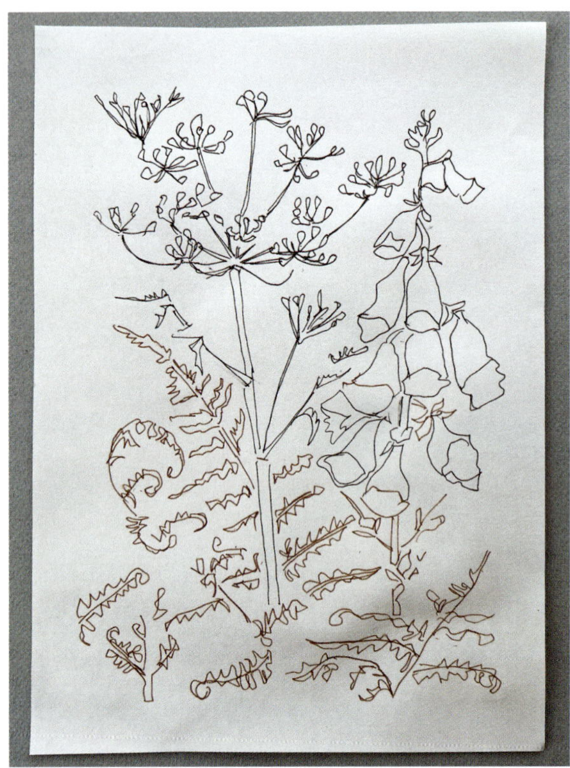

The information you need on the block consists of the lines for the cutting tools to follow. The drawing should include the outlines of your botanical forms and any details on the inside of the shapes such as veins, petals, stamens and the centres of flowers.

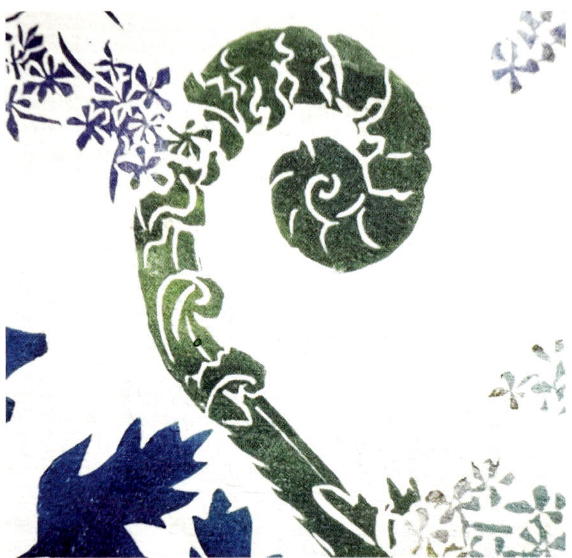

Remember that certain details of the pencil drawing will print as fine white lines, such as on this curled-up fern – something to bear in mind at the design stage.

requirements. The pencil lines of a drawing that denote details 'within' your subjects print to give the appearance of light, which has caught and illuminated the forms of your subject. It takes some consideration to decide how much information to include there.

Using Composition Frames

There are many ways to come up with a composition. Try making simple paper frames as a devise to help visualise and identify potential designs. Cut the 'window' of the frame to correspond to your lino block. The paper frame helps to visually eliminate any noise from elements that are not included so you can focus and get an immediate sense of the final look of the print. On an iPad device, scale an image up and down by using your fingertips until you happen upon a composition you like.

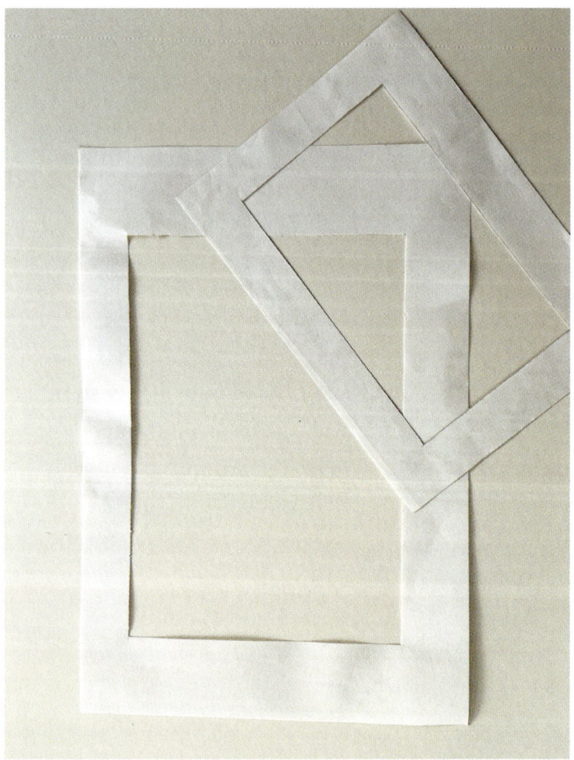

Use paper frames with A4-size and A5-size windows. Place them on top of drawings in your sketchbook or illustrations to find a composition you like, blocking out other visual distraction.

Arranging a Design from Separate Elements

Rough charcoal sketches on inexpensive layout paper are all about composition rather than accurate botanical drawing. It can be fiddly to assemble separate sketches into a design, especially if you want to use tracings rather than redraw them. Tracing paper can also be 'swapped out' to try an alternative design element.

Drawing with Charcoal

Drawing with charcoal can be useful at this rough, 'fluid' stage because it is easily rubbed out on tracing paper or newsprint; no need for a putty rubber, just

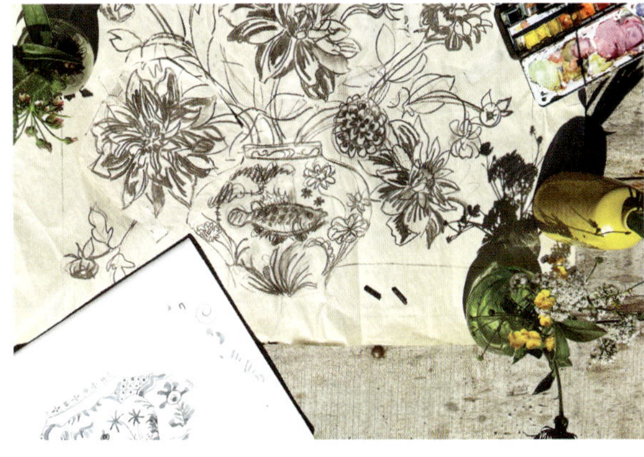

Chop up and move elements around to where they look most pleasing. I enjoyed painting an alternative vase so I could decide which would look best with the dahlias. The rejected vase drawing could be worked into another print.

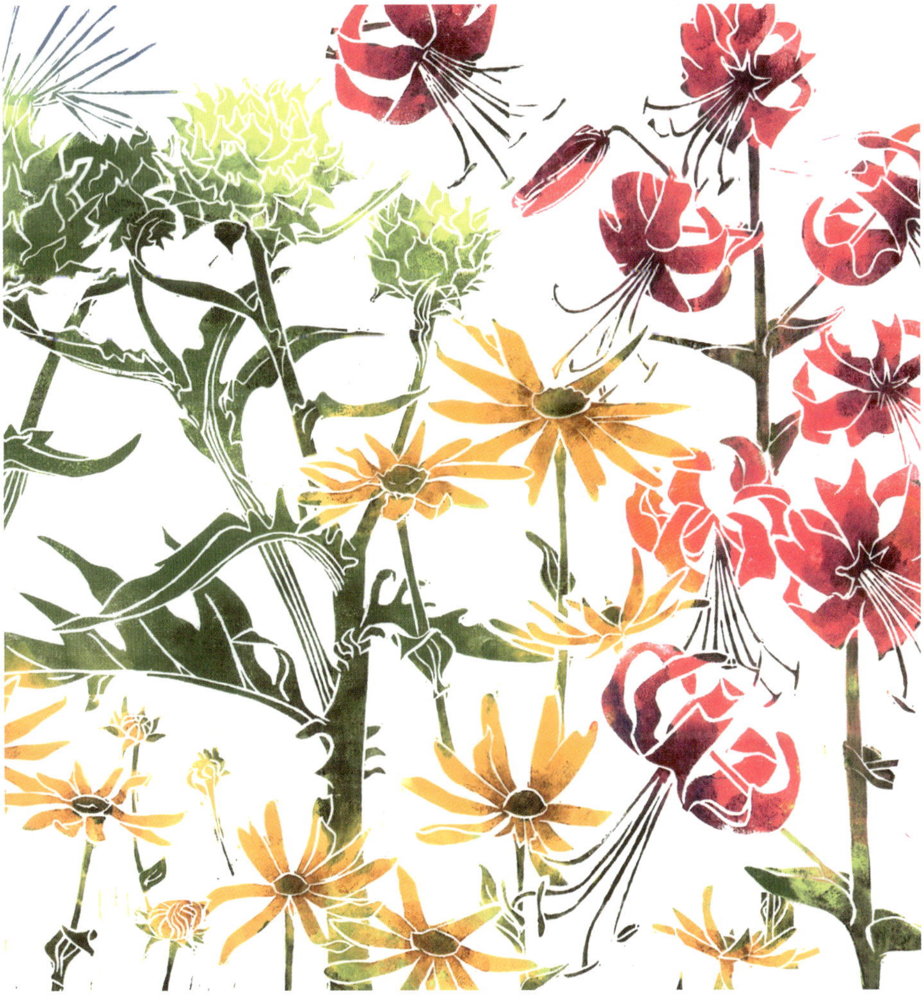

The design components for this print were assembled from a few separate line drawings in my sketchbook. I drew them on a visit to a special garden here in Cumbria, the home of John Ruskin, where I found the stately cardoons, rudbeckias and lilies growing in different borders.

use your fingers! Lines drawn in charcoal are never too delicate; it gives an appropriate thickness to cut out of lino.

Tracing

If you are not confident in your drawing ability, feel free to trace. Photos can be a good starting point, but tracing entirely from photographs can lead to disappointing results. More often than not, some part of the image will need improving. Trace or draw from them, perhaps improving them to exaggerate elements for better impact.

Tracing elements of your design, from illustrations in books, magazines or internet searches, is also an option. Images from the internet can be either printed off on a home printer or traced directly from your device. An iPad can act as a kind of light box; its screen is a useful A5 size. There are even apps available for the iPad that mimic a light box, keeping an image still while it is traced. Simply lay a piece of tracing paper over your device, using masking tape to hold it in place, and trace over lightly with a soft pencil.

You will be surprised how distinct and original the final print will look from the separate elements you used to compose it. After all, the arrangement of the composite elements is all your own. There may be some subjects you can trace and other perhaps smaller or simpler motifs that you could add in by freehand drawing them. My message is don't be afraid to use tracings but equally try not to restrict yourself by only tracing.

One advantage of working with tracing paper is that you can turn your images over and judge if they fit into your composition better that way. You may even find that you can use an individual element more than once in the same design. By flipping a tracing over you can reuse it, perhaps scaled up or down. Once reversed, the fact it's a copy is not at all obvious. Once you have decided on a composition it may require only a small amount of 'new drawing' to fill in any little gaps.

Resizing

It is often a necessary to scale an element to a more appropriate size. An iPad or phone is a useful tool

When planning a design, remember how the finished image will appear on a larger sheet. However, avoid unnecessary work by only trimming the block down to size after the design has been cut. For now, place the drawing so that it fits comfortably in the centre of a large block.

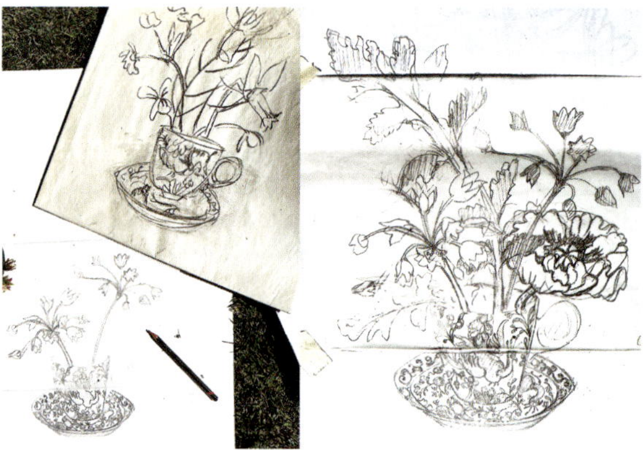

Rough working out for a large print. Having decided that the teacup was definitely going to feature, I could play with different compositions. Here the teacup sketch remains while I overlay a fresh sheet of tracing paper to try out another design.

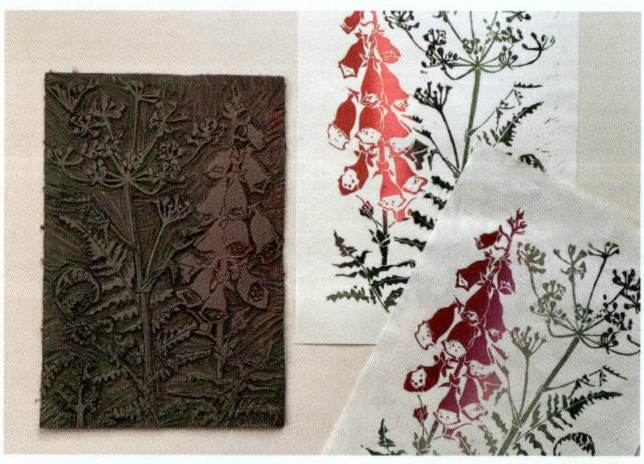

Trim excess lino only after the cutting process is complete – it is easier to cut a larger piece of lino and trim it afterwards. Working with the tools, you will find that the edges are fiddly and harder to work on than the centre.

for enlarging images to the size you require. Tiny designs on small pieces of lino are usually too fiddly and not very effective as prints. Scale up your drawings or images to produce a successful design. The images you scale up could equally be photographs of your own sketches or something you found through an internet search.

The traditional method of doing this by hand is a little time-consuming, involving using a grid of squares laid over the resource image. Draw up the same grid of squares, only larger, on your paper, then transfer the drawing square by square onto the larger grid. Use this method or technology – whichever is quick and easy.

DESIGNING AN INVERTED PRINT

Also referred to as a reverse or negative space print, this type of design differs from what we have explored so far. This time, the subject matter is cut out from the background, while the background is left in.

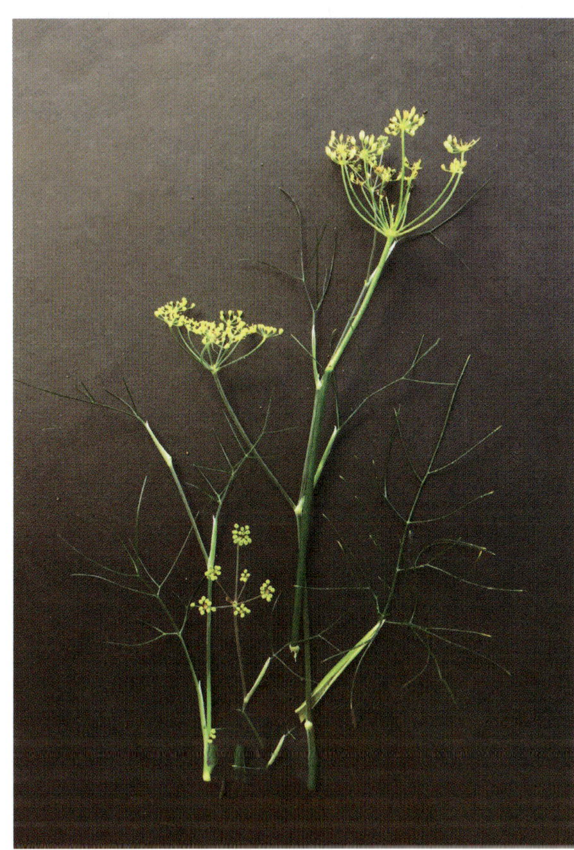

Making an inverted, reverse or negative space print calls for a different approach at the planning stage.

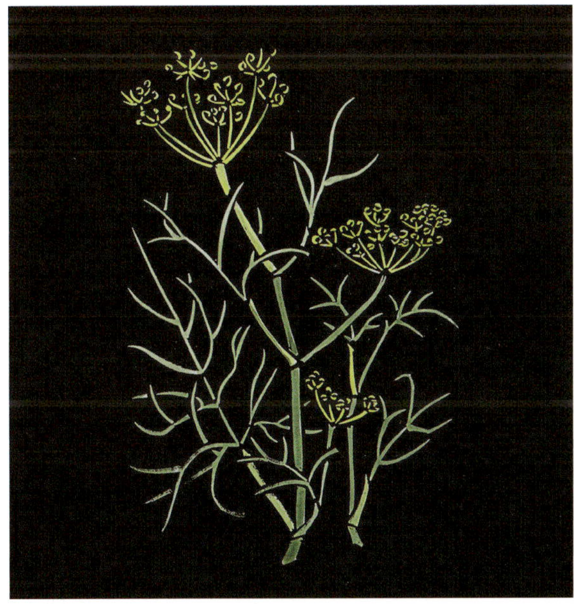

Wild Fennel is an example of a print designed using negative space (*see* Chapter 6 for more details).

To design an inverted print, lay the plant material on a dark surface so it more closely resembles the finished print. It is quite difficult to think in reverse – by looking at a white background and imagining it as dark – so this solves that difficulty.

To add watercolour to prints such as these is not always necessary. If extra colour is required, the correct Japanese machine-made paper must be used, which is smooth, medium-weight and designed for wet media. Ordinary watercolour paper would require a press to supply enough pressure to achieve a solid black ink background on heavy textured paper. For hand printing on an alternative to the Japanese paper, look for papers that are around 120gsm in weight with a smooth surface, made for wet media.

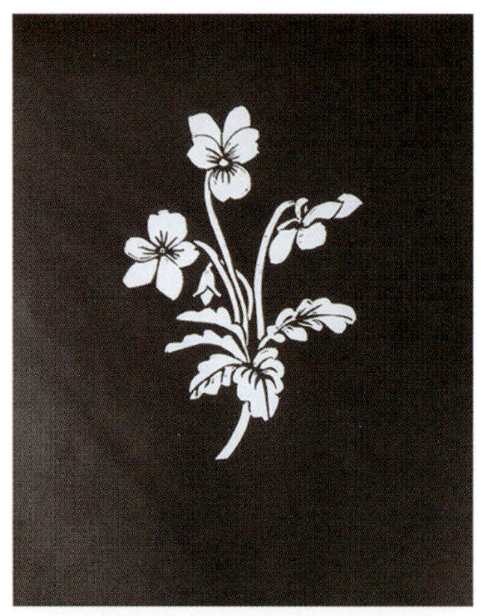
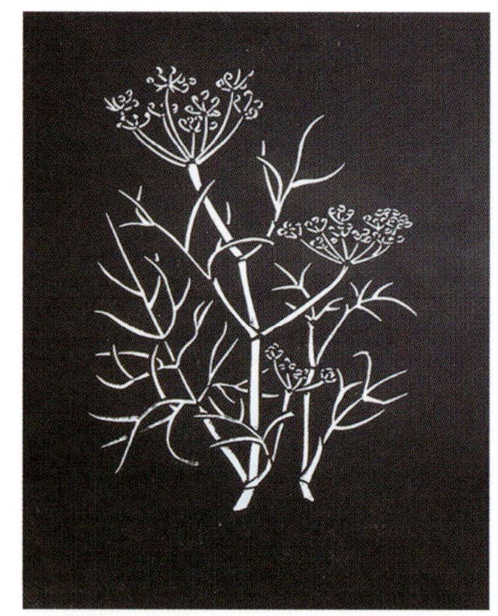
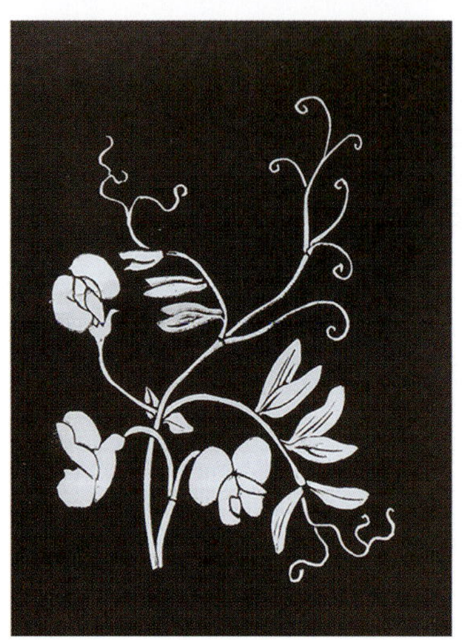
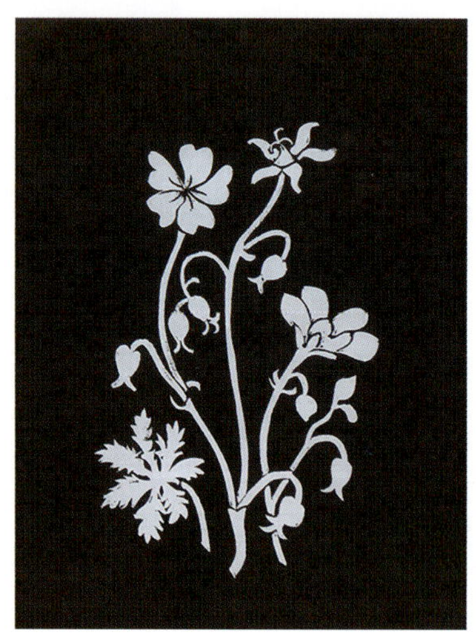

These inverted prints look completely unfinished at this stage. Once dry, watercolour is applied to the blank areas with a brush to finish them.

CREATING A BANK OF INSPIRATION RESOURCES

Keep a sketchbook of observational drawings from the garden to compose into a design. I might draw honeysuckle in various stages of flowering, from bud to full flower, and from different angles. Pay close attention to the details of the structure; how leaves are arranged and how side shoots meet the main stem. The details you include in your study will bring a print to life.

Imagine your design in black and white in order to focus on the forms alone, rather than relying on colour. Thinking in monochrome means you can zero in on shape and leave other details aside. For example, curling and twining shapes are always interesting and contrast well to large, flat plate-like leaf shapes.

Cut and arrange plants onto the floor or a large surface so that you can comfortably observe and draw them. Think like a designer. William Morris did not restrict himself to a faithful rendering. Decide if a stem that stands bolt upright might look better with a sinewy curve. From my bank of drawings, I can consider which to combine. I will bring together forms that are the most extreme contrasts.

Consider mass and overall balance. A solid mass contrasting with something of equal mass but made

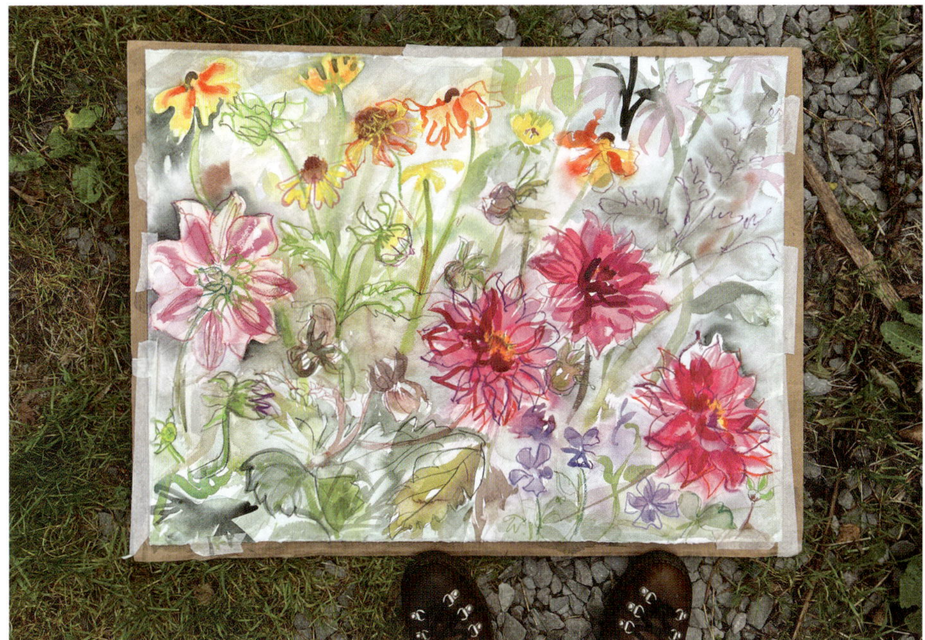

This watercolour is on the largest watercolour paper available and was made sitting on a camping stool in front of a border. Such instant gratification is a great antidote to the planning involved in printmaking. The practice can feed into your prints as a ready source of inspiration and helps develop familiarity with your subject matter.

up of lots of tiny elements will give broken and unbroken areas of colour. Chapter 7 will look at these issues further.

You may also wish to enliven your botanical designs with garden birds and insects – snails and beetles are great favourites. Birds can be very difficult to draw from life, but a bird feeder at a window is great for making studies. Some details are best found in photographs or illustrations.

Once you get into printing, you will find you pay more attention to the world of botanically themed print that surrounds us, such as high-end packaging for toiletries as well as fabrics and wallpapers. An image bank on your device of screenshots or photos is a ready supply of ideas to spark your creativity.

COMBINING WATERCOLOUR WITH LINE WORK

As noted earlier, all you need is a simple line drawing for the block – no colour or shading is required. However, to get to know your subjects and for the sheer joy of it, watercolour can be a wonderful complement to your work, providing a valuable colour reference too. Combining watercolour with drawing materials, such as artist-quality colour pencils, water-soluble crayons, watercolour pens and acrylic paint pens, means you have a great resource that could be transformed into prints. For coloured line work, artist-quality materials have great strength of pigmentation. There is a growing selection well worth experimenting with.

To improve your drawing, challenge yourself by making quick portraits of family members or whatever is around you. People on devices stay still enough to draw, even if their poses aren't particularly interesting. Not confining yourself to botanical imagery and using different media such as paint, pastel and charcoal could feed into your printing in unexpected ways. The practice could lead you in new directions. Using charcoal and watercolour are the results of my experiments. Explore to discover what you most enjoy.

Now that you have a design that excites you and that you think has the best chance of success as a print, the time has come to become acquainted with the lino itself.

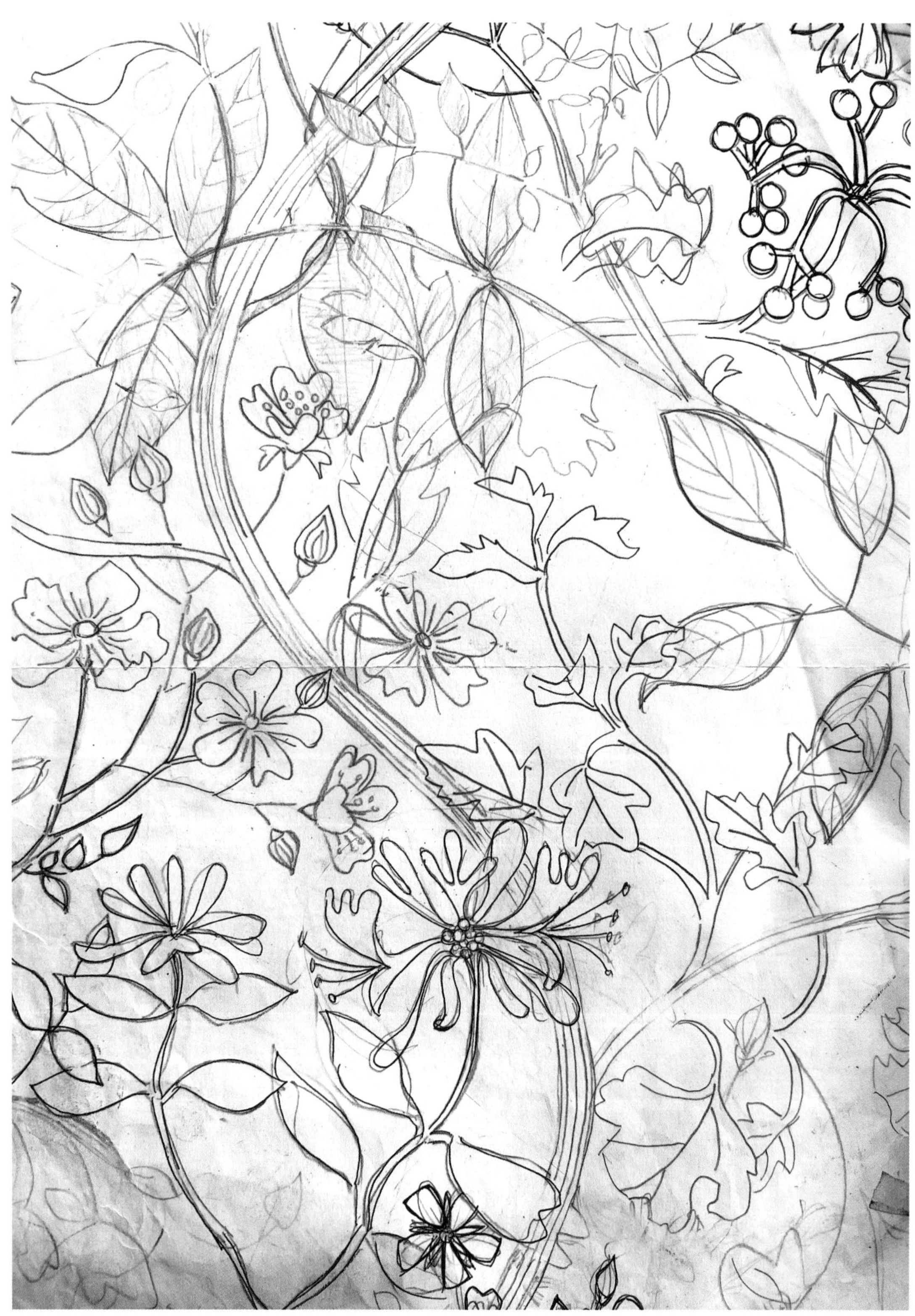

A detail of the line drawing design for *Hedgerow Tangle* pattern wallpaper.

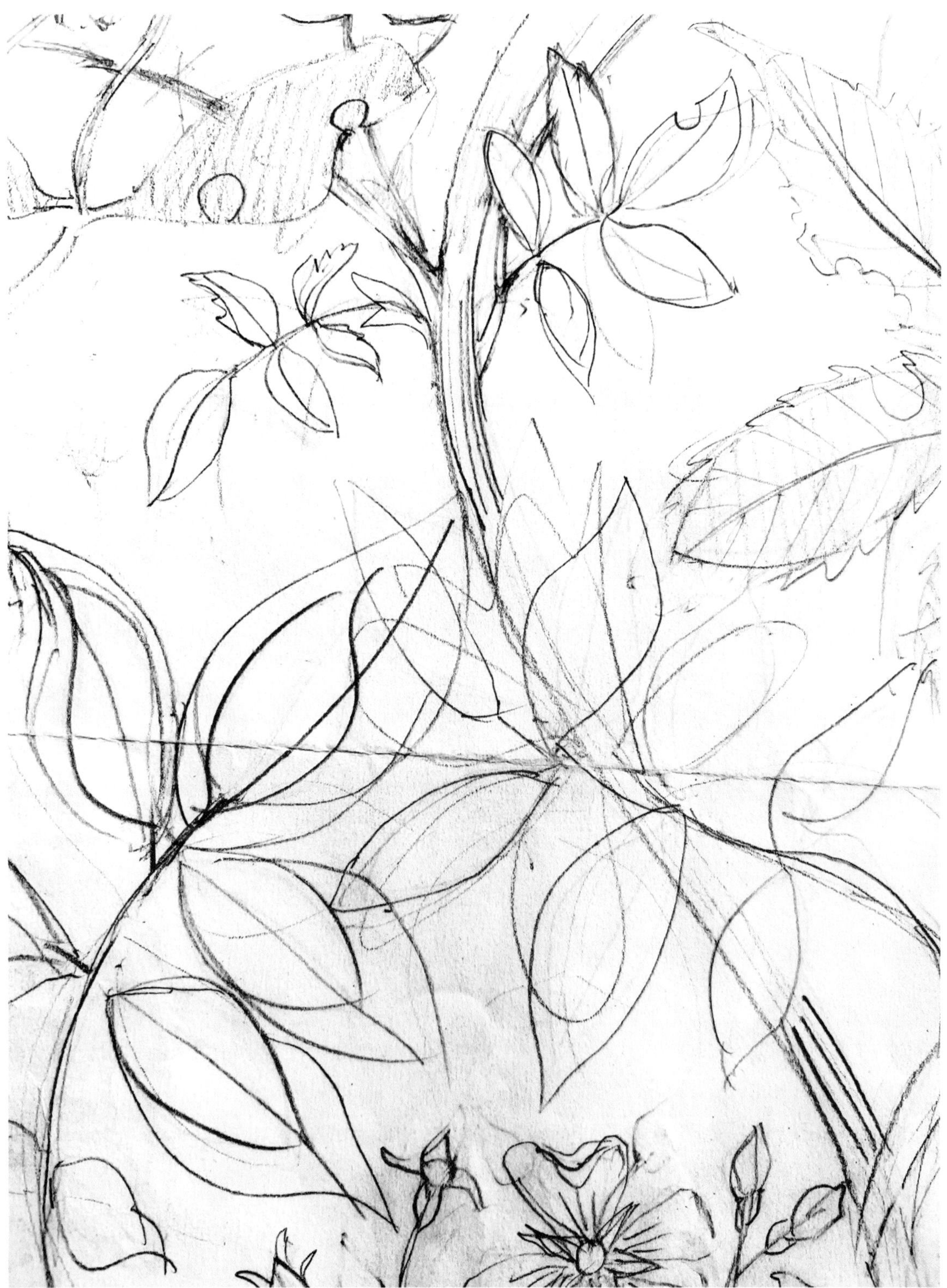

A detail of the drawing showing how the exact positions and sizes of elements are fluid as design takes shape. The drawing can be adapted according to how well the different elements relate to each other.

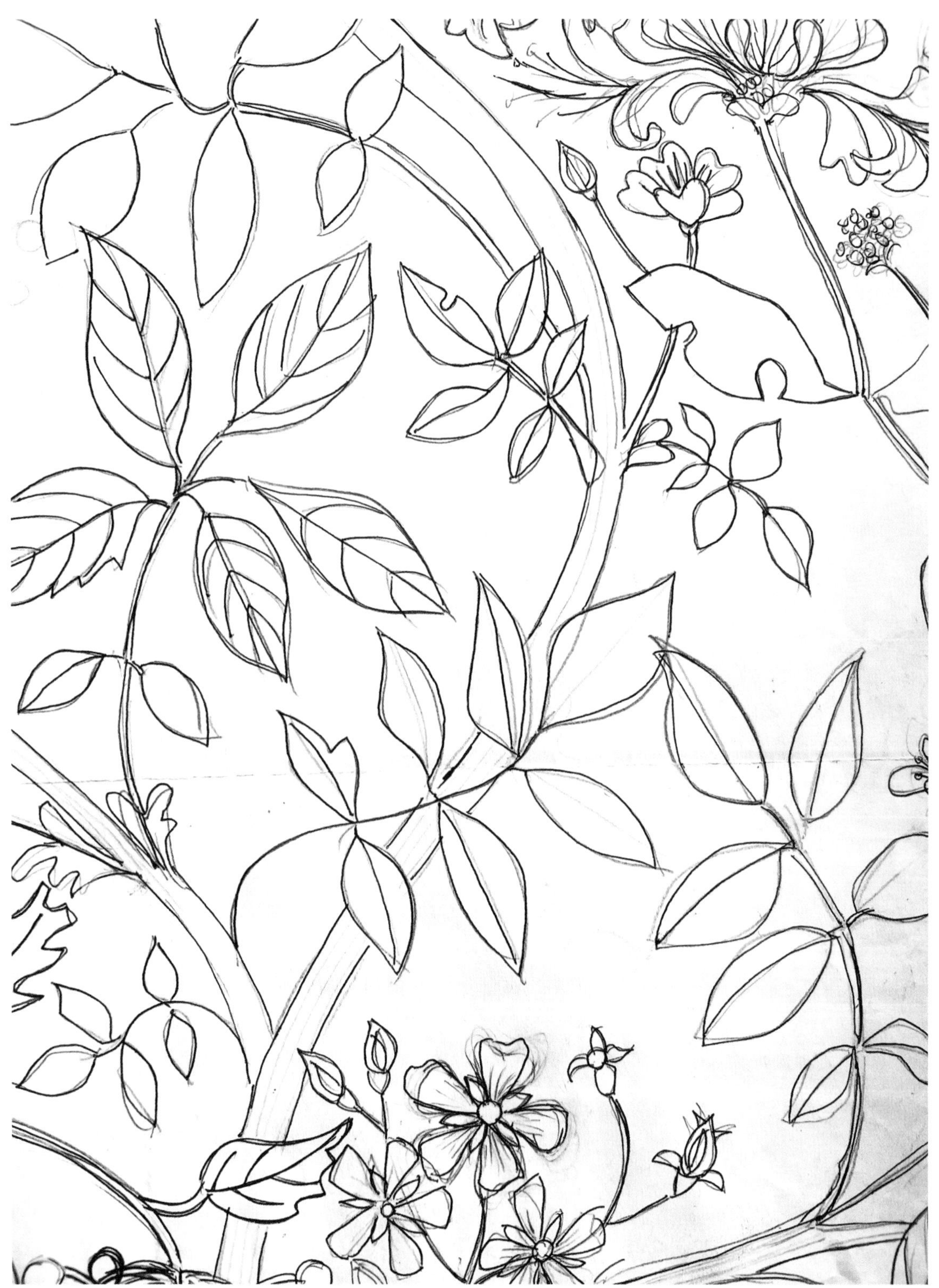

Once the sketched design is firmed up in pencil, it may help to draw over it in pen to define and clarify the lines.

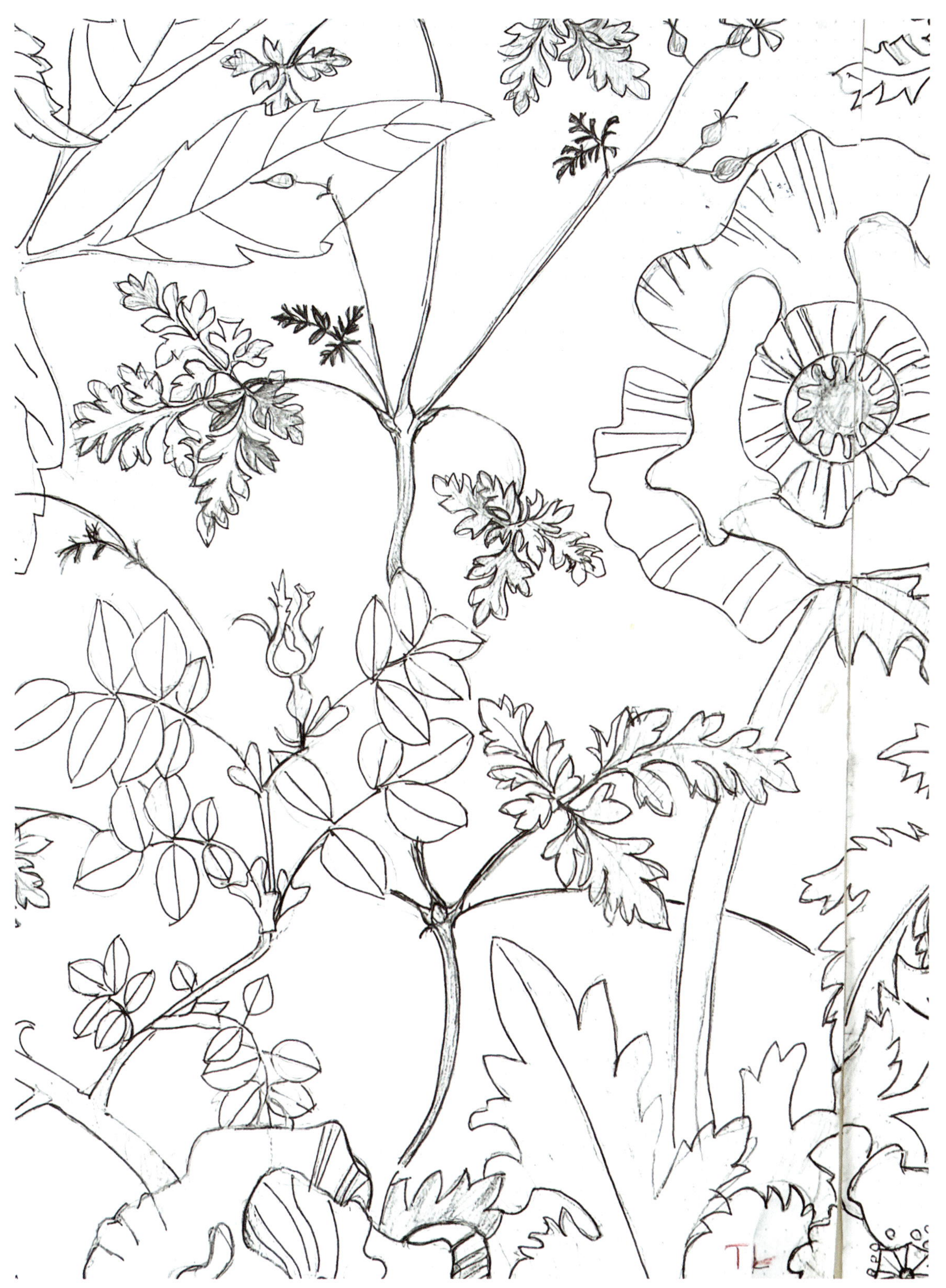

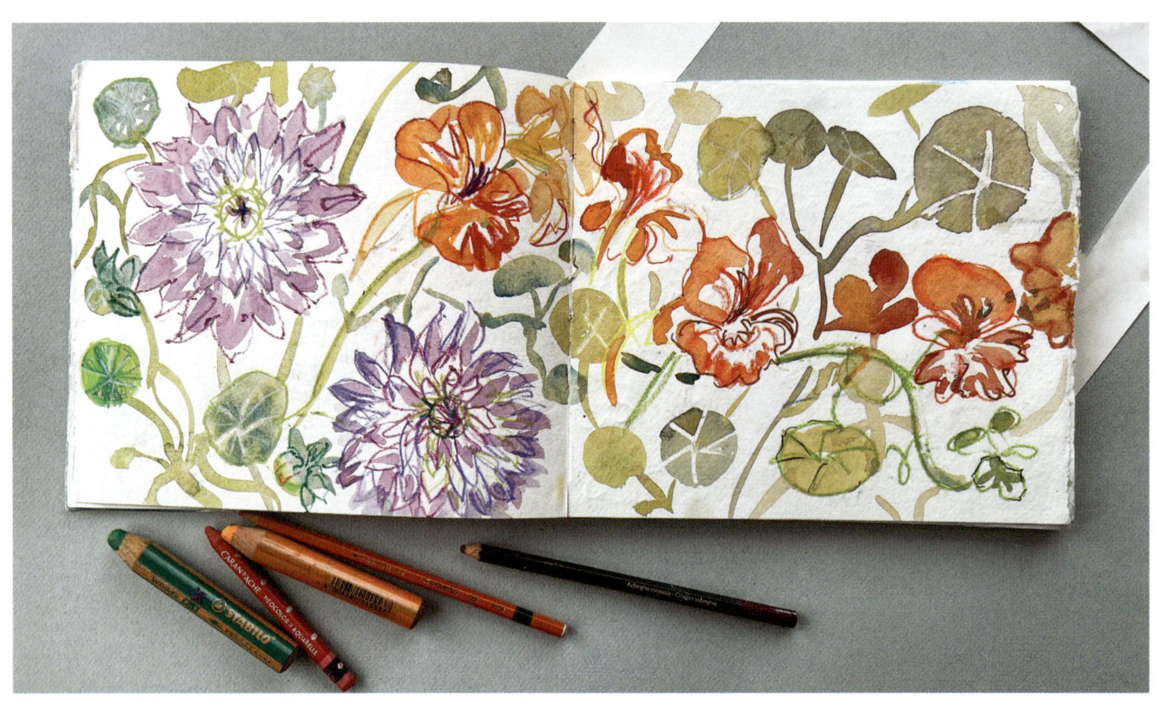

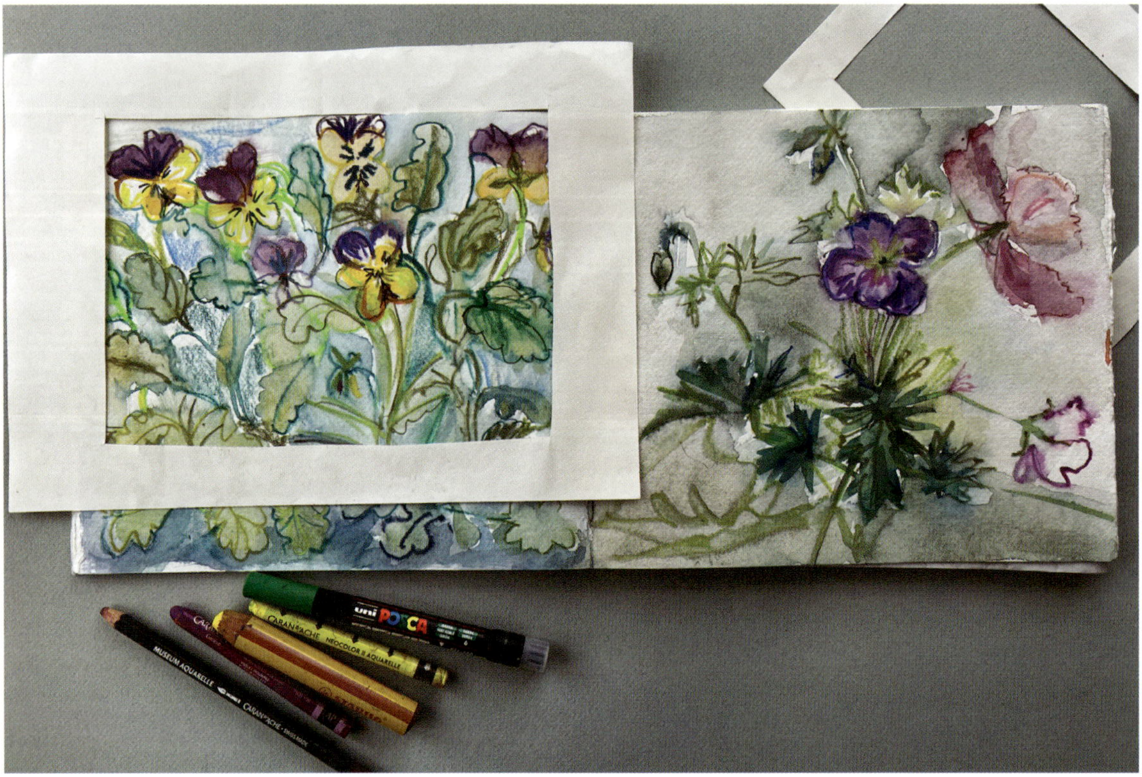

Sketchbook pages.

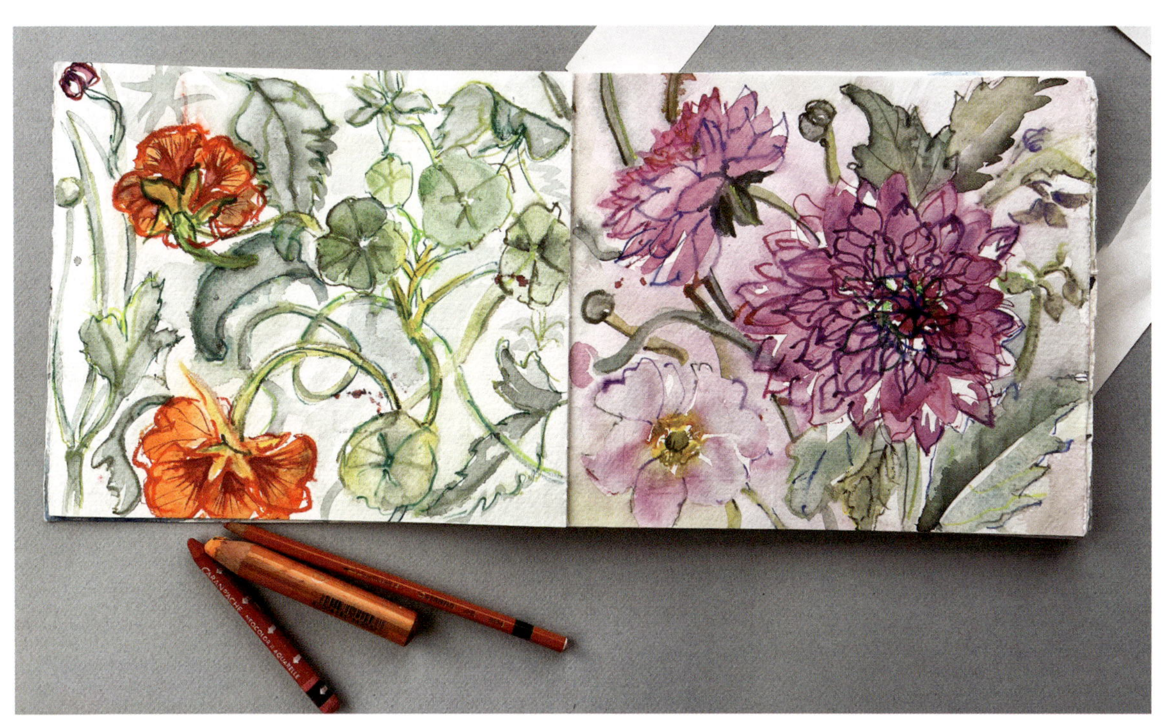

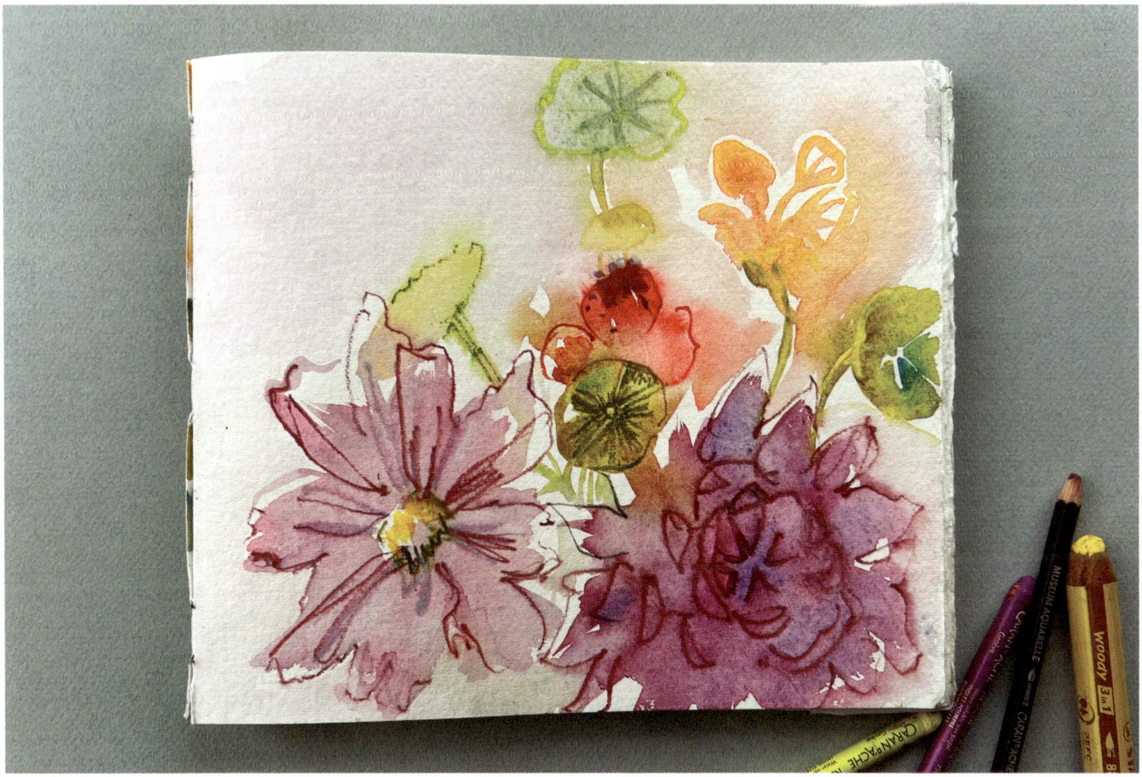

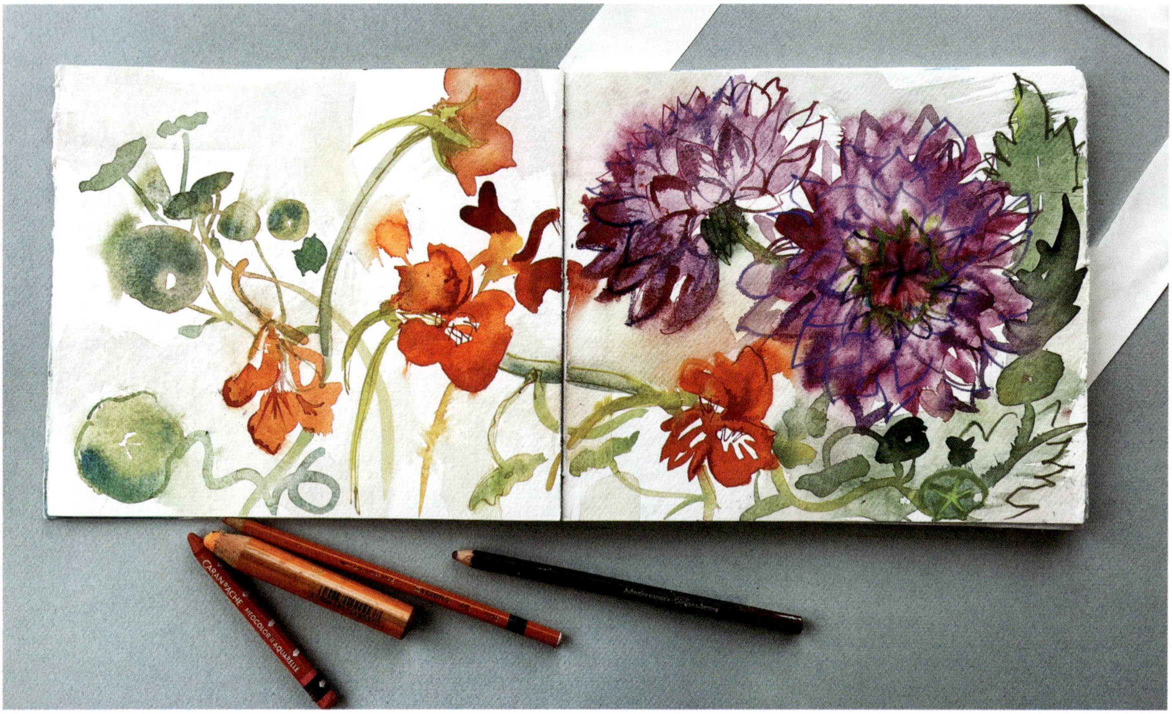

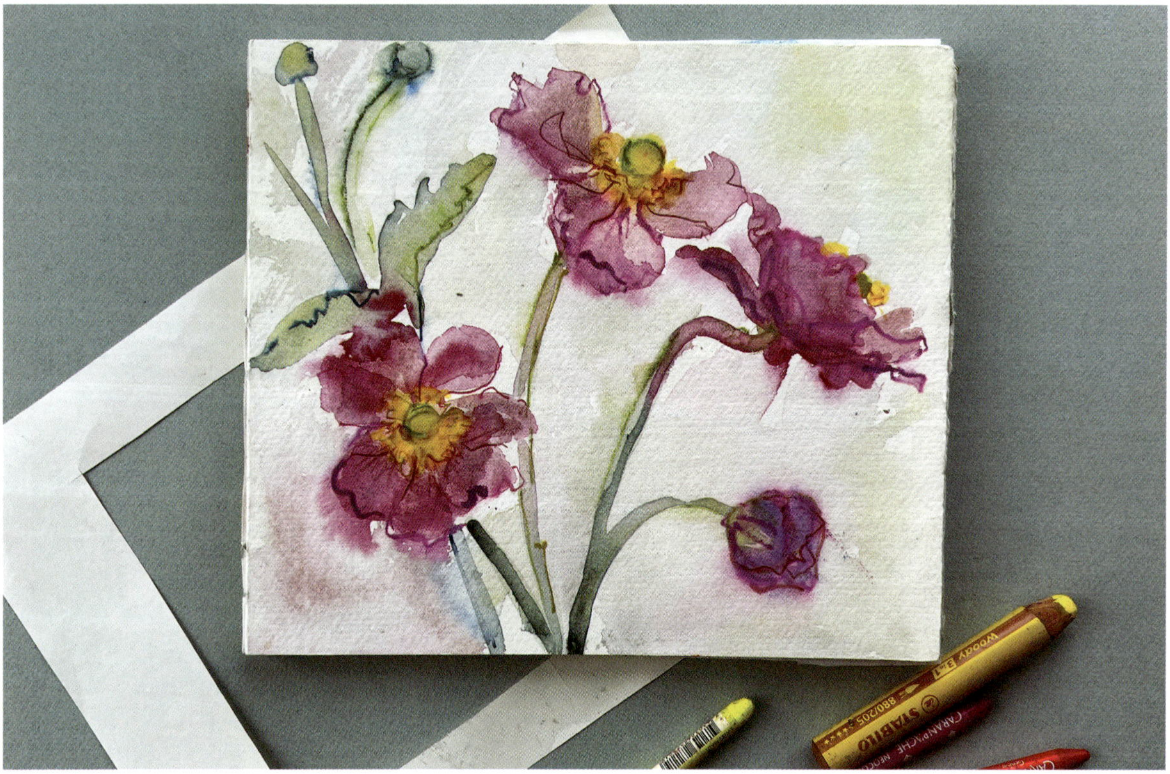

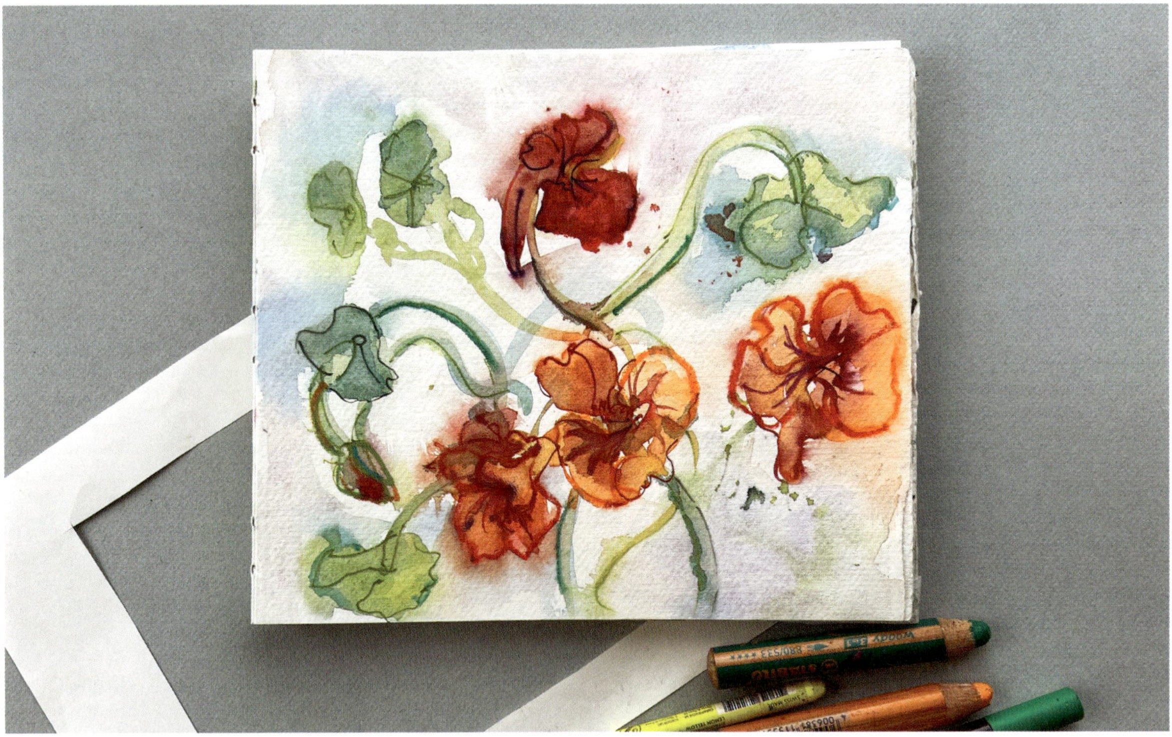

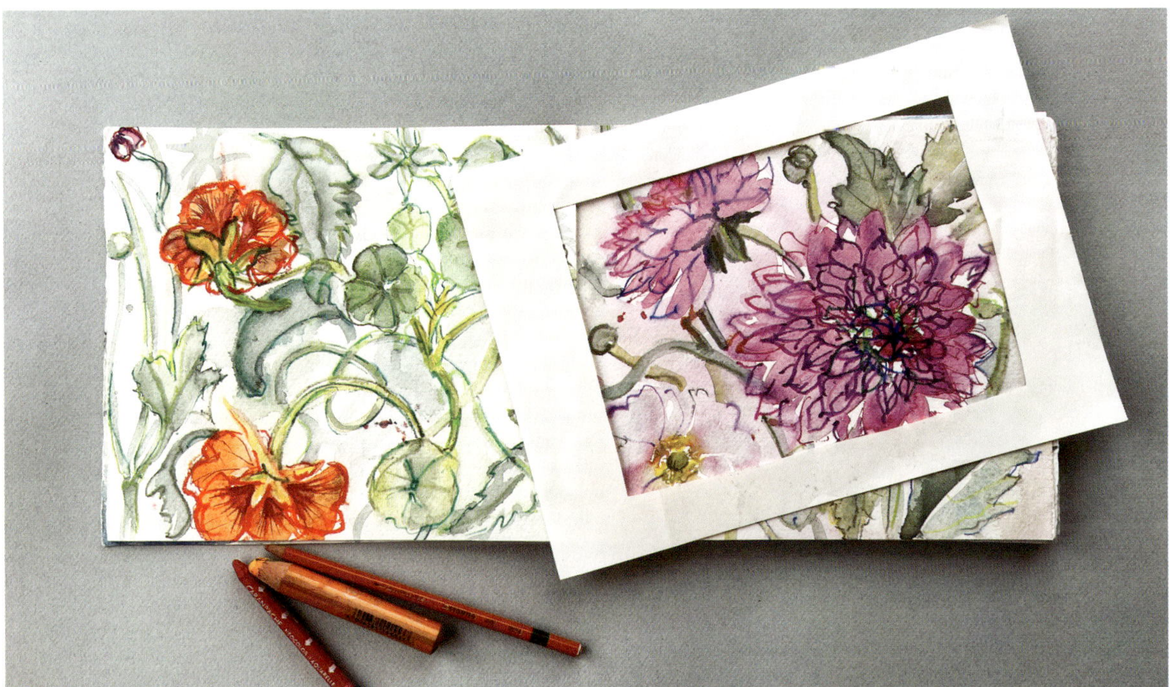

Trace over full-colour images to synthesise them, extracting the most important lines to transfer to the block. The paper frames are used to investigate potential compositions. The practice of keeping a colour sketchbook is exciting – a refreshing alternative to amassing simple pencil line drawings.

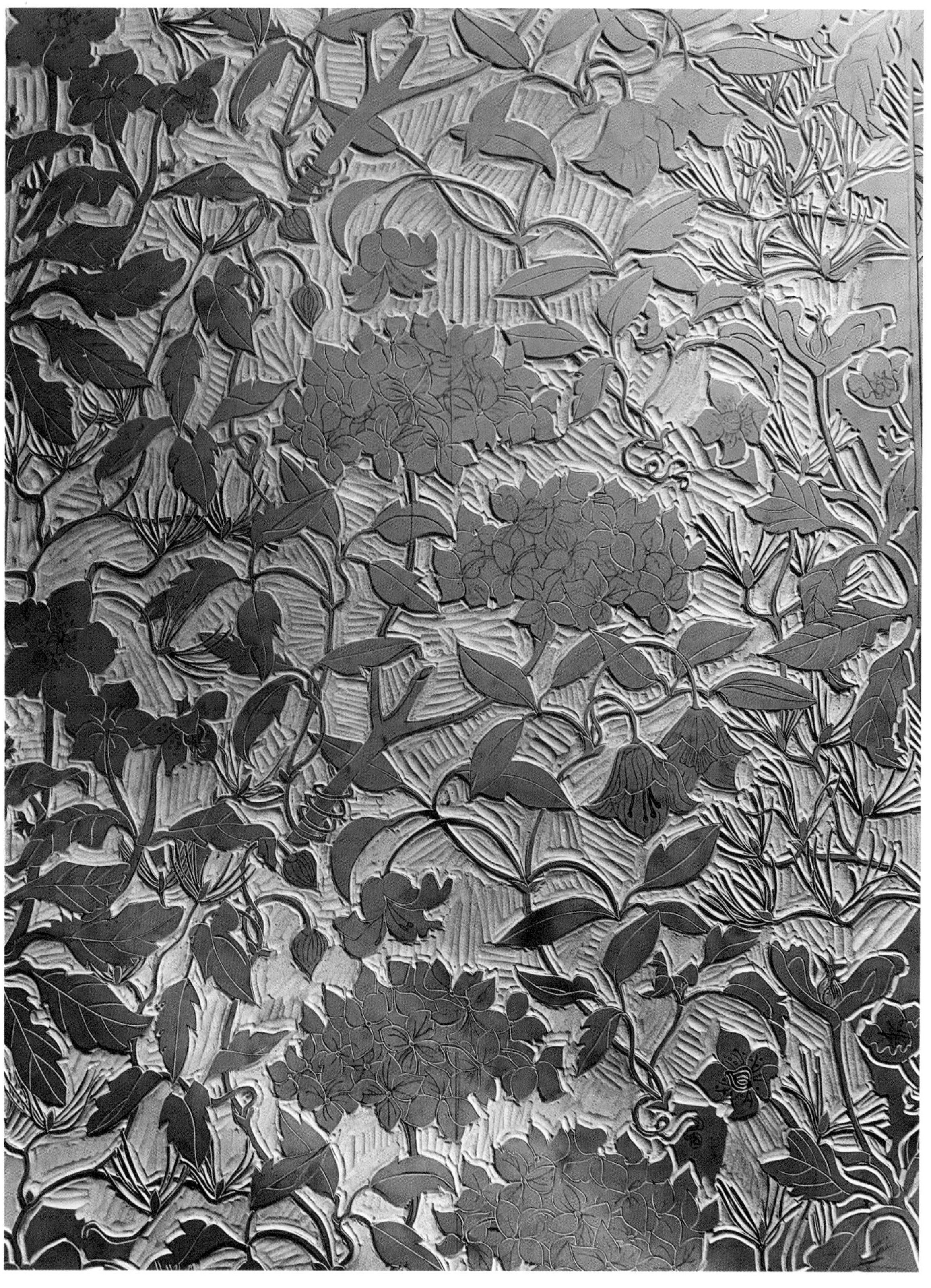

CHAPTER 3

CUTTING

With the help of the previous chapter, you now have a design on paper or tracing paper that you are – relatively speaking – happy with. Now we get to work with the lino itself, our chosen medium. In this chapter we will look in detail at how to copy the drawing onto the block and how to cut the lino so it is ready to ink up.

PREPARING YOUR DRAWING

Flipping Your Design

There is one extra step before you can copy your design onto your block. Bear in mind that a print is a mirror image of the block. For a print to be the same way round as the drawing, you will need to flip it over. To do this, trace the design onto tracing paper so that you can simply flip the tracing paper over before copying it onto the block.

A shortcut is to trace on the back of the cartridge paper. If you have a light box, use it. If not, turn the drawing over and attach it to a window with masking tape. The daylight allows you to see the drawing through the back of the paper.

This step is not always necessary. If you judge your design is just as handsome the other way round then you can save yourself the trouble. Decide this by turning your paper over and holding it up to the light so that you can see through it. Occasionally,

asymmetric or randomly placed botanical designs 'read' just as well either way round.

Placing the Drawing

Placement for a single-block print is not so crucial. As mentioned in the previous chapter on design, centre the drawing on the lino so that only after all the cutting out is complete you can trim away any excess. Trimming offcuts is quicker than gouging with tools, so this will save you extra work.

To trim lino, score the front surface and then fold the lino back on itself. This is best done in straight lines, from one edge to another, so it can be folded back. Run a Stanley knife along the fold to cut the hessian backing.

Note, later chapters will show you where to place your drawing on the block for a multi-block print, where precision placement for correct registration is required.

Demonstration: *Poppies* – The Cutting Technique

The following demonstration shows an A5-size detail from *Poppies*, a wallpaper design. The small section features large Virginia creeper leaves contrasting with the diminutive wild cranesbill. I have reversed this image so that it is easy for you to compare the print to the block; bear in mind that normally the block would print as a mirror image.

Part of the *Winter Garden* block, cut and ready to print.

Use carbon paper to copy the drawing. One simple method of transferring the drawing from paper to the block is to use carbon paper. 'Trace Down' is a brand of artist-quality graphite copy paper, although cheaper carbon papers work just as well.

1. Attach the flipped-over tracing or drawing securely with masking tape to a fresh piece of lino that you have cut to size.

2. Sandwich a sheet of carbon paper, inky side down, between the drawing and block.

3. Go over all the line drawing, using a sharp tipped pen or pencil. A pen helps to keep track of your progress to completion.

4. Once you have used your pen to go over all of your pencil marks you can remove the drawing and carbon paper. The surface of the block will now show the image ready to cut.

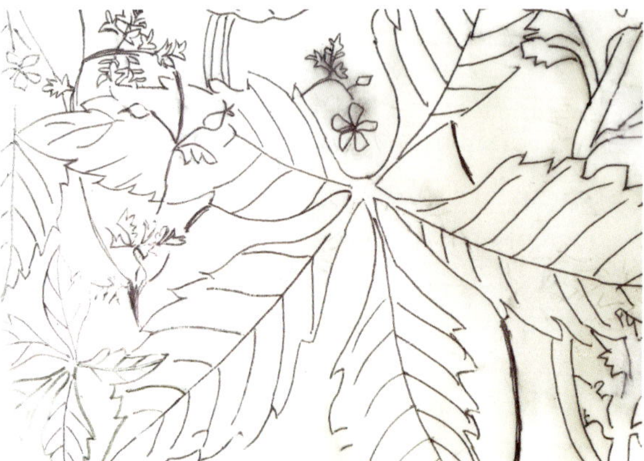

Turn the image over so it prints the same way round as your drawing. Remember that if you wish the print to be the same orientation as the drawing, you will need to transfer it to the block 'in reverse' – a simple matter of turning the tracing paper over.

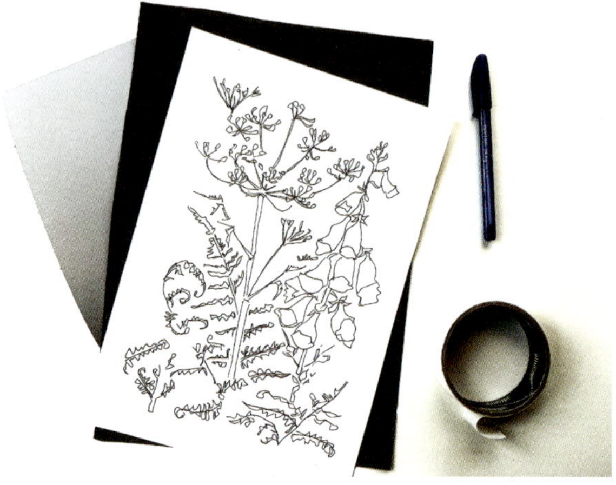

A sandwich of drawing, carbon paper and block.

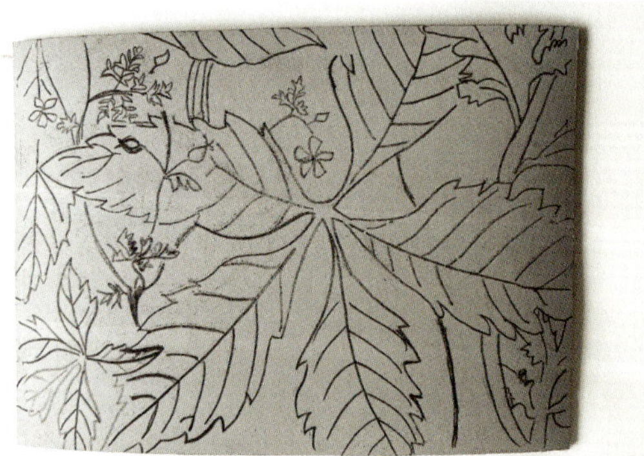

Notice that this block does not lie completely flat. It has been cut from a large roll and will need to be flattened under a weight such as a book. Just visible in the top left-hand corner is a stray piece of hessian string protruding from the backing mesh. Trim this before you ink the block to avoid a fuzzy mark on the edge of an otherwise perfect creation.

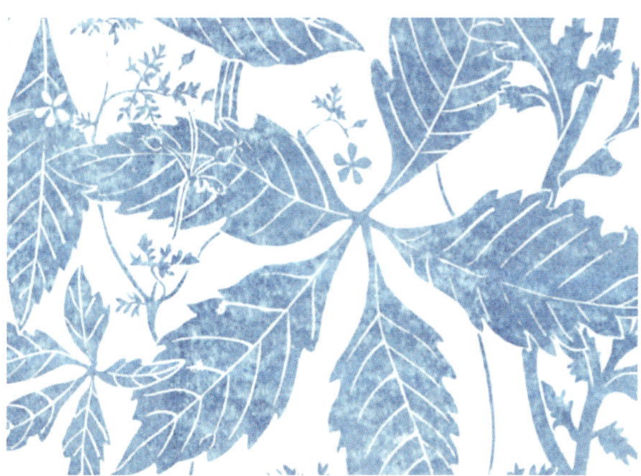

This image has been flipped so it is easier to compare it to the block. As described previously, the most important thing to understand is that the flat surface receives the ink. A roller is used to apply it. The areas that are cut away lie below the surface and therefore do not receive ink and expose the paper.

THE CUTTING PROCESS

You have now reached an exciting stage where you are ready to cut out your design. You will need three tools for this. I suggest you buy either an economy woodcarving set or three professional tools.

5. Begin with the fine V-shaped tool (Pfeil no.12) – the cutting edge is the point of the V. Use the index finger of your most dexterous hand (my right in the photograph) on the metal part of the tool and clasp your fingers around it. Put the index finger of your free hand in front of the index finger of your working hand, close to the tip of the blade, to help in guiding and controlling the tool by pressing down on it.

You need to be able to constantly adjust the angle of the lino to make cutting it comfortable. The other fingers of the helping hand are gripping the lino, and, importantly, turning it as cutting proceeds. (A bench hook device for keeping lino still is not needed.) The hessian backing prevents unwanted slippage.

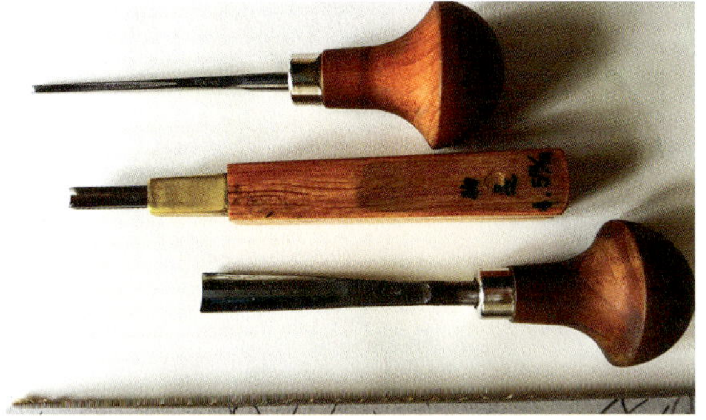

The array of different shapes and sizes can be confusing when it comes to buying tools. All of the prints in this book can be made with just three artist-quality tools: Pfeil fine V tool no. 12, 1mm (912) (top); Komasuki 4.5mm or Pfeil large U-shaped tool, 5mm (909) (middle); and the clearing tool, Pfeil large shallow gouge no.7, 10mm (908) (bottom).

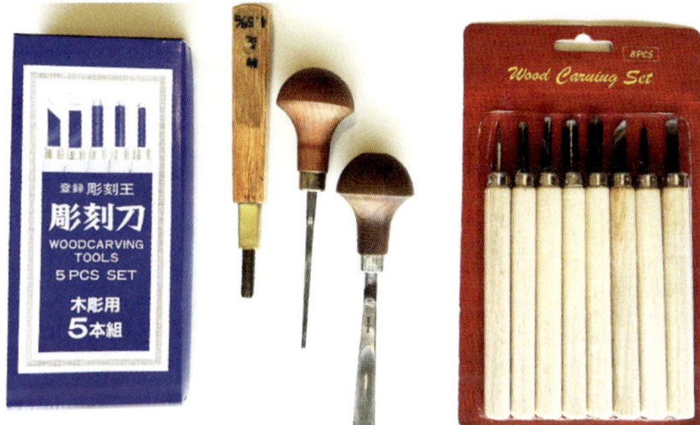

The three artist-quality tools alongside cheaper alternatives.

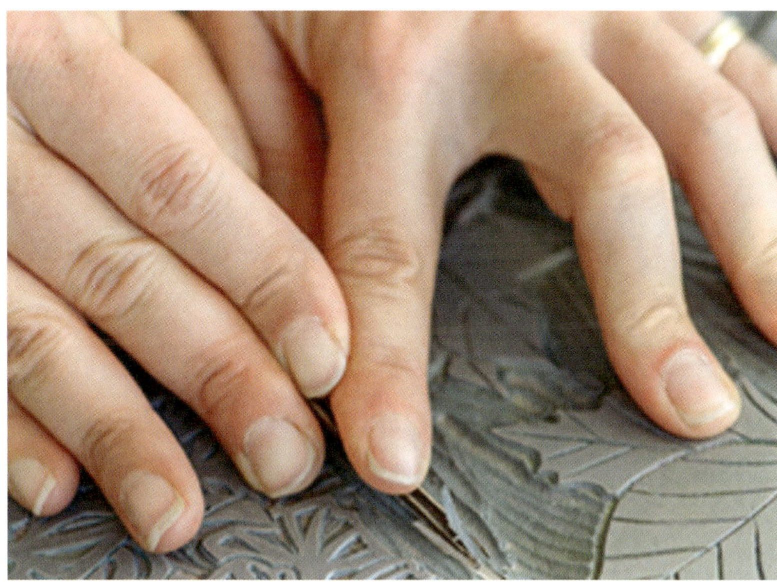

The Swiss-made Pfeil mushroom tools have long metal blades. The economy, pencil-type cutters have only a short length of metal to accommodate both fingers.

6. The fine V-shaped tool is first tool you will work with on your block. It is your workhorse, so get well acquainted before moving on to the other tools. Use it to outline all shapes. When everything is outlined, use the same tool to take out the fine lines within your shapes, such as the veins of the leaf.

7. When using the fine V-shaped tool, you will usually remove the pencil line itself, rather than working to one side of it, but there is one exception.

When cutting a slender stem, there is a danger of removing too much and taking out lino that is wanted. To print a stem, a slither of lino must remain intact. In this case, it is wise to make your cuts either side of your pencil lines.

TAKE CARE

When the helping hand is not on the metal part of the tool, keep it out of harm's way, behind the working hand, to avoid cutting yourself.

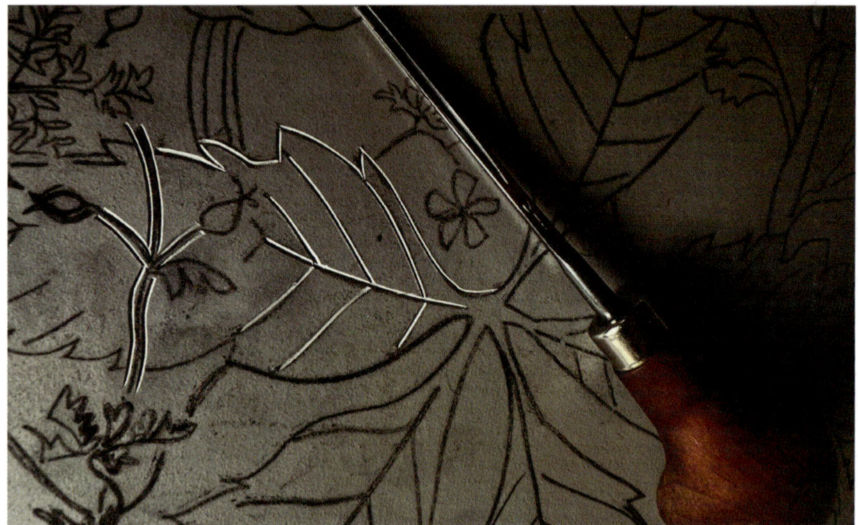

The white areas of the image show the cuts the fine V tool makes. A single pencil line on the drawing to depict a stem or stamen may be too fine to cut, but here the stem is of sufficient width to use the tool either side of it.

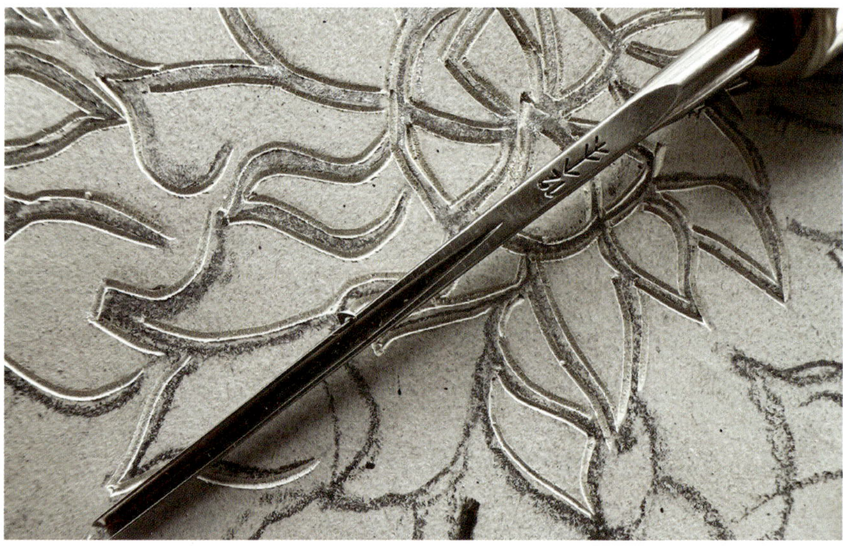

Begin by going around all of the design with the fine V tool. As a rule, follow the pencil line, removing it as you go. However, when cutting either side of slim shapes be careful. Allow yourself a margin and run the tool to one side of the pencil line instead, that way you won't remove it altogether.

8. Once everything is cut with the fine tool, switch to the U-shaped gouge Komasuki, 4.5mm or Pfeil large U-shaped tool, 5mm (909) and outline where the shapes meet the background. This creates a wider channel from which the clearing tool can be worked without damaging your design. Follow with the U-shaped tool to one side of the fine grooves you've already made.

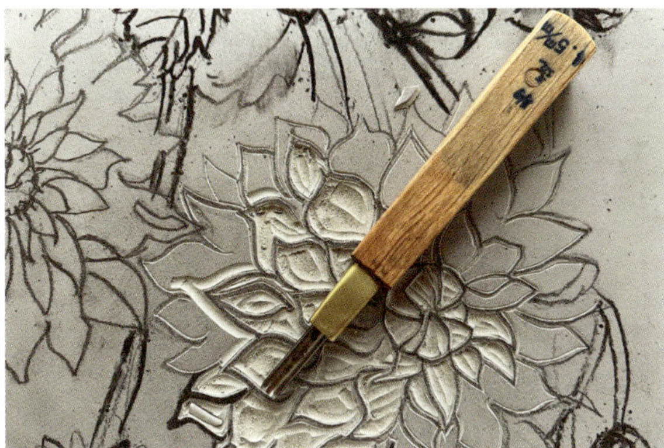

The U-shaped gouge–Komasuki, 4.5mm, or Pfeil large U-shaped tool, 5mm (909)–makes a wider channel for protecting shapes and is also useful for removing small internal areas.

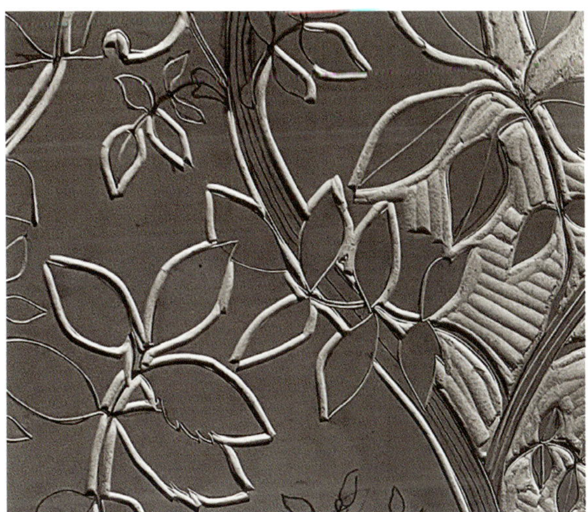

Select the right tool for the job. Start with the fine V-shaped tool going round all shapes and 'internal' fine line details. Next, 'protect' the outside of the shapes with a wider U-shaped gouge. The leaf and the striped side shoot (bottom right) show the marks made by the fine V-shaped tool. Finally, the wide, shallow clearing tool removes the background with cuts that are at right angles to the shapes in relief, seen here as a sets of short parallel lines.

9. Finally remove all background areas with the wide, shallow clearing gouge tool to expose the paper. Work this tool at right angles, starting in the U-shaped grooves and working outwards, away from them. Avoid strain when using this tool and do not try to work it in one continuous motion; it is better to make a set of short parallel cuts that break off easily with the thumb of the free hand.

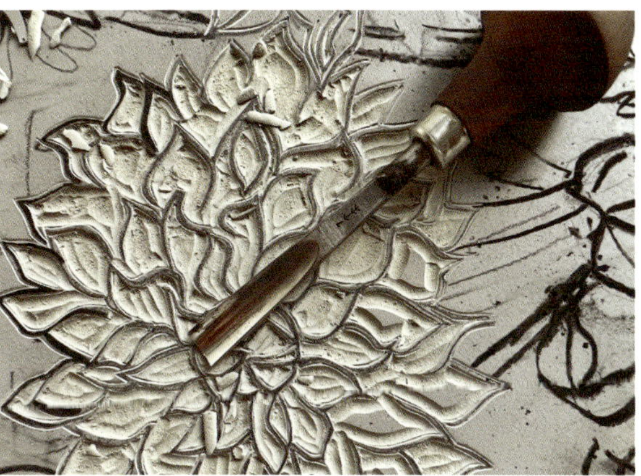

Cut away the areas that will not print with the Pfeil large shallow gouge no.7, 10mm (908).

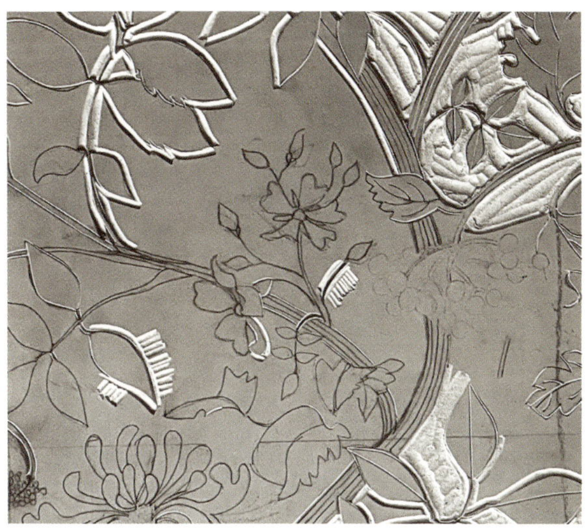

Compare the different marks made with the three types of tool. Notice how the wide, shallow tool removes the background with cuts that are at right angles to the shapes in relief, seen here as sets of short parallel lines.

CUTTING TIPS

Practice First

Before you tackle your design, get yourself a spare piece of lino so that you can draw a few leaf and stem shapes to practice on. Practice on an A5 piece, as blocks any smaller than this are more difficult to cut. You need space for both hands to hold it firm while you work.

Cut away from the body at a 45-degree angle. Avoid sticking your elbow out to cut towards the body, which is awkward, uncomfortable and will

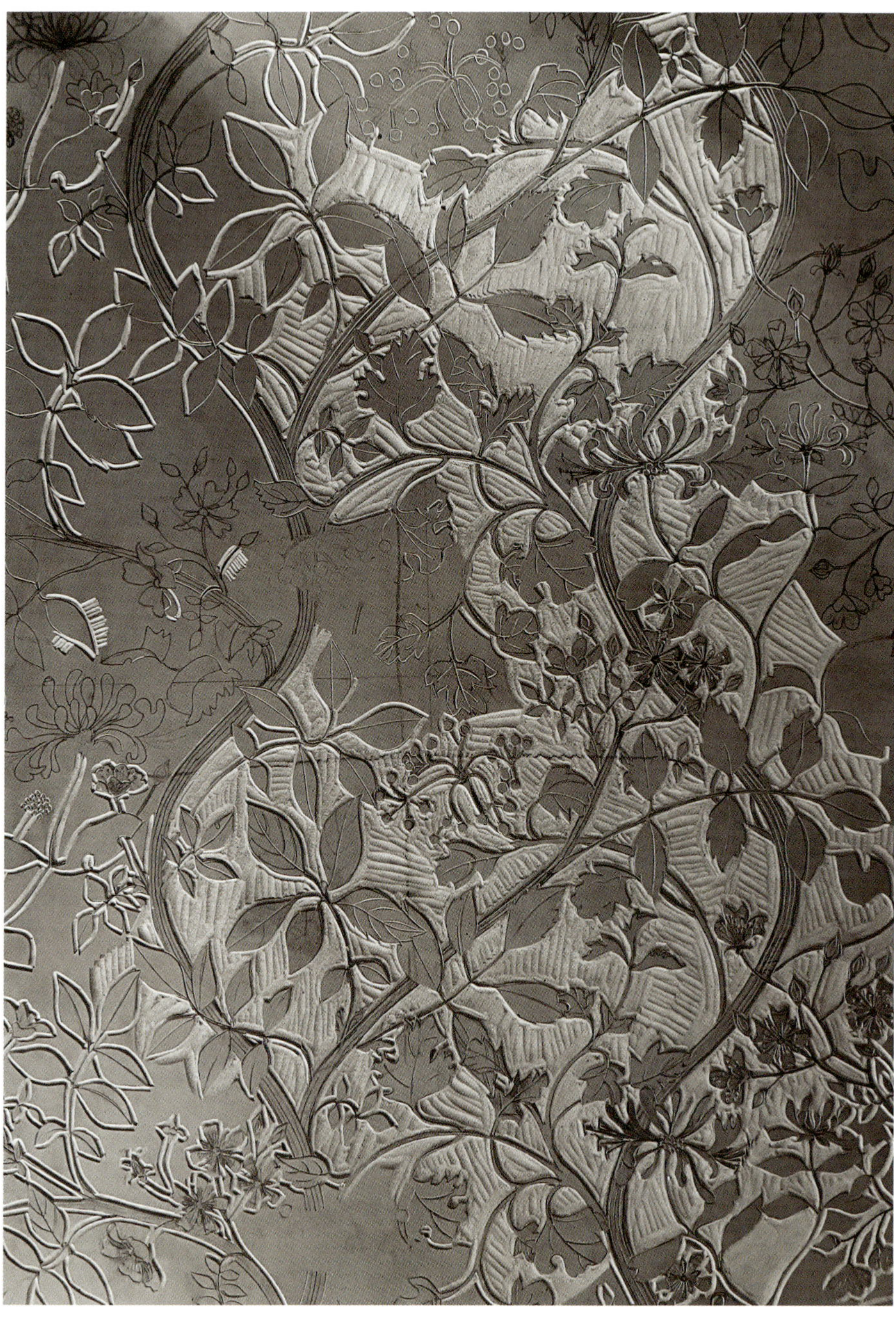

The half-finished block for *Hedgerow Tangle*. (For the finished print, *see* Chapter 7.)

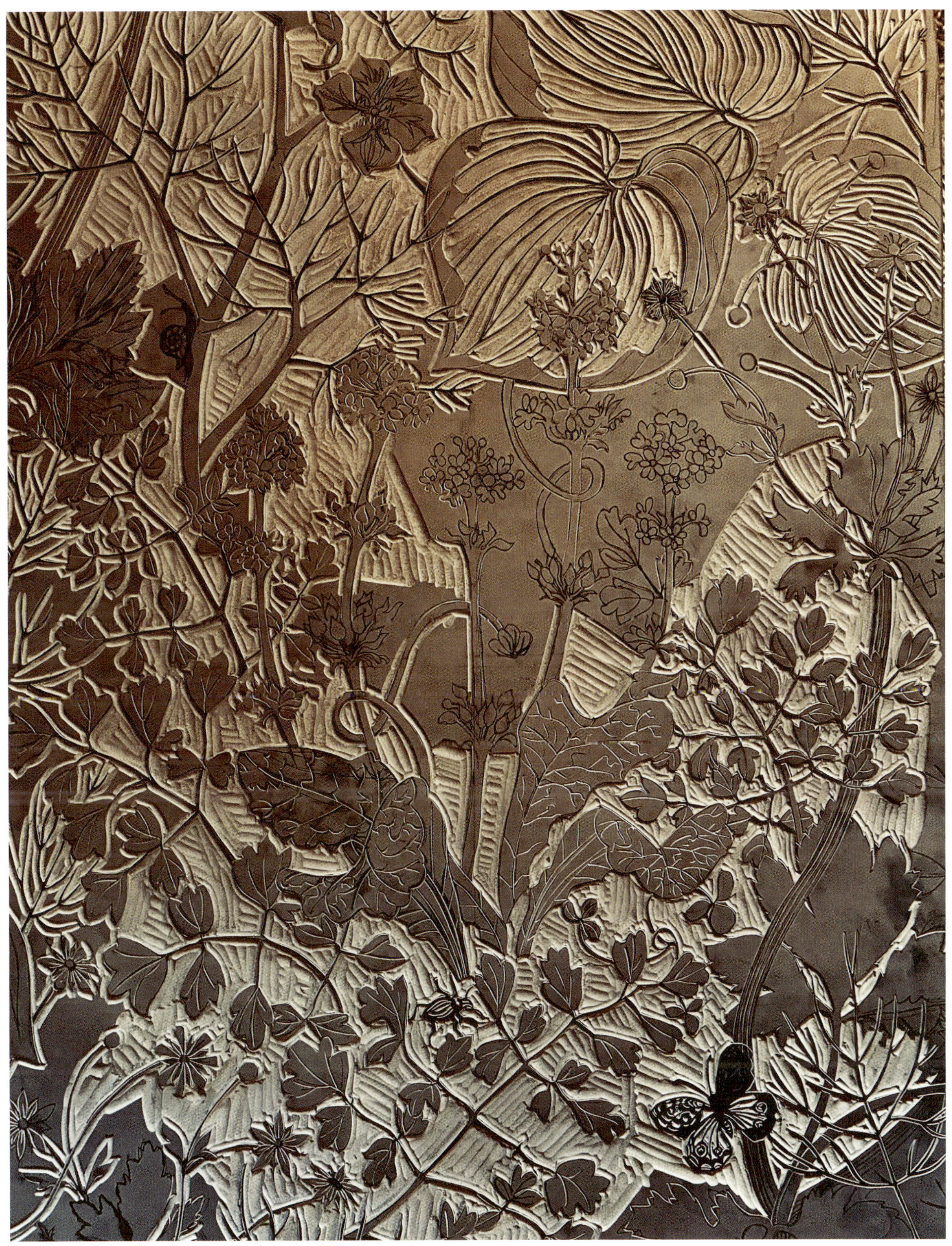

The block for *Bog Primrose*. For the finished print, *see* Chapter 7.

soon cause tension. It is best to keep the lino moving instead, continually adjusting it with your fingertips as you progress along a curve or as the angles change in your design. I have found a swivel office chair to be useful as I can adjust the position of my body. The Japanese method of holding tools uses the thumb of the helping hand to apply pressure to the top of the tool. I find this especially useful for gouging out the background, relieving extra pressure from the shoulders.

How Deep is Deep Enough?

Keep the angle of the tools shallow; it is not necessary to go very deep. Once you can make confident marks,

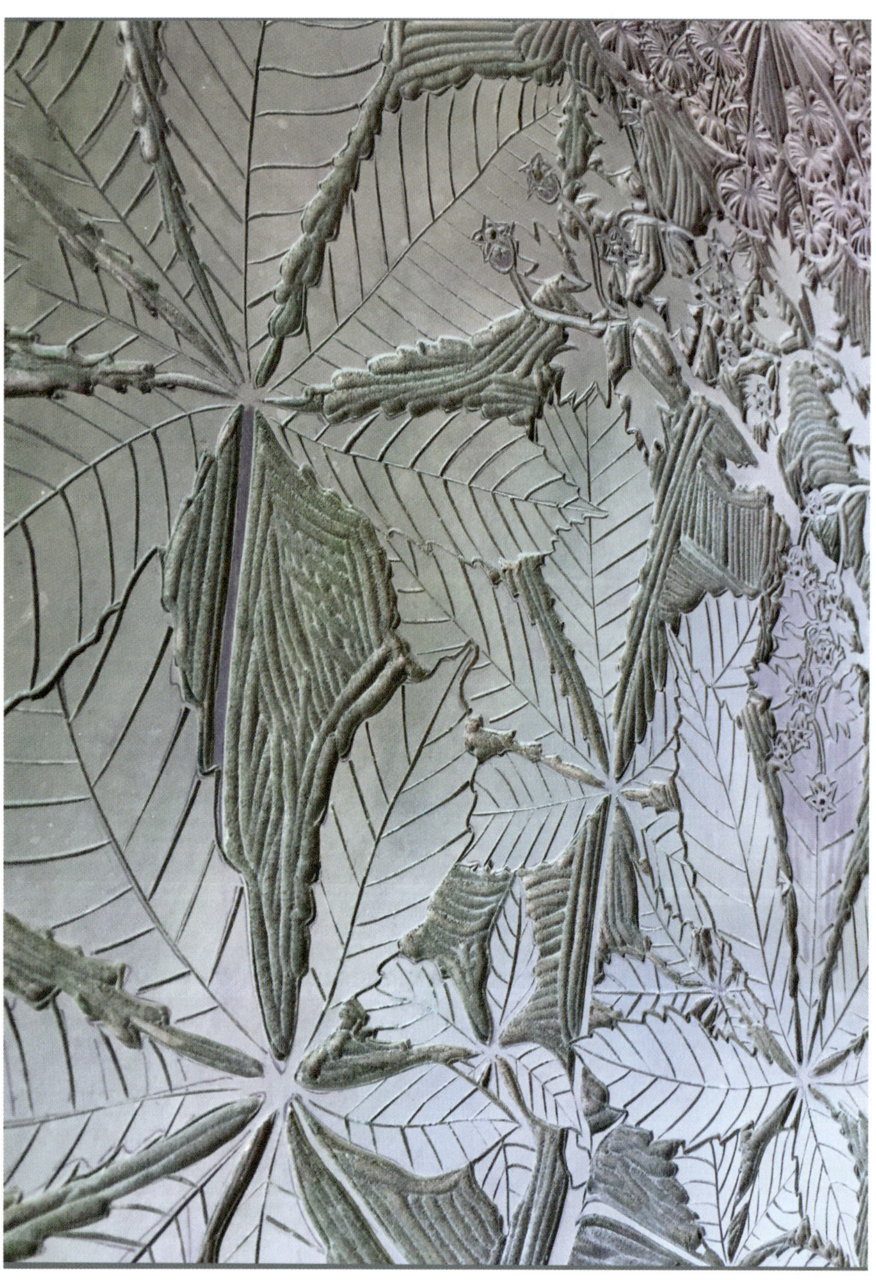

Close-up detail of the block for *Horse Chestnut*.

return to the fine V-shaped tool to cut any remaining details inside shapes. These print as fine white lines; the veins of leaves or edges of petals, for example.

The cutting process can be therapeutic, especially if you give yourself plenty of time. It is easy to scrunch your shoulders and cause tension, so from time to time relax. Keep your feet firmly on the floor.

Cutting lino takes time to complete, though it is quite addictive and hard to put down! In Japan, with its time-honoured tradition of wood block printing, it is conventional for one artisan master on take on the cutting while another undertakes the printing part. Apprenticeships last decades!

What If I Make a Mistake with the Tool?

A common fear is making a mistake with the tool by slipping or taking out something you intended to keep in. Be assured that this usually does not matter. It can be your secret. After all, only *you* can compare the finished print with your original design.

A mistake could be more obvious on a print made with a coloured background, such as those described in Chapter 5. Go carefully and keep your tools sharp – sharp tools are less likely to slip. If the tool does slip and cut into the background, it will be visible but not disastrous. Refer to your original drawing frequently when cutting so that you don't remove a crucial detail by mistake.

FINAL CHECKS

When you have finished all of the cutting, check that some of the ridges in the non-printed areas are not too prominent or they will print. If ridges look prominent, go over a few again with the background-removing tool.

Some directional marks can look dynamic in these background areas. Many artists intentionally include them; Mark Heard's work is an example. Depending on the design, a clean look might be appropriate.

Before you start to roll on ink, hold up your lino block, wave it around and bash it a few times, like banging a drum, so that any crumbs will fall out and be clear of your block when you come to print. Clear the working area so it is completely free of clutter and crumbs. Stray crumbs that appear harmless can be scourge later on. It is surprising how the tiniest crumb prints in a very obvious way. (A flaw or an indication of the hand-printed nature of the work, depending on your view.)

After a well-deserved rest, you are ready to move onto the fun and excitement that comes with playing with colour. Printing your masterpiece is positively a high-octane affair, so take a celebratory cup of tea at the very least.

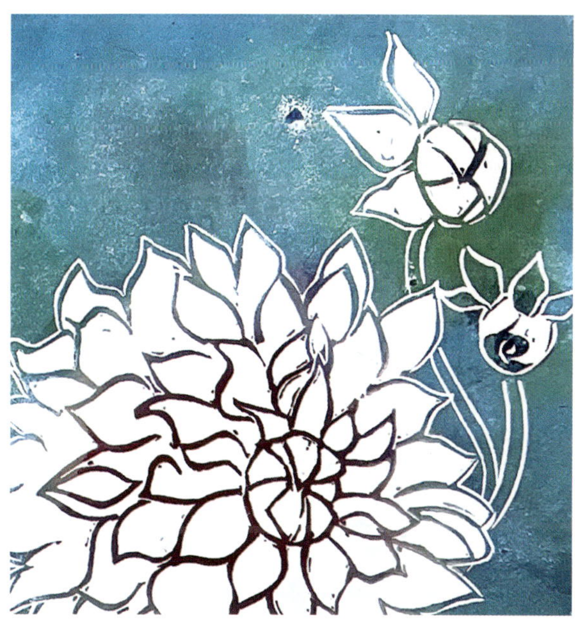

When a crumb of lino gets stuck in the ink, it will print as an obvious 'flaw' because of the white halo of paper around it. This shows the handmade nature of the work.

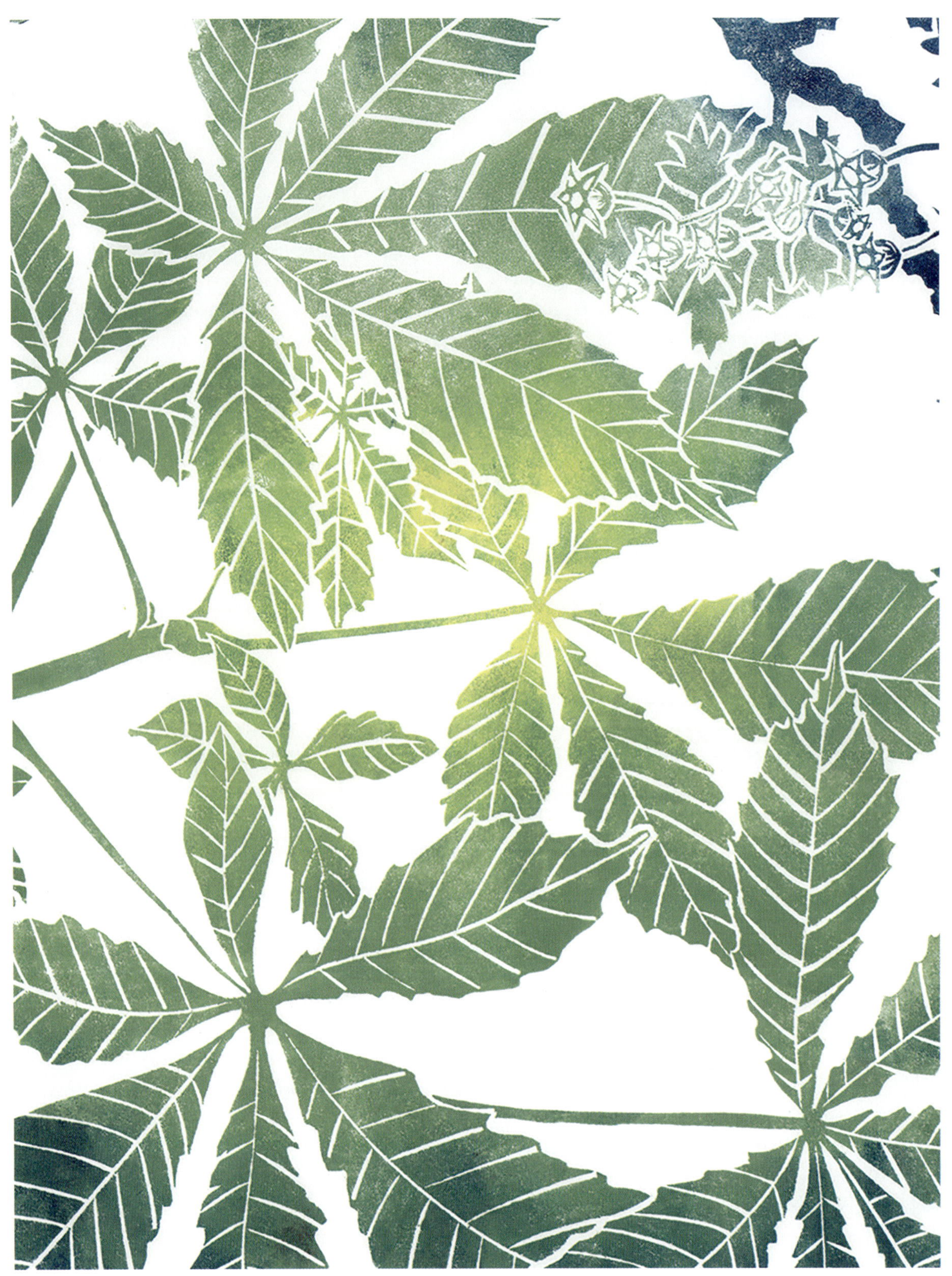

CHAPTER 4

INKING

Now we reach a thrilling moment. The design has been cut and the lino is ready to be brought to life with colour. Before we cover that process, let's look at how to choose and mix ink to create the perfect palette to work with. Oil-based ink is stiff and sticky, like treacle, so it is quite difficult to work with and takes some getting used to.

All the prints in this book are made using oil-based ink (*see* Chapter 1 for recommended brands), which must be cleaned with white spirit. In its favour, the 'colour payoff' is unlike any other sort of ink. Oil-based ink is the best for the technique we are using; applying many colours, all in one go, to the block.

You will need a basic set of six inks:

- Three primary colours: red, yellow and blue
- Black
- White
- Colourless extender (sometimes called tinting medium)

This set is the minimum number of inks you need – all colours of the rainbow can be mixed from just these six. You can add to your set as you become more familiar with colour mixing.

It can be tricky to decide from the vast array of colours available. From each hue, choose a tone that sits in the middle of the range; a tone that is neither on the cool nor the warm side. That way, from each of the three primary colours, you will be able to mix the broadest range of colours. For example, when picking a red, go for a true red rather than a crimson or an orangey red. From the Intaglio Printmaker range, choose Poppy Red, Primrose Yellow and Ultramarine, for example.

MIXING INKS ON THE PALETTE

Ink is mixed on a palette, which needs to be quite large to accommodate everything. You can use a tile, a mirror, toughened glass or a thick piece of Perspex. I often use a tabletop, which I cover with strong sticky-backed plastic. This saves me having to clean the palette, as the self-adhesive plastic sheet can be peeled off and thrown away at the end of its use.

Blending the colours is one of the beauties of this technique. Each print becomes unique and part of a so-called 'varied edition'.

Preparing the Rollers

Prepare one roller per colour, ready to use on the block. Squeeze out the ink in a row along the top. Make another row below this of ready-mixed colour, each diluted with plenty of extender. Use a palette knife, or improvise to save expense with half pieces of old plastic credit card, to help you.

Dip a roller into one of the wells of colour you have mixed. Stretch it out by rolling back and forth in the space closest to you. Do this until each one is evenly coated with ink and within easy reach.

For convenience and speed, I often touch the rollers straight into the pigment, without the need of an extra implement such as a palette knife, and proceed to stretch it out on the palette to coat the roller evenly, then apply it.

Making Tints

To start to understand colour mixing with inks, you will need to make tints with them. Making a tint simply means mixing with white. With the addition of white, a colour appears paler but it will also change the colour from translucent to opaque. If a translucent tint is required, add extender to tint you have made. This 'waters down' its opacity, giving off a watercolour effect.

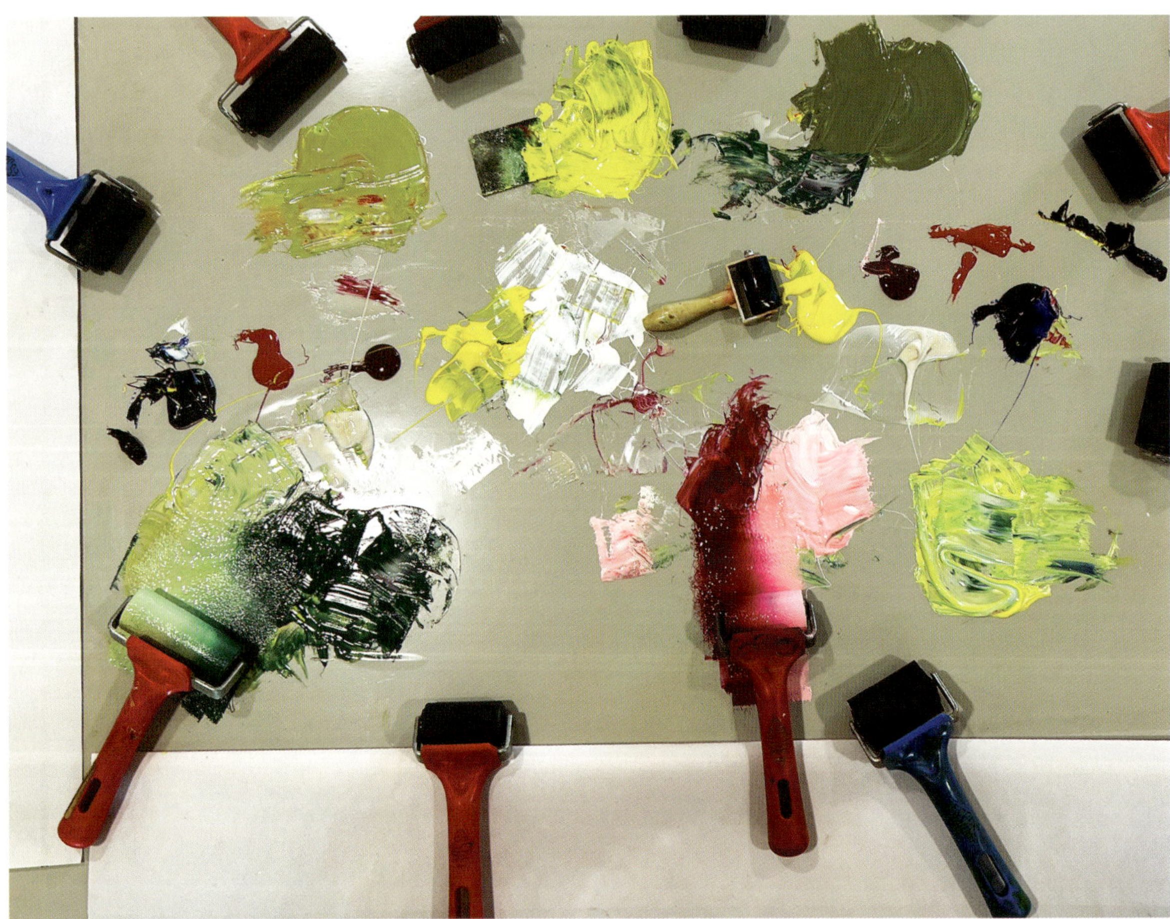

A palette with ink rollers prepared from wells of pre-mixed colours. Notice the top row of ink straight out of the tubes. On the left, the amount of white ink and the colourless extender is more generous. From left to right: a warm and cool yellow, a warm and cool red (crimson) and warm and cold blues are laid out. The rollers are prepared, ready to use with a two-tone pink/crimson, a two-tone yellow/red, a plain blue and a plain green.

Yellow is usually an opaque colour, appearing already somewhat tinted with white. Most other pigments are translucent; they appear very dark straight out of the tube.

From the thick reservoir of colour mixed on the palette, it is sometimes difficult to judge how it will appear on the print. This is especially true when there is not much white in a colour or if it is very concentrated. (If the palette itself is not white, this adds to the difficulty.) To judge colour mixes accurately, take a gloved finger and smear a thin stripe of ink onto a piece of paper to give you a better idea of what a thin layer of ink will look. Do this for all your mixes to ascertain how well they will sit together in the final print. You can then make adjustments accordingly.

How to Use Extender

You may be wondering why you need extender or a tinting medium. This colourless binder is non-pigmented and identical in make up to the base of regular, coloured inks. Some colours, such as Ultramarine Blue, are stiffer than others and adding extender makes the inks easier to roll out. Adding up to 30 or 40 per cent extender to your inks will loosen them. Extender also speeds up drying.

Most interestingly, extender can be used to create a more translucent watercolour effect to your mixes. The more you use, the more translucent the ink layer will become so that, in effect, you can see the paper through the ink. Later, when you come to explore multi-block printing, this translucent quality can be exploited when two layers of ink are printed one on top of the other. The more opaque bottom layer will remain visible after a translucent layer of ink is applied over the top. The uppermost translucent layer alters the appearance of the base colour, resulting in a new colour effect (*see* Chapter 5).

When making tints for pale tones, always use much more white than you might expect; just a dab of coloured ink will achieve the colour. You can add but you can't take away. This saves wasting ink, as you will find that the pigments are strong. If you add too much colour at the outset, the only remedy is to squeeze out extra white ink – more than you need – to return to the colour you were aiming for.

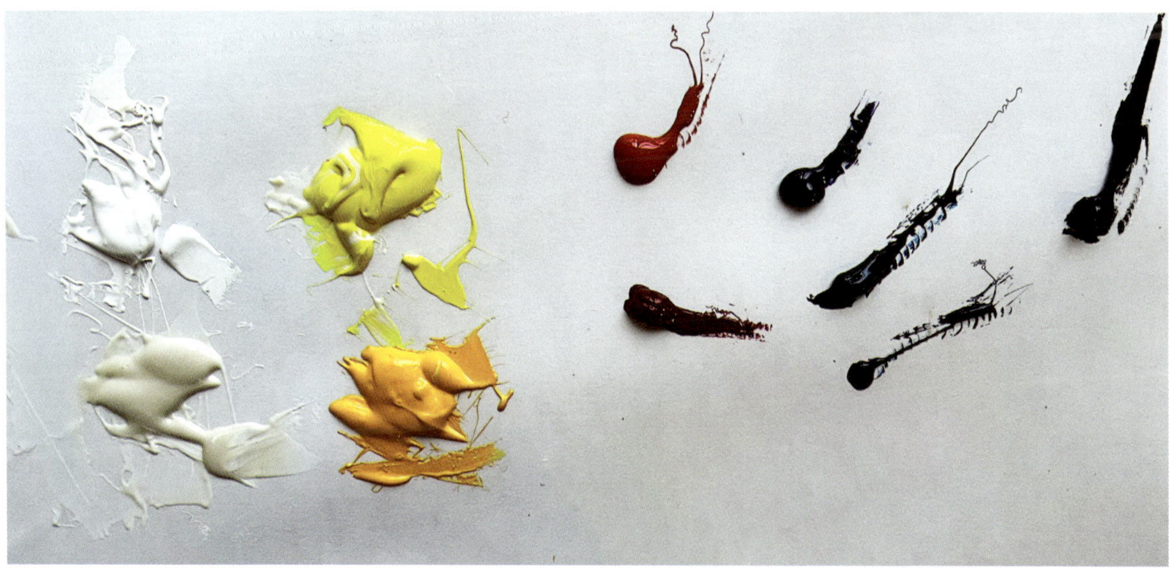

Mixing tips: to a large proportion of white and extender, add just a dab of colour. Notice how dark the other pigments are. To tint white, much less colour than you would expect is needed. Build up with tiny dabs, assessing as you go if you need more for a deeper colour.

For a deep translucent colour, you may not wish need to add any white at all (or very little). In this case, use the extender with your ink – up to 60 to 70 per cent extender is possible. Again, use the finger dab test and smear a stripe on to some paper to understand the type of effect you'll be getting.

Creating Two Tones on One Roller

This can be two tones of the same hue, i.e. a very light green with a very dark green. It pays to exaggerate the contrast when mixing, otherwise there is the danger of creating two middling tones and inadvertently losing the effect. For example, to create two tones of green, mix one light pastel or bright, fresh yellow with a rich, dark, translucent blue-green.

Mixing Greens

As a botanical printmaker, you'll need to have good array of greens in your repertoire. Experimentation, trial and error is the best way to learn. Ready-mixed greens from a tube are usually alarmingly vibrant. Known as 'palette killers', they are often made from phthalocyanine blue. Your own mixes of yellows and blues will make more natural greens.

If your greens are still too vibrant, try a dab of red to 'dirty' them. Yellow and black can also result in a naturalistic olive green, which can be left dark or tinted with additional white to give a soft natural sage.

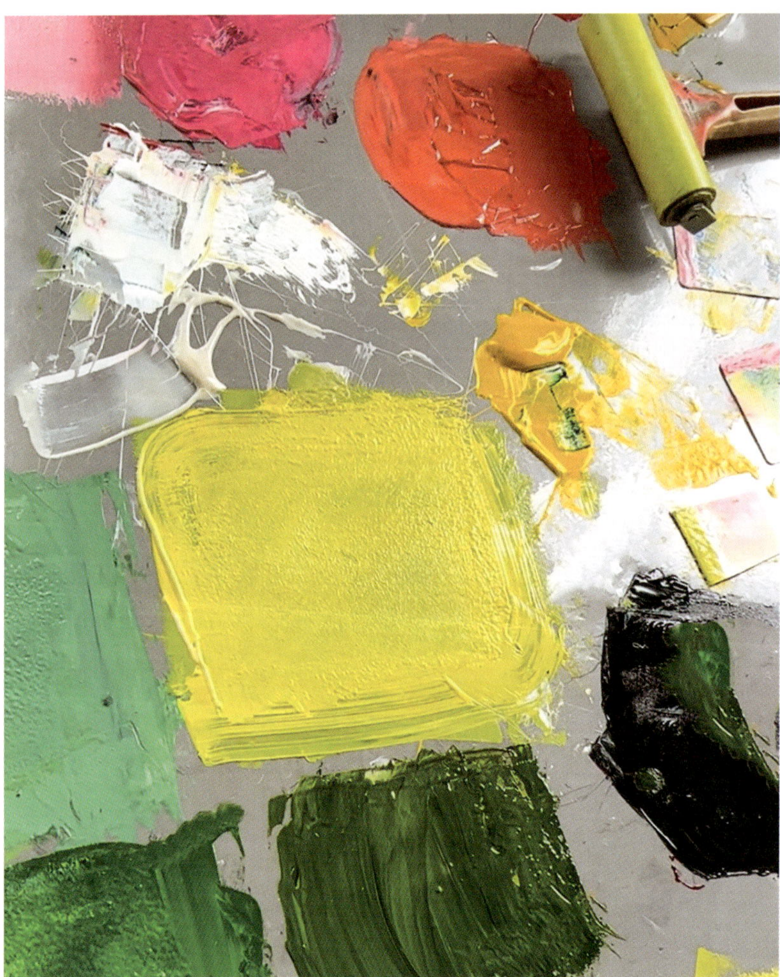

Ready-mixed greens from a tube are usually unsatisfactory. As green is essential to the botanical artist, learn to mix your own. To achieve a good layer of ink, reload the roller frequently from the pool of mixed colour. 'Stretch it out' on the palette first, then apply it to the block.

Neutralising Too-Bright Mixes

If your mixes still seem overpowering and bright, you can neutralise or 'muddy' them in one of two ways.

The simplest is by adding a little black so that you will be 'greying out' your colour. Go easy with this and proceed with tiny dabs of black, mixing thoroughly before you decide to alter further.

Another way to tone down the brightness of your mix is to neutralise it with a complementary colour. The complementary colour to green is red; just a tiny dab of red will 'muddy' a green mix. It is surprising how tiny this amount of complementary colour needs to be to achieve the result you're after.

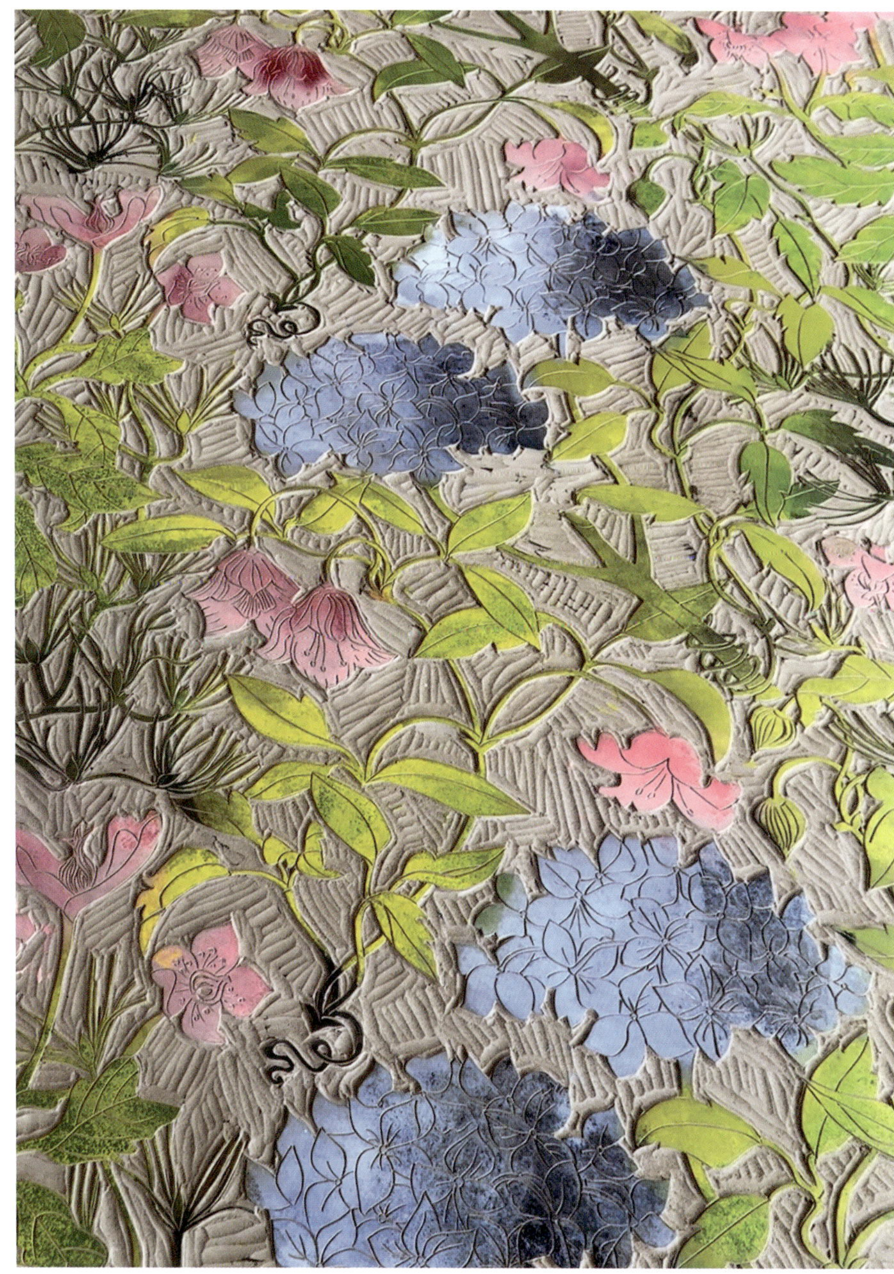

One of the virtues of good-quality highly pigmented oil-based inks is that all the colours of the rainbow can be applied to one block, with no need for traditional methods of cutting and printing a separate block for each colour used.

INKING UP THE BLOCK

To make a print from a single block, all the colours are applied at the same time and the block is printed just once. (For inking multi-block prints *see* Chapter 5.)

Preparation

Squeeze small amounts of ink from their tubes and mix them. Make tints as described earlier so that you have reserves of all the different colours you plan to use on your print.

Load up a roller – one for each colour – by rolling it in the ink mix. Then, moving to an area alongside so that you can reload as necessary, 'stretch' out the colour to coat the roller evenly.

Depending on the subjects you've chosen to depict, you will want a couple of rollers prepared with two tones of colour: one with tones of green, another with the tones of your flower colour (perhaps deep magenta fading to pastel pink).

Essdee red- and blue-handled rollers are cheap and perfect for this method. The 5cm (2in) ones are useful. Use those with a good-sized gap between the roller and the handle to make cleaning easier.

Applying Colour with Two Tones on One Roller

The order in which you roll your colour onto the block will depend on your design. For this *Foxgloves* block, I start with the pink before moving on to the greens.

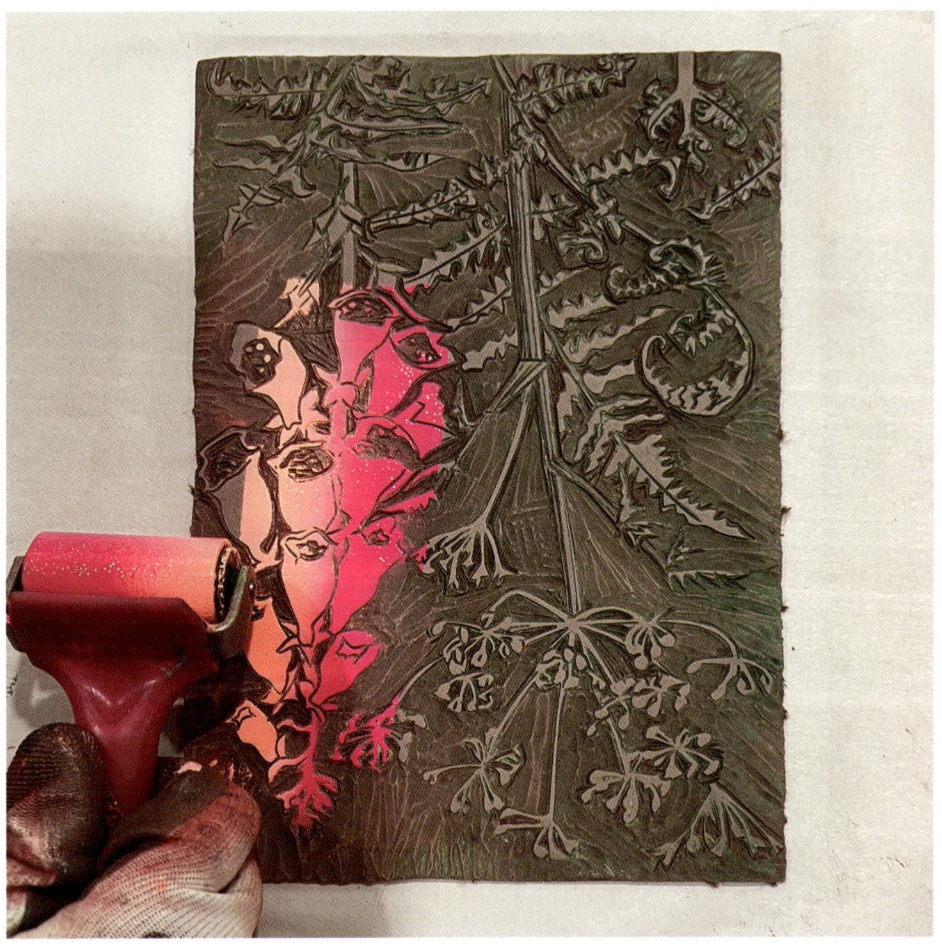

Apply the ink in a back-and-forth motion in one direction, then turn the block 180 degrees, as shown, to repeat the application alongside until you have a good, even coating. Recharge with ink from the palette as often as necessary.

Take care when using a two-tone roller to keep the direction and position, back and forth, the same. If you roll on ink in an arbitrary manner, the dark tone will cover over the light and thereby lose the effect. Instead, rotate the block itself and move the position of the roller to build up a wide stripe of the matching tone alongside.

For this *Foxglove* print, the first stripe of ink was applied with the block the right way up. I then rotated it 180 degrees to fill in with the same colour, extending the pale pink all the way to the edge of the flower.

Be Generous

Add all the colours until you have a generous coating. A print with too little ink applied, and not enough pressure applied to print it, will look blotchy and patchy and will lack the crispness and clarity of a well-inked print.

For the best results, make a thick, even layer of ink and reload the roller regularly. At worst, a layer of ink that is too thick will fill in a fine incised line of detail. This will not detract from your print – only you will know that this tiny detail is missing, after all. Your print will still appear crisp, even and perfectly printed.

Roll on colour according to where you need it (no need to be overly precise) and continue until you have an even coating. The inks blend extremely well and the gaps between printed areas create natural barriers that separate the different elements, e.g. leaves from flowers.

Masking

If you do need to keep colours separate in a particular area of the design, you can use small pieces of paper, held in your free hand, to mask one colour from another. There is no need to overdo this; use it judiciously. Instead, apply colour without worrying about when, say, some pinks overlap a green – let the colours layer over each other. Where they overlap, a third, neutral colour results and, in fact, helps to add more realistic tones and shading to the overall effect. Win.

This is most easily understood by practising. Have fun applying colours and notice how well they merge and blend happily at the edges where they overlap.

BLENDING OUT ROLLER LINES

Use a gloved finger to blend away any harsh or obvious lines created by the sides of the roller.

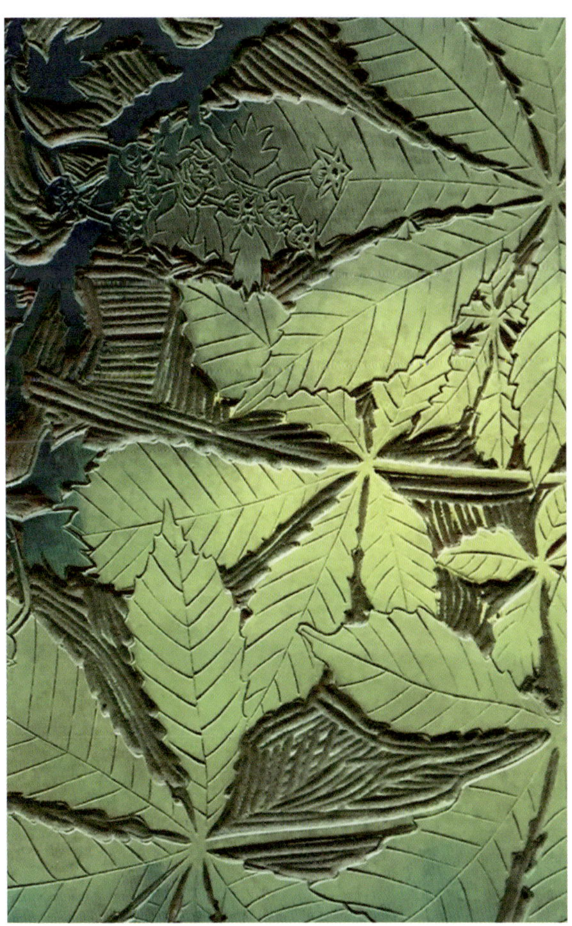

A close-up detail from the large *Horse Chestnuts* block. I have used different greens here, using a roller that has been prepared with two tones: a light and a dark. Where they overlap, the inks blend to create happy accidents that look intentional.

FINAL ASSESSMENTS BEFORE PRINTING

In good light, scan the entire block to assess whether all areas are covered adequately with ink. They should look glossy. Notice if some areas have less ink coverage than others and take your time – this is the final hurdle. Reapply where necessary, remembering to err on the generous side.

Increase Tonal Contrast for Impact in One Sweep

Have you achieved your desired tonal effects? It's not so easy when the ink is on a grey lino block rather than on a white surface. At this stage, I pick up a roller and select the darkest tone (black or a translucent dark blue with a tiny bit of extender). With a light touch, I sweep it across the area that needs darkening, in one direction, away from me. This technique is

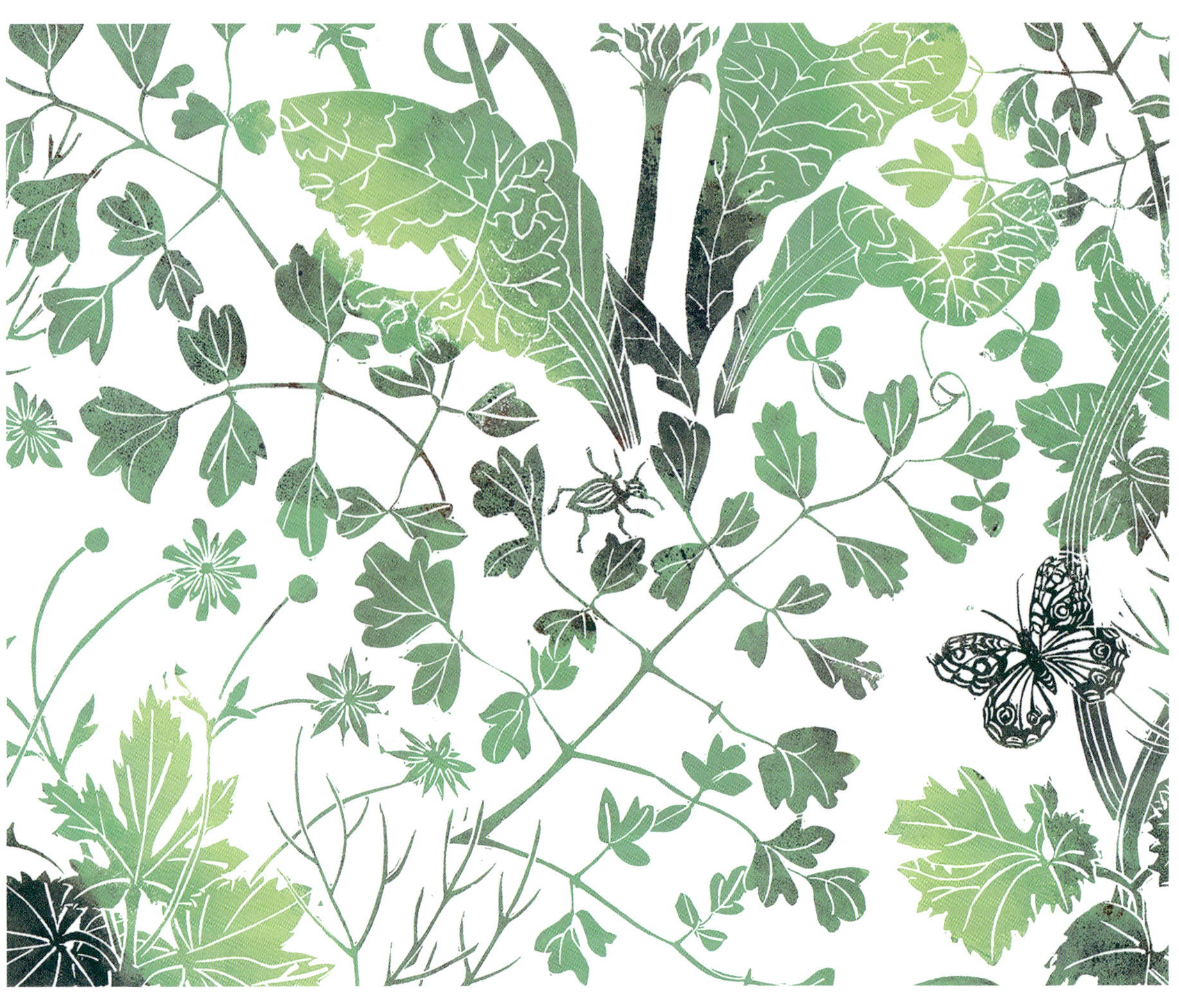

To achieve the effects in this section of *Bog Primrose*, two separate rollers are used. One is light with mid-green over the entire area. The final flourish will be to go over selected areas with a second roller in the darkest green-blue. Apply deep tones like this in one light sweep away from you – the result is a pleasing mottled effect. The lightness of touch will prevent any obvious signs from the straight edge of the roller.

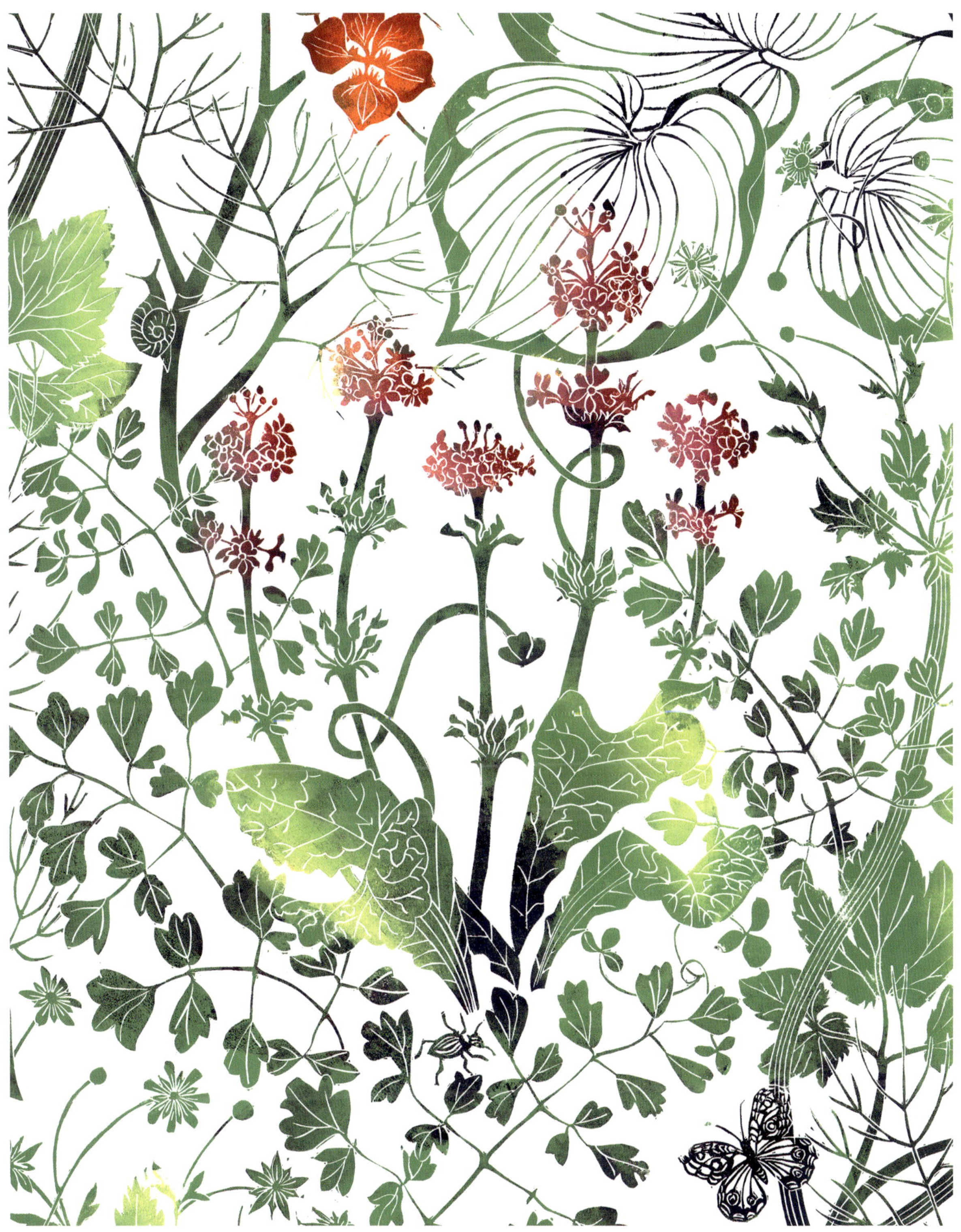

Bog Primrose: with so much green on this large print, the full tonal range is needed. The contrasts from lightest to darkest green prevent it looking too flat.

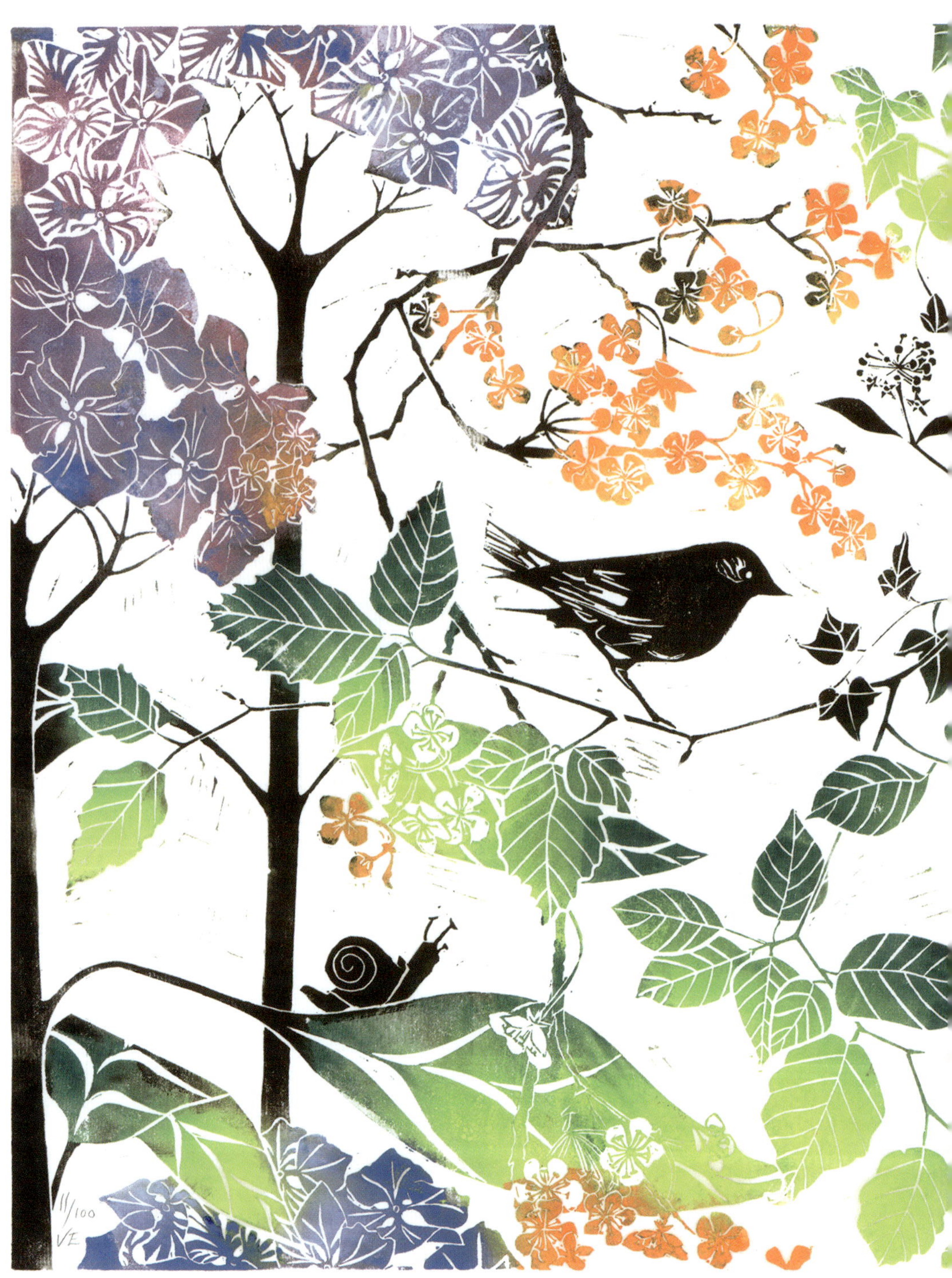

Hydrangeas: Reapply colour without cleaning the block between prints. You can adjust colours slightly from one print to the next to achieve a variation within a run of prints. It keeps things exciting for the printmaker, too.

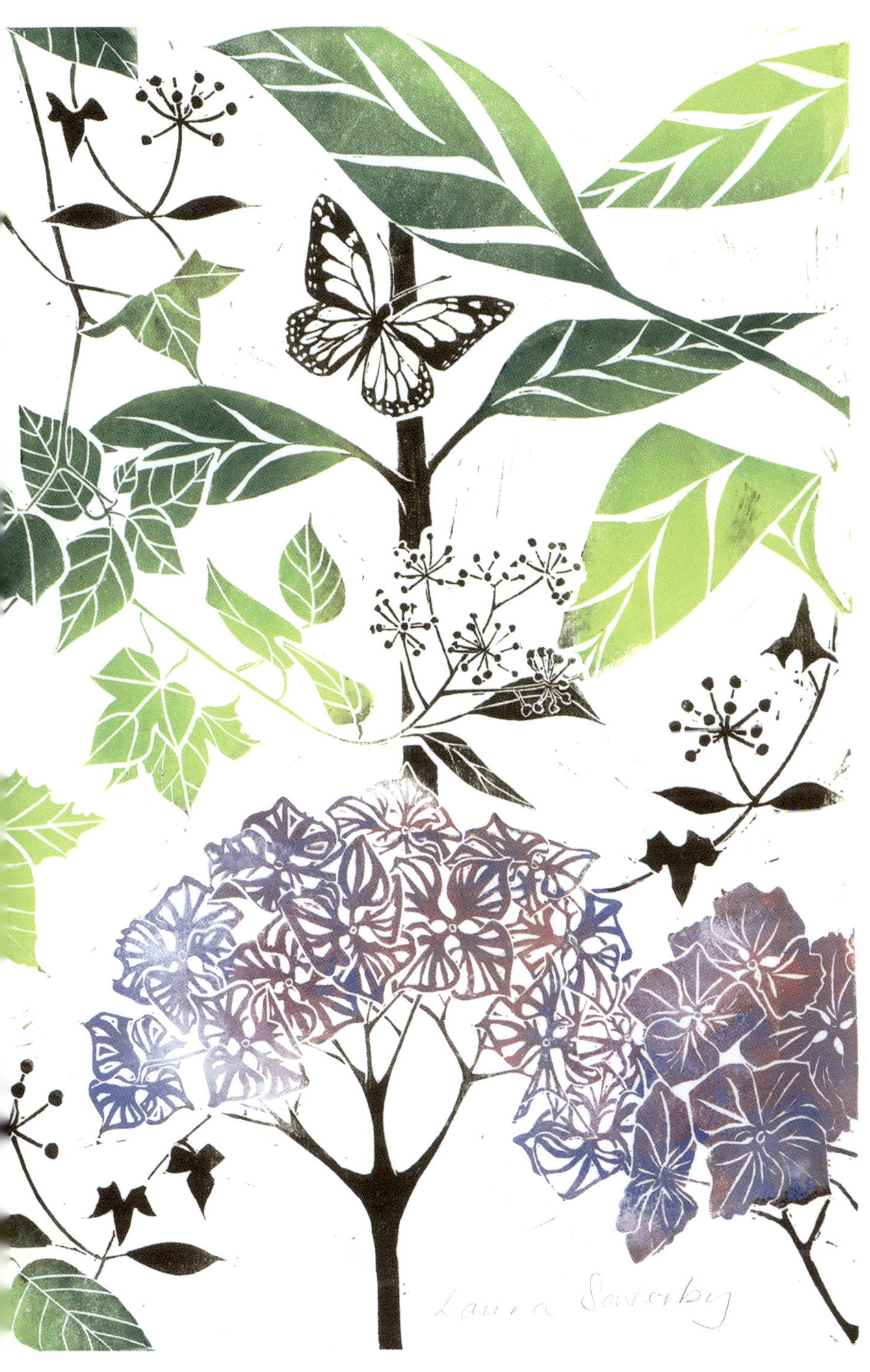

effective to exaggerate form and avoid everything appearing as one boring, flat, middling tone with little contrast from light to shade. Forms can look flat, unrealistic and lifeless, so try adding a very dark tone like this as a final flourish in a few well-chosen places.

PRINTING

Create the print bed, as already described in detail in Chapter 1. Print and repeat. After you have made a print, move straight on to making your next. There is no need to clean off any residue ink between successive prints – the printing process will have removed most of the ink. You may find it easier to ink up after the first time, as the remnants of ink act a guide, showing you where to put down the colour again.

Printing the Same Design in Different Colours

The same print can look very different when printed in different colours. Adjusting colour in this way produces a great deal of variance within an edition. This block is easy to roll up with the different-coloured inks. The cut-away areas in between the elements provide ample space to avoid getting the wrong ink on a neighbouring shape, where you don't want it.

After printing the single-block version of *Hydrangeas*, I wanted to see what would happen if I included a coloured background. This involved cutting a second block to create the arsenic green background and the white 'inverted' hydrangea head. The second block provides the coloured background and the opportunity to try out some other changes to the design. These differences mean I have to ink

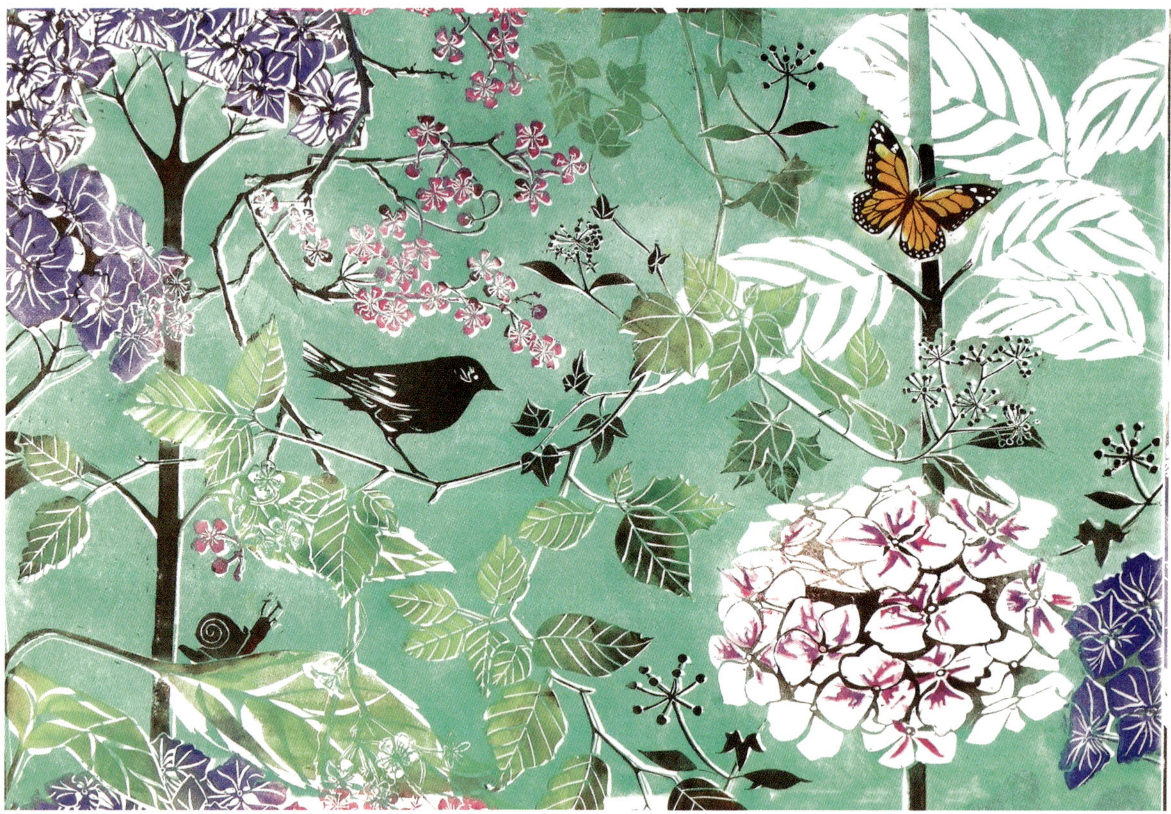

Another example of the *Hydrangeas* print, this time made with two blocks instead of one.

it up carefully to avoid inking elements that do not feature in this multiple block version. (*See* Chapter 5 'Making Prints from Two Blocks'.)

Here we have another alternative to explore; an inverted print. The block is completely inked in white and printed onto coloured paper. I made the textured effect of the blue background by hand using a Japanese watercolour block printing technique called *moku hanga*.

If you want to make your own, stippling, dagging or rag paint techniques could be explored as long as your chosen technique produces a relatively smooth surface and the paper is not too heavy in weight (maximum 120 gsm for hand printing). You could seek out coloured papers to print onto – wallpapers have a similar effect.

Ink Drying Times

Oil-based ink is prized for its ability to stay open, i.e. stay wet while you work. The method we are using to apply ink can result in some relatively thick layers that can take a longer to dry – a few days to a few weeks, depending on the conditions.

When you have finished a printing session for the day, you would usually clean up using white spirits. However, if you want to continue working on subsequent days, the stay-open quality is useful. I have left a palette and rollers for over a week. It's not best practice, but it has suited my 'come and go' working patterns.

Extra force is needed to remove semi-dried-on ink, which can be hard work. Always clean your lino block at the end of every session, so you don't risk ink drying on your precious work.

This really is a cause for celebration; time to appreciate the fruits of your labour. The following chapters take you further, but for now, having come so far, the best approach might be to take stock of what you've learnt. So print, repeat, print, repeat!

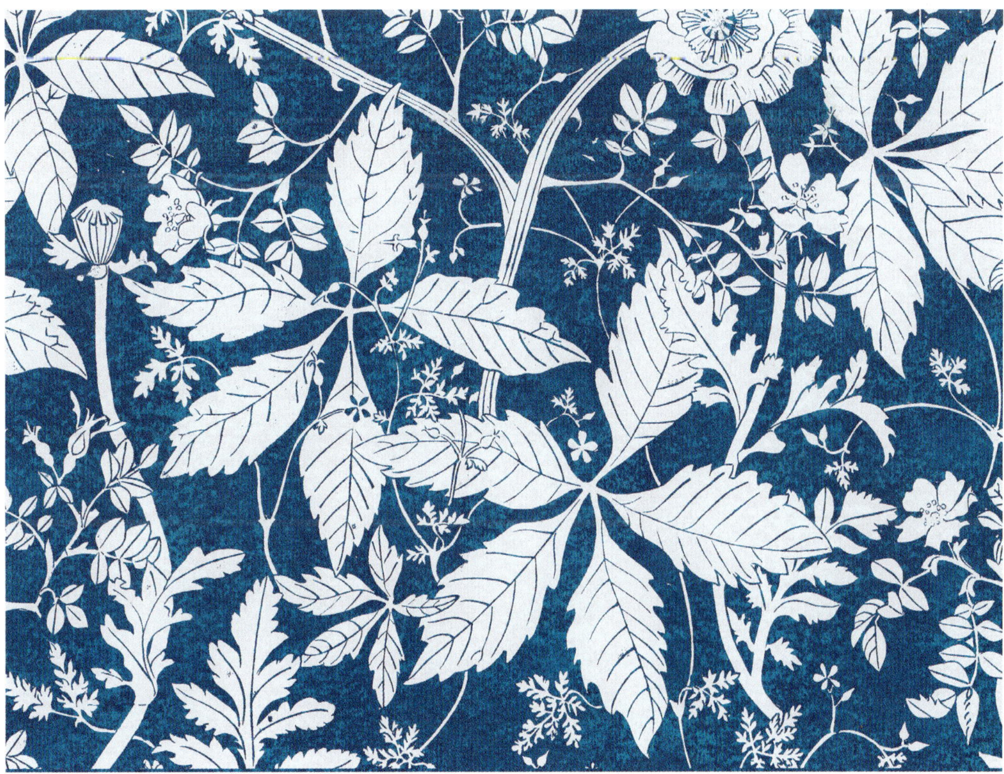

Another version of *Poppies*, this time a type of inverted or negative print. Ink block in a white and print onto a coloured paper to achieve this.

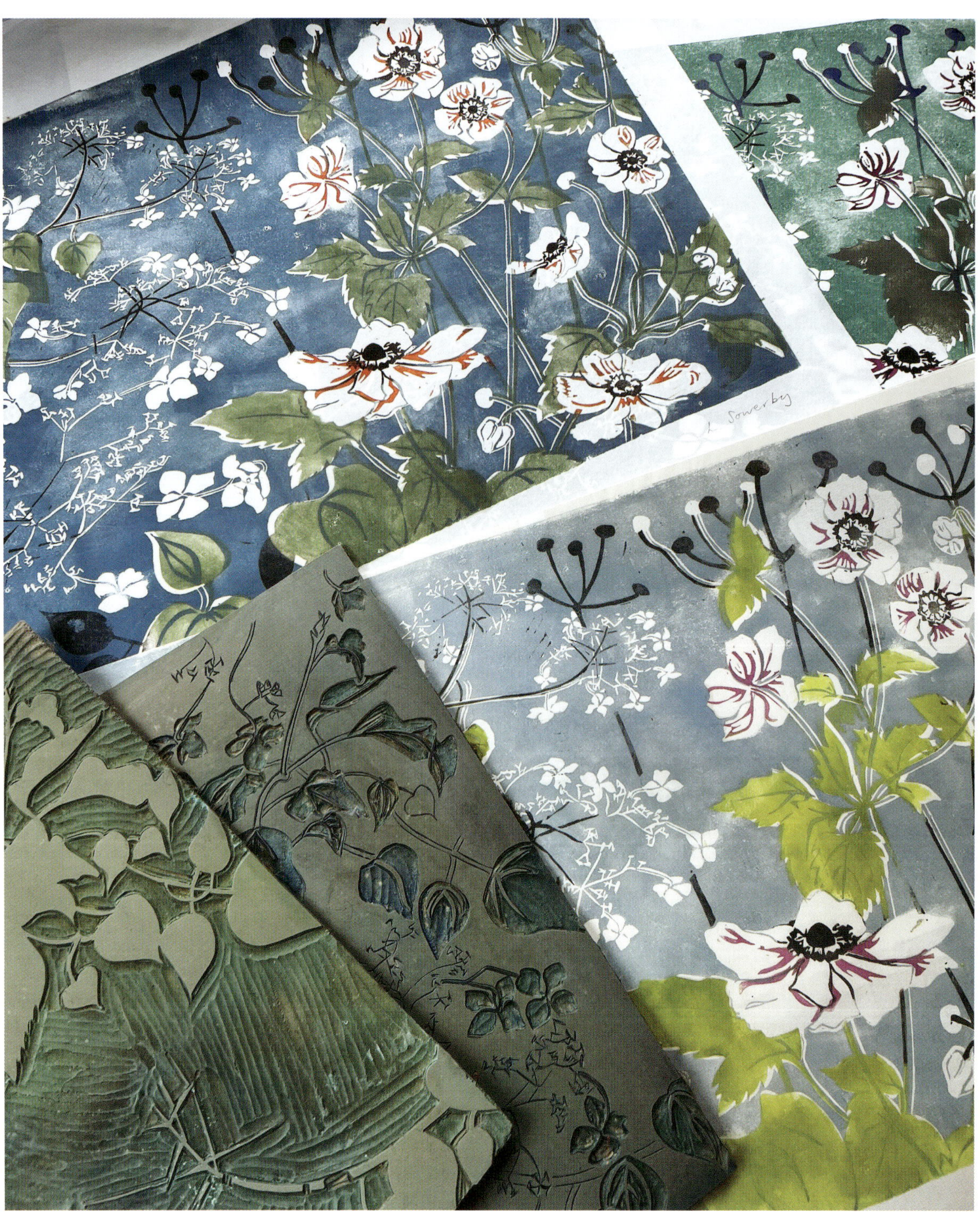

Windflowers print, shown in Chapter 5, is made from the two blocks shown. Notice how the various colours are successful to different degrees. In the example seen in the top right corner, the green I mixed for overprinting the leaves was too dark and too opaque to reveal the leaf veins below.

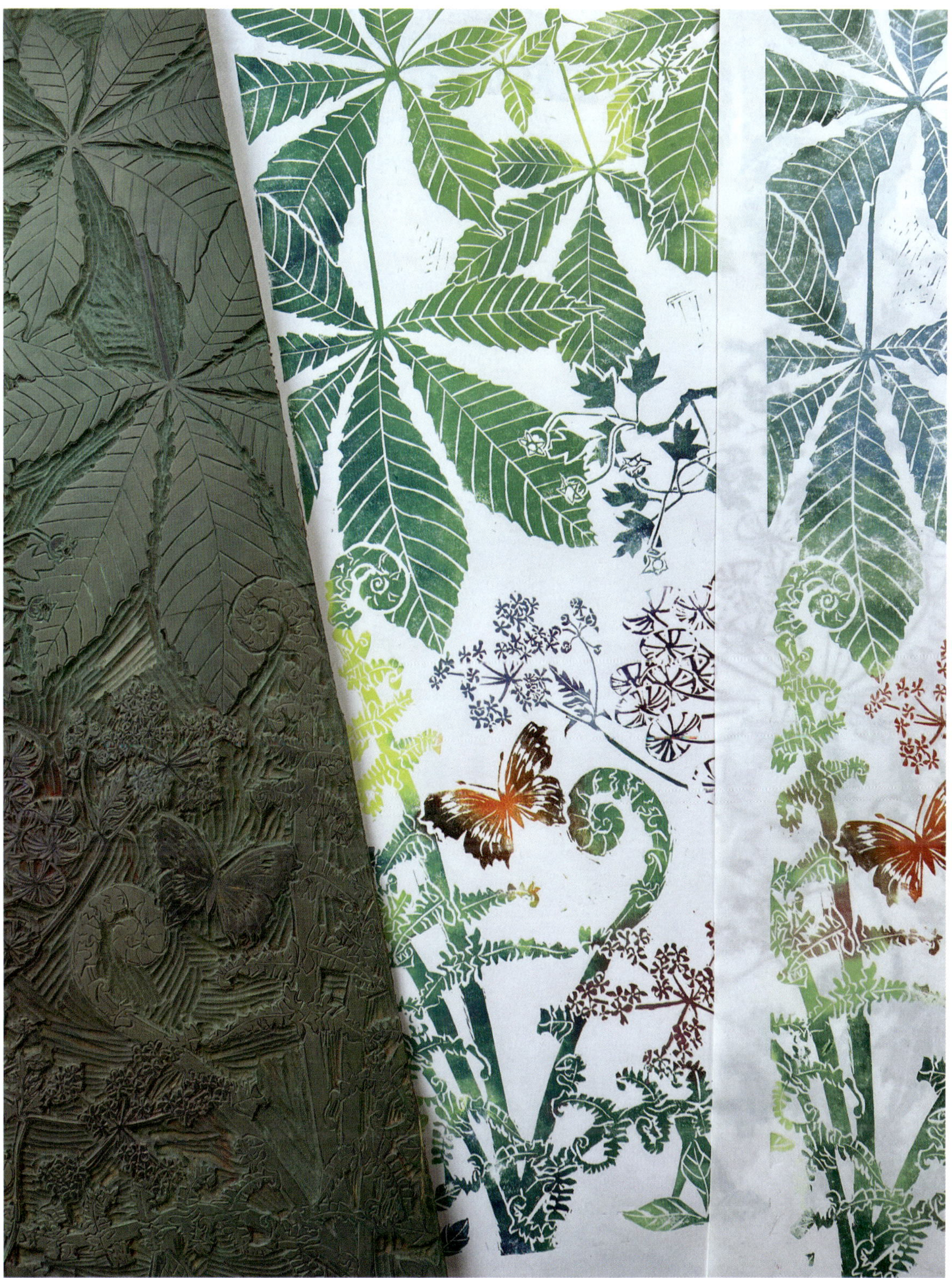

The *Horse Chestnut* block with two prints made from it using different coloured inks. Variation helps keep me motivated. The repetitive work involved in printmaking is rewarded with new and surprise results.

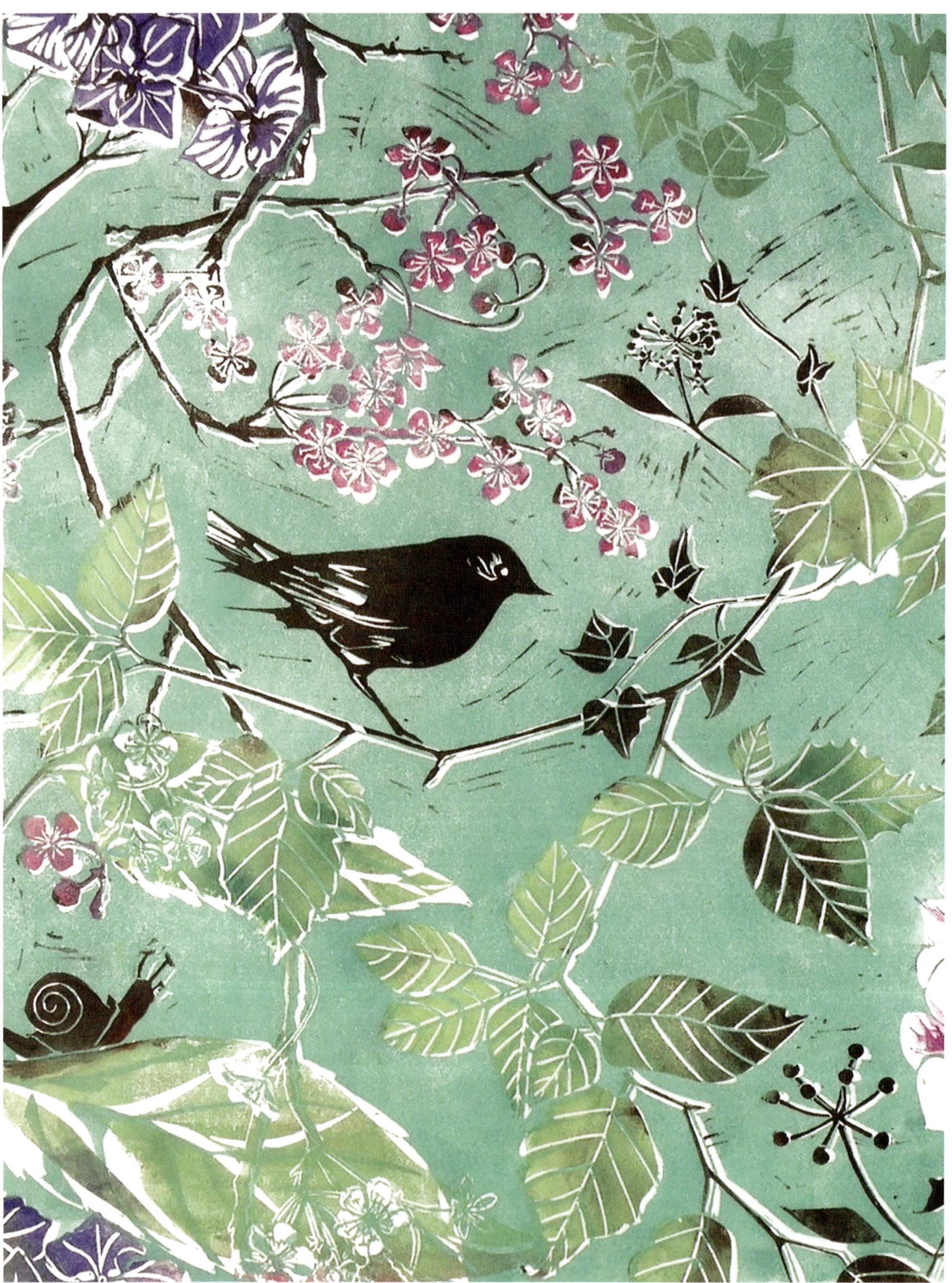

CHAPTER 5

MULTI-BLOCK PRINTING

This chapter takes you further, as we will explore making a print from multiple lino blocks. We will look at the design process in detail, as well as the steps involved in the actual printing method.

Multi-block printing brings a new layer of complexity. It can seem demanding at first, but it's a step well worth taking. In my own printmaking, I never use more than two blocks, as I find more than this unnecessarily labour-intensive and allowing too much room for error, but there's no reason not to extend to more if you wish. As you become familiar with printing from a single block, it's great to go on to challenge yourself further. You will start to appreciate the novel opportunities and potential that adding a second block can bring to your printmaking.

Previously, we explored creating a finished print in full colour from a single piece of lino. We inked up this block with all the different colours needed and printed it once to give the final result. Printing from a single block in this way is an efficient method and may be all you ever need to achieve the results you are looking for. It is also very accessible to the beginner. Before you attempt to follow the instructions here, first make sure you have had a go at creating a print from a single block (*see* Chapters 1–4).

Learning how to print from more than one lino block means you are free to produce all sorts of images that single-block printing does not allow. In effect, a single-block print simply shows botanical silhouettes in colour on a white paper background. Using two blocks opens up new possibilities and pushes the limits of what can be achieved. With a second block we now have the opportunity to add a coloured background, to exploit what happens when two colours and shapes are layered on top of each other, to cut out forms from the background to allow the white paper to show through, or to over-print these areas. It may not necessarily be a better method – the choice of technique would depend on the image you have in mind and what you are trying to depict in print.

Before we get into specifics with step-by-step instructions, we will study an example of a print made from two blocks to understand the potential of this layered technique.

This version of *Hydrangeas* is made from two blocks instead of one.

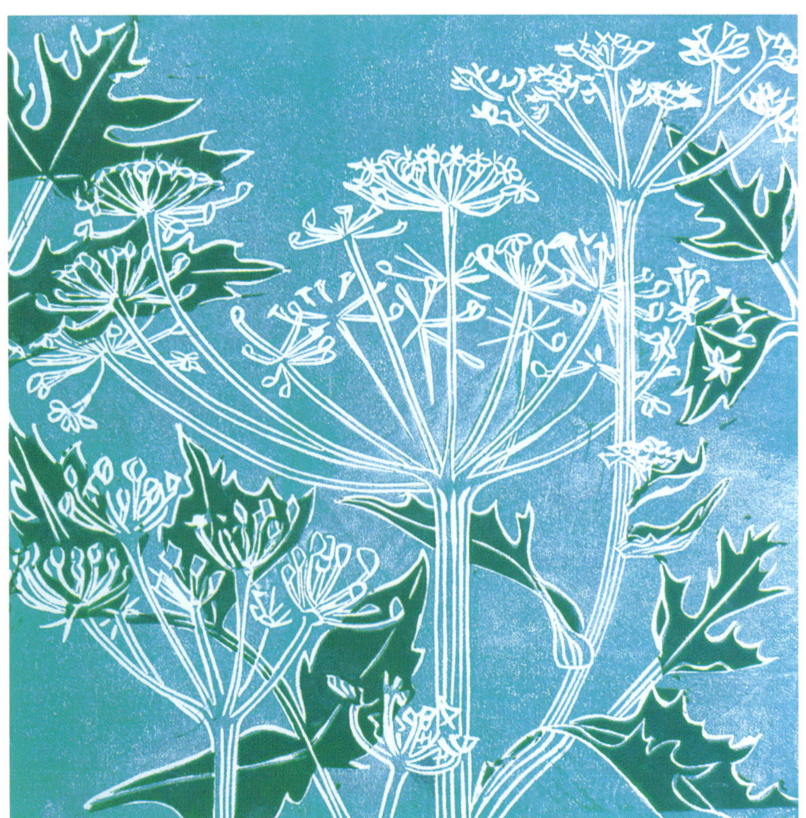

Winter Cow Parsley print. A monochromatic design made from two blocks. The design is a negative or inverted image – that is the block is left intact and the line drawing is cut from it, giving white lines when printed. A second block is overlaid to fill in the leaves and create a sense of depth.

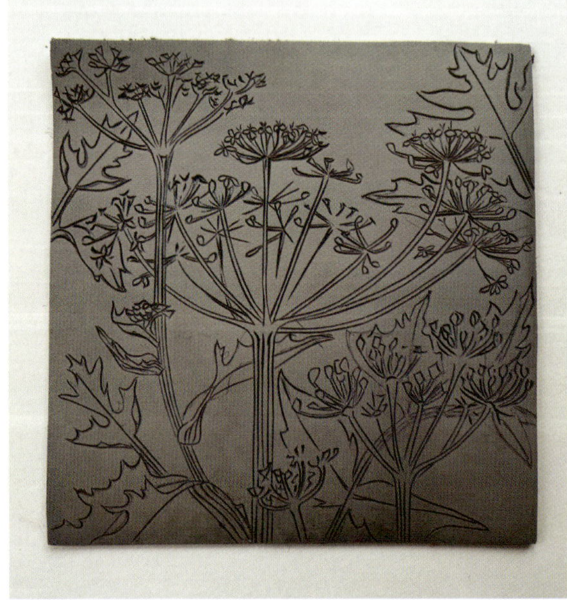

On block 1 the background remains intact with the lines of the drawing cut from it using a v-tool.

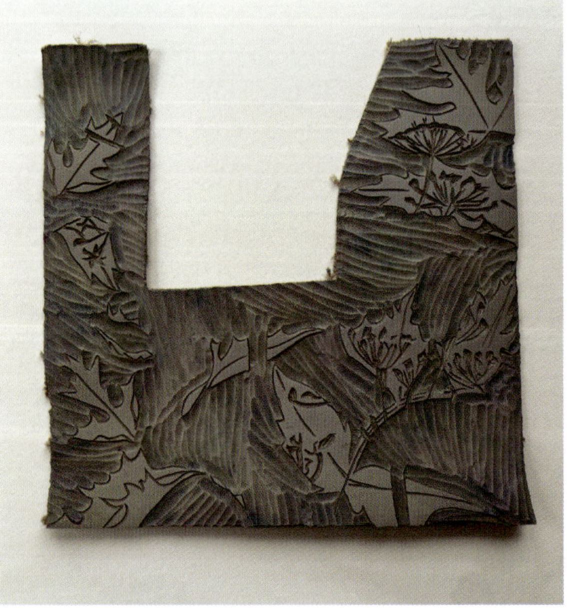

Block 2 consists of the leaves as flat shapes. Notice how they are placed behind the flower heads and stems providing the design with a much needed sense of depth.

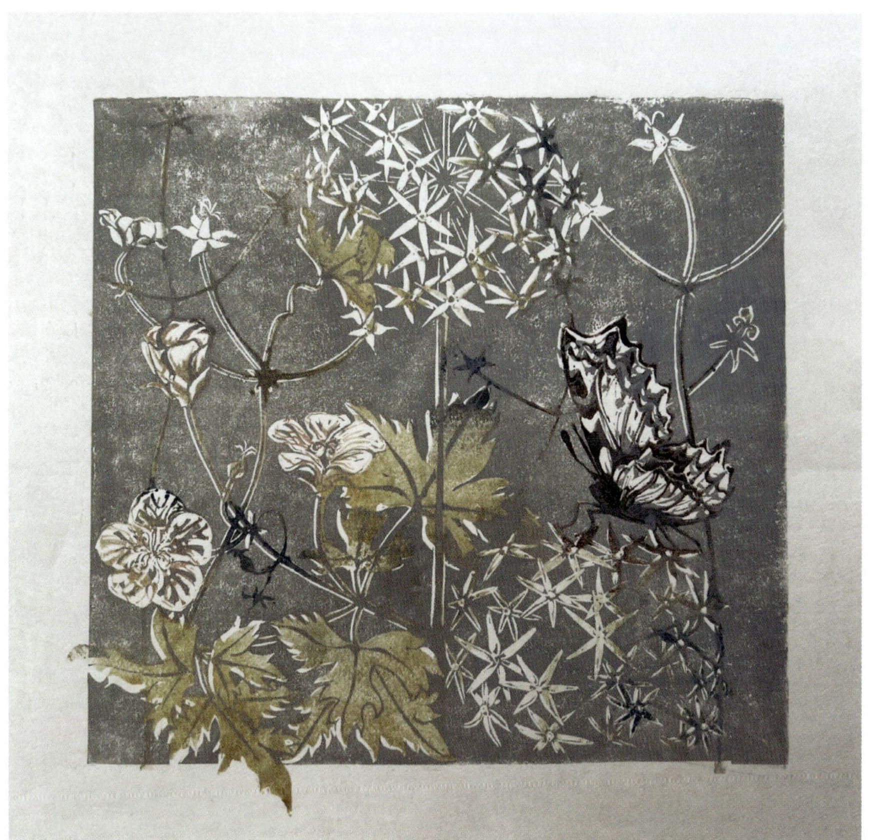

Wild Garlic and *Cranesbill* print. Another example of a print made from two blocks. Block 1 consists of the drawing cut out of the background, which is otherwise largely intact. This is overprinted with a second block which fills in leaves, flowers and the focal point, a butterfly.

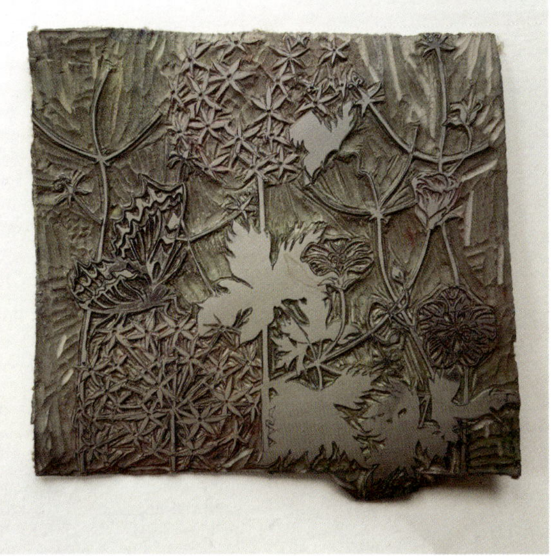

Block 2 containing the 'infill' subjects.

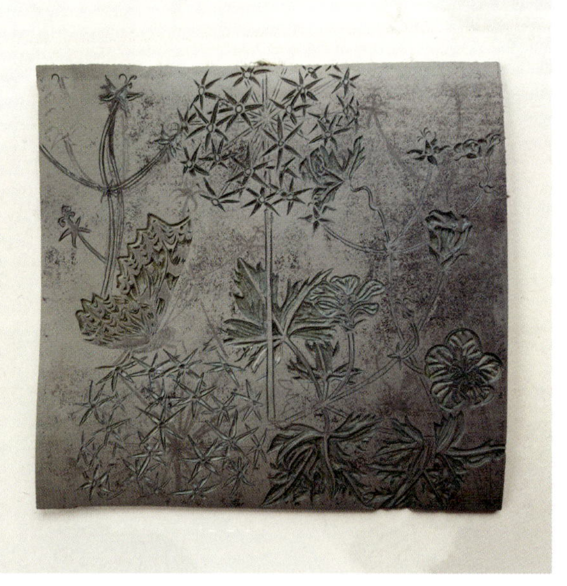

On Block 1 all the lines of the drawing are cut. Some shapes are removed for overprinting or to be left for the white of the paper to show as part of the design.

DESIGNING AND PLANNING

Just as the single-block printing technique takes planning, the multi-block method also takes some careful prior consideration. Work out what type of image is best-suited and how to exploit the two blocks at your disposal. Obviously, by creating two printing blocks you are effectively increasing your workload – cutting two blocks and precisely matching the two images so that they become one when printed, one overlaid over the other. This process of accurate alignment is called registration and it is crucial to get it right at two stages; when transferring the drawn image to both blocks and again at the printing stage. So why bother? When might two blocks be better than one?

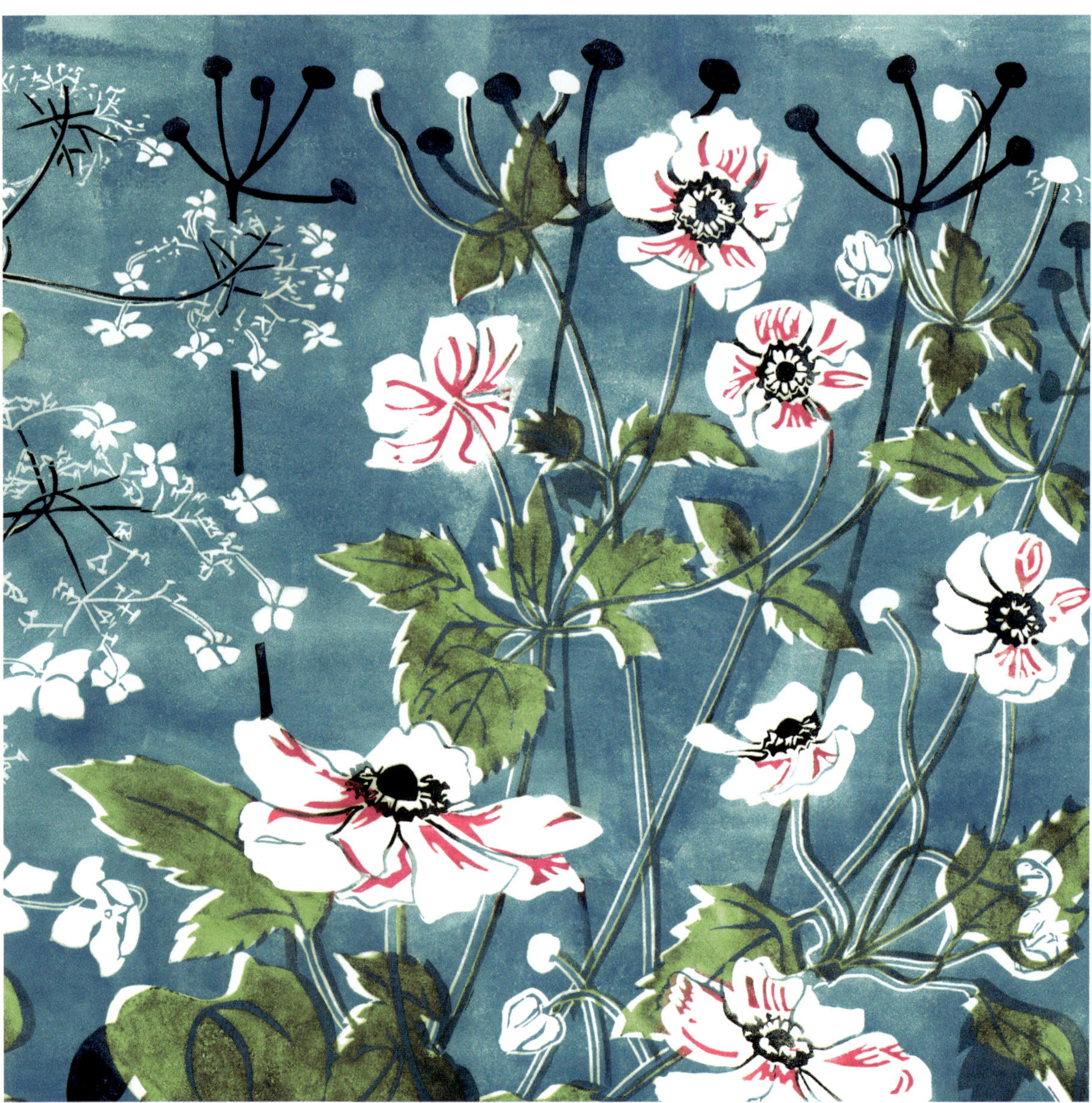

This example, *Windflowers*, shows the different ways to use this layered method of printing. Two layers make up this print: the background layer (Block 1) and the shapes layer (Block 2).

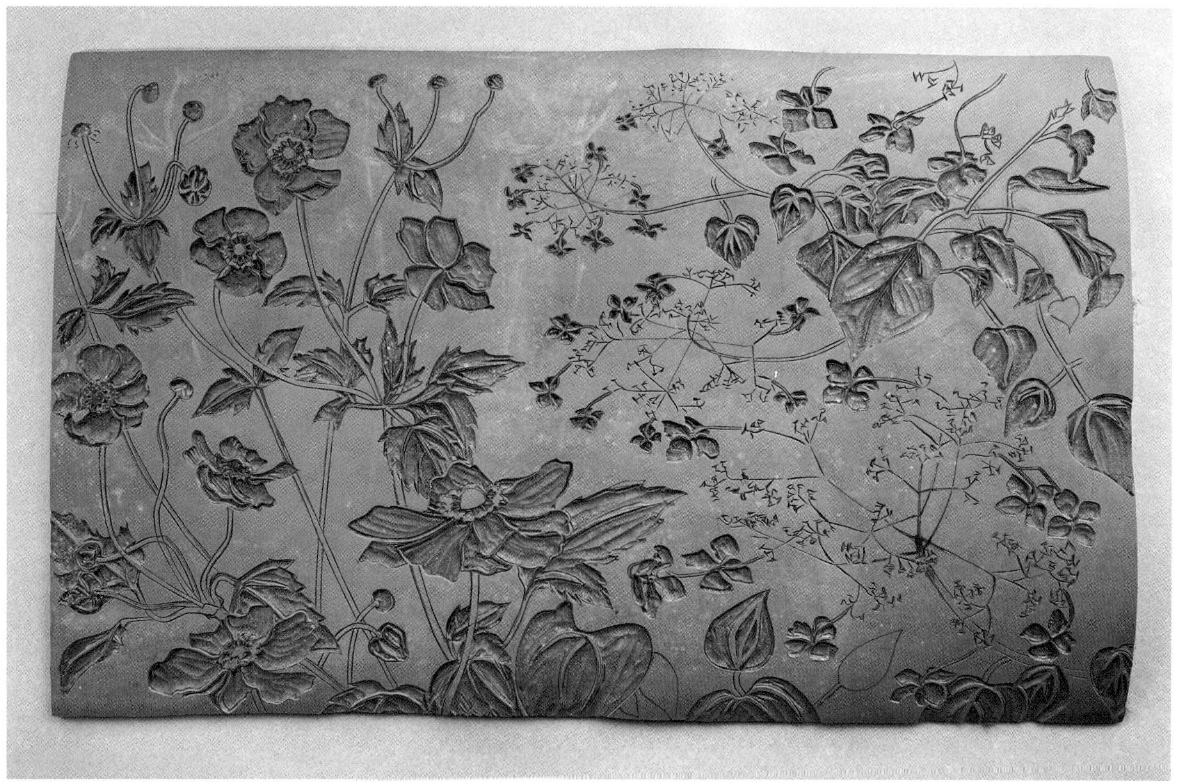

The first layer, or background block, used to create *Windflowers*. The blue areas form the background layer, which is printed first. We can see that the surface area of this block of lino is mostly intact and negative spaces have been cut out from it – these negative spaces are then either overprinted with coloured shapes of the second block or left so the white of the paper can show through.

It may help to think of Block 1 as the background block, which remains largely intact and from which negative spaces are cut. Print this first. The result is a coloured background that can be overprinted with the 'shapes' (flowers, stems, leaves, etc.) of Block 2.

The second block features the main subject matter with all of the background cut away; the sort of scenario we have been more familiar with up to now. The silhouettes and 'positive' shapes of the main features – flowers, stems and leaves etc. – are all on Block 2.

With the first 'background block', exploit the white paper in a different way than we have up to now. More like an inverted design, think of Block 1 as 'the coloured background block', although it serves as much more than that. Now it is possible to flood the composition with colour and have the

botanical forms cut out of it, creating, in effect, little windows through which the paper below can be seen. These windows allow either the paper to show through or for overprinting with a new, translucent colour provided by the second block.

With *Windflowers*, I used these windows of white paper in several ways. I cut out the white flower petals of the Japanese anemone and the climbing hydrangea from the background block, leaving the white paper to show through, without overprinting it. The white paper becomes white petals. Similarly, the complex fine lines and filigree structure of the lacecap hydrangea heads are also cut from the background block, again exploiting the white of the paper.

As ever, choose forms for their contrasts. Pair subjects for their contrast of shape, size and relative

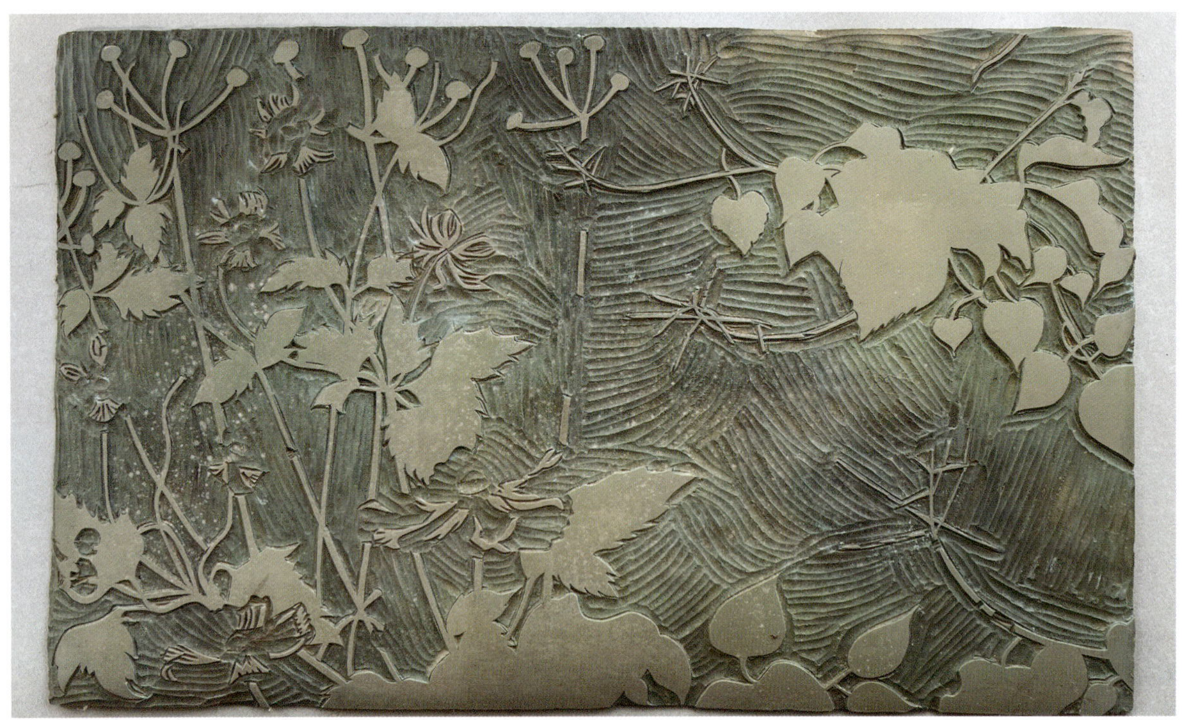

A second layer is printed on top of the background. It contains all the shapes that are to be overprinted in the windows cut out of the first block. This block includes the positive shapes in relief; the background is entirely cut away.

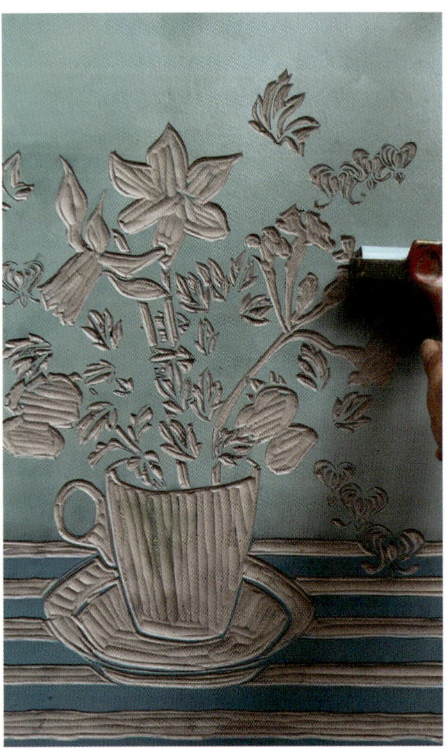

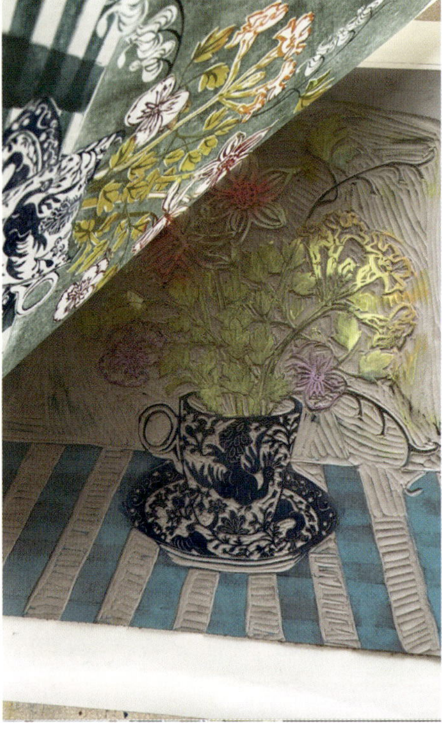

The two blocks used to create the print, inked and ready for printing: the 'shapes block' (right) with the background cut away and the 'background block' (left) with much of the surface area intact. As we have seen in earlier chapters, the flat surface area of a lino block is the part to which the ink is applied by means of rollers; the surface that prints. The cut-away parts will not receive ink and will therefore not print – these reveal the white paper or can be overprinted.

complexity. In the example, the fine-cut lines allow the paper to show through to become white intricate areas of the interior structure of the flower. These make a nice contrast to the comparatively large, white spaces of the anemone's saucer-shaped petals. If you prefer, overprint these areas and instead of white petals, make flowers of any colour. Cut the negative spaces of your leaf shapes, then overprint these as I have done here. Overprinting is possible by including the entire flat leaf shapes on Block 2. In *Windflowers*, the veins of the leaves are left intact on Block 1 and overprinted so that they show through the translucent ink.

When you look hard and notice the different ways used to print the botanical forms – at times allowing the white paper to show through, at others overprinting and layering one shape onto another – you can start to get an appreciation of the different effects and take these into account at the planning stage. The planning aspect of printmaking may lack spontaneity, but it can be satisfyingly inventive – cerebral, even. A challenge to find all the different ways you can create form and colour effects by combining just two layers.

With the botanical forms combined to make a pleasing arrangement and an understanding of how to use the two layers in interesting ways, you are ready to make a final drawing. As well as the information above, Chapter 2 has a wealth of information on designing to help you.

Demonstration: *Daffodil, Cowslip Primrose and Bleeding Hearts –* The Printing Process

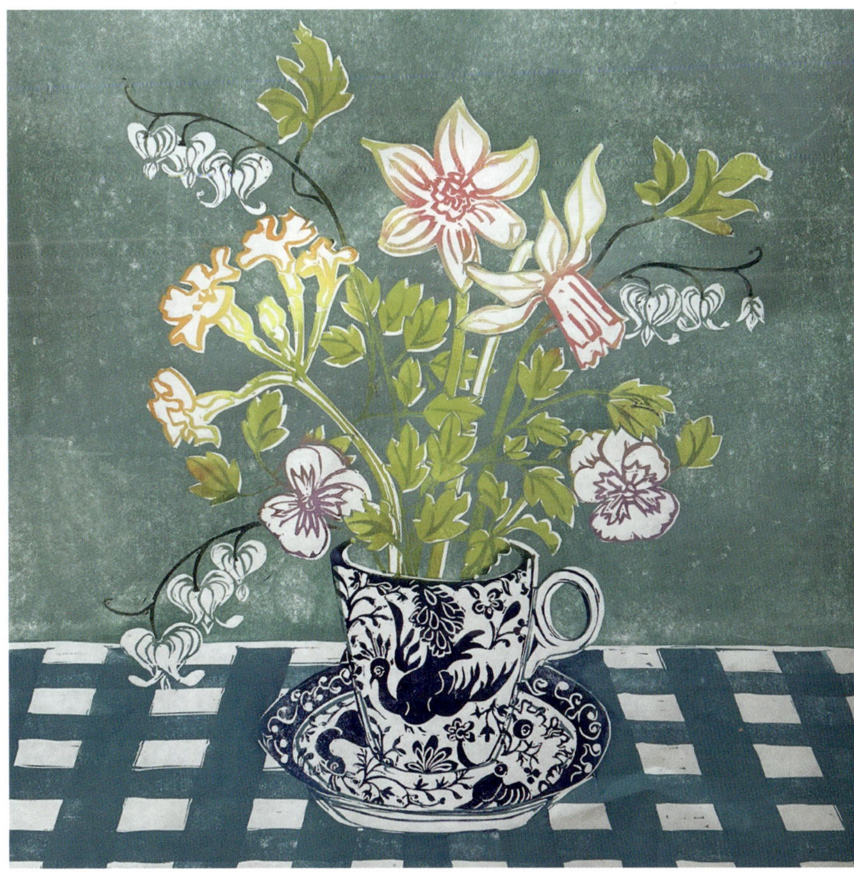

Daffodils, Cowslip Primrose and Bleeding Hearts. The printing stage is complete. Watercolour is added by hand as a final embellishment (*see* Chapter 6).

1. To transfer your drawing to the two blocks, make sure your drawing is placed where you want it on your drawing paper, as the outer edges of this sheet are the outer edges of your composition and final print. Start by cutting two blocks to fit your image from your roll of lino or purchase two machine-cut blocks of lino of the appropriate size – you can easily trim it to fit your design (*see* Chapter 1).

The two blocks must be identical in size. If you are cutting these yourself from a roll of lino, accuracy is key to this process. Measure diagonally from corner to corner and check that both measurements are the same. A sharp pencil and fine pen will make crisp tracings from the original drawing.

2. When a print is taken from a lino block, it is a mirror image of the original design. Reversing your drawing is easily done – there are several methods to choose from. To recap, lay a piece of tracing paper over your drawing and trace it. Then turn the tracing paper over and the drawing will be clearly visible on the reverse. Alternatively, use a light box and lay the drawing right-side down on the surface to trace over the back. Or improvise; I tape my drawing to the window in my studio. Daylight shines through, allowing me to trace on the reverse.

You may decide that reversing the drawing is not necessary – it may work just as well as a mirror image. By turning the drawing over and holding it up to the light, you will have an idea of how it will look if you skip this step.

3. Now we will transfer the drawing onto Block 2 – the block that will have your main shapes of botanical forms retained and the background cut away. It will be printed second, on top of the background.

To transfer the design, the first method is to secure the reverse drawing accurately and firmly with masking tape. Line up the bottom-left corner of your paper with the bottom-left corner of the piece of lino. Sandwich in a sheet of graphite carbon transfer paper, inky side down, between the drawing sheet and the block. Trace over the relevant areas. Go over all the outlines of the shapes that you plan to include on Block 2, for example solid leaf shapes, solid stem shapes, solid silhouettes of seed heads and any flowers you intend to overprint. Also include abstract shapes that denote areas of shading or details within a flower structure, such as a flower centre. Retain these and plan to cut away the rest of this block.

When complete, remove the drawing and repeat the process. Trace the relevant parts of the drawing onto Block 1, the background. Switch to a different colour pen to help you distinguish which motifs are relevant to Block 1.

4. If I want a really accurate match between the two blocks or the freedom to draw directly onto the lino using charcoal, I use an alternative method. First I transfer my drawing to Block 2. Rather than moving on to do the same to Block 1, I begin to cut it with the finest V-shaped tool instead. This way, I will have the opportunity to enhance my design with charcoal.

I make a crayon rubbing of the fine lines of Block 2 and use it to transfer the design to Block 1. The advantage of this is that a rubbing or 'proof' is more accurate than the original drawing. Proofing is like taking a brass rubbing – making a picture by placing paper over a brass plate, usually from

NEVER MOVE THE DRAWING
Avoid moving the drawing during the transfer process or the overprinted shapes will not line up with their respective windows and the print will be misaligned.

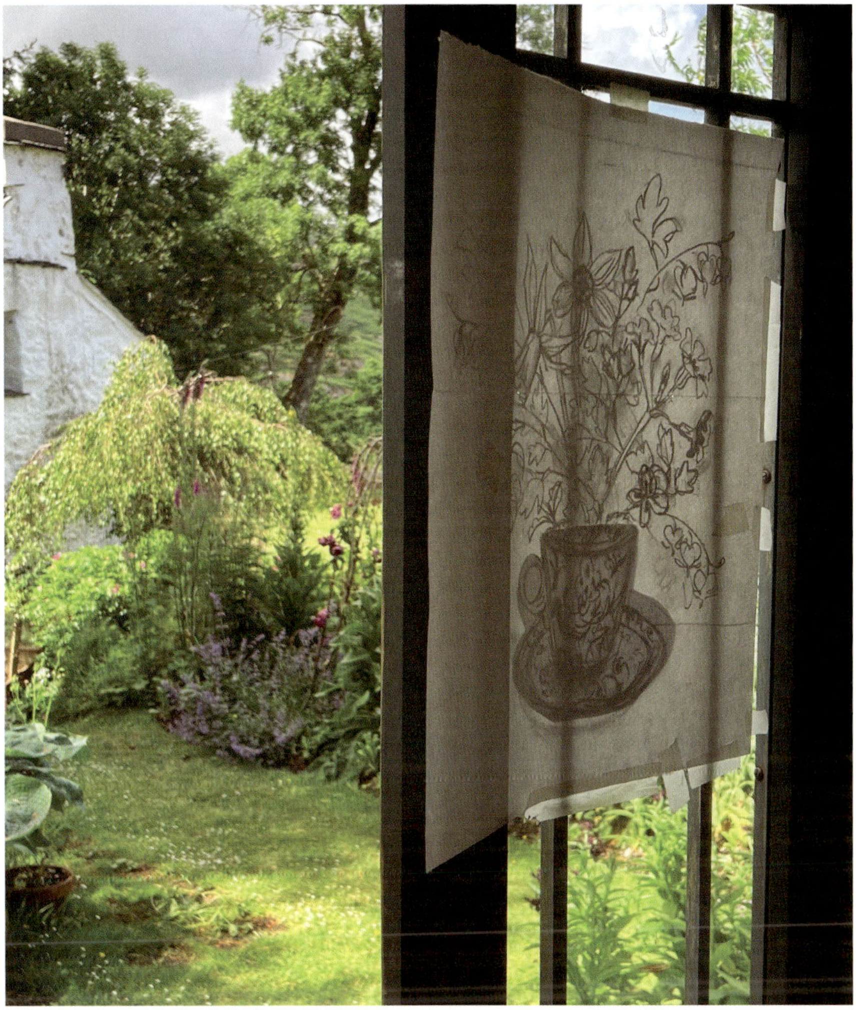

Using a window as a lightbox is a great way to quickly reverse a drawing.

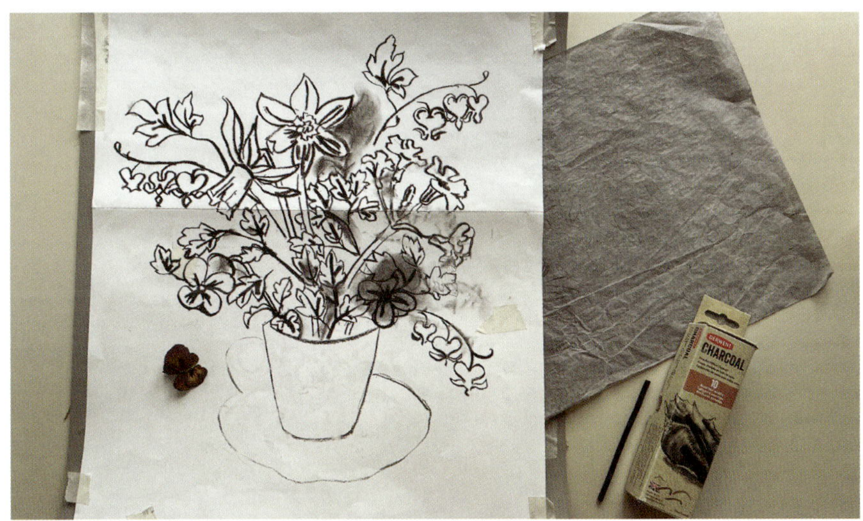

Using a pen helps to see where on the drawing you have yet to trace over. That way there is no need to disturb the drawing itself by checking your progress underneath.

plaques found in churches, and rubbing with a wax crayon. Make sure the paper you use fits your design so you can match the bottom-left corners of the block with the paper to keep everything aligned.

5. You can draw directly over your tracing onto the lino. I love to draw with charcoal. Use hairspray or artist fixative to fix the drawn charcoal lines in place – if you skip this step, all your careful drawing will become a smudgy mess!

The beauty of using charcoal is twofold. First, the lines it makes are relatively thick so they will translate well when it comes to cutting your block. (Tiny, fine pencil lines are in danger of disappearing as you cut either side of them with the tool. It is easy to cut and – whoops – the sliver that you intended to leave behind has been inadvertently removed.) Second, drawing directly onto lino with charcoal means I can develop my initial design further. It allows me to draw freely, making the lines more expressive and sinuous, reminiscent of calligraphy.

Once you have transferred all the information to both blocks, you can remove the tracing and start cutting.

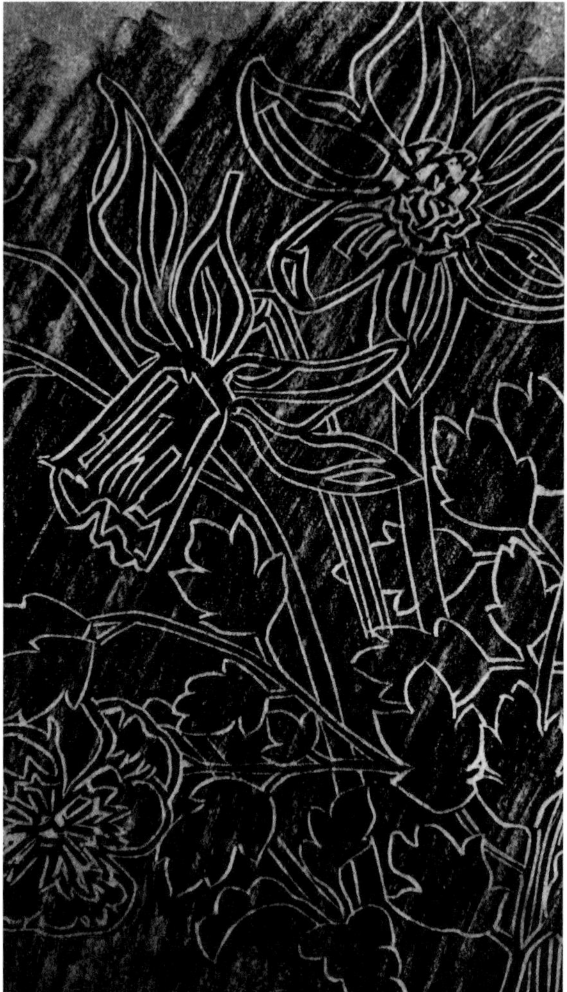

Having transferred the drawing to one of the blocks, here I move directly to cutting it with the fine V-shaped tool. I will do no more than go around the shapes. Here I made a rubbing or 'proof' in crayon on newsprint. Spray mount can be used to attach it.

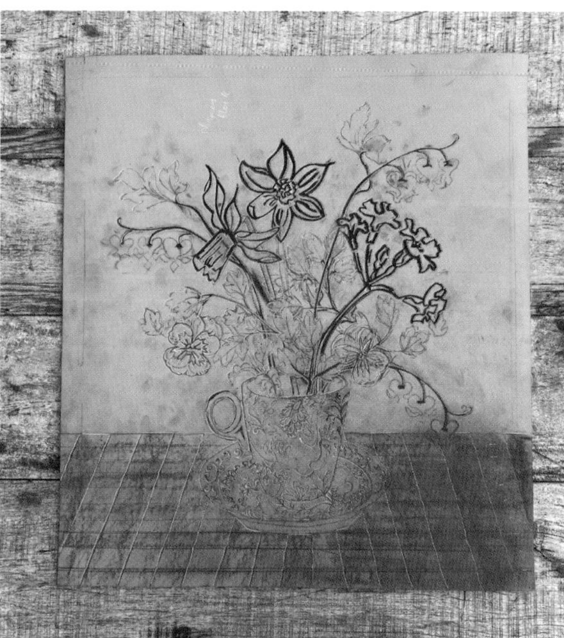

The block with the tracing enhanced with charcoal. The design was cut with the finest V-shaped tool. Notice that the only elements not cut are the white flowers of the bleeding heart plant. This is because these are to remain white – achieve this by cutting them out of the background block for the paper to show through. There is no need to overprint them.

6. The cutting technique is outlined in Chapter 3. To recap, starting with Block 2 and the finest V-shaped tool, cut around all the elements that you have planned to include in this layer of the print. Refer to the drawing as a guide. Next with the medium U-shaped gouge, cut around the outer edge of these elements again. You can follow in the grooves made with the V-shaped tool.

7. Switch to your widest, shallow U-shaped tool to cut away all background and the blank areas within and between your shapes.

8. On Block 1, most of the lino is intact and windows are cut out for shapes such as flowers, stems and leaves. Start with the fine V-shaped tool and cut the outline of all of the shapes to be removed. Then, as before, switch to the medium U-shaped gouge and cut around the fine lines again, following their inside edges. Remove the excess lino from inside these shapes.

The tool for this job depends on the size of the areas to be removed. In the example, I have left in the veins of the leaves so some of the lino to be removed is quite tiny and will require a tool commensurate in size. The area to be overprinted with a daffodil is a large blank space so I use the large, shallow U-shaped tool. (For more about purchasing the minimum number of tools and how to use them, *see* Chapters 1 and 3.)

With blocks ready, prepare paper and a printing area. The messy job of laying out a palette of inks comes later to avoid ruining work with inky fingerprints.

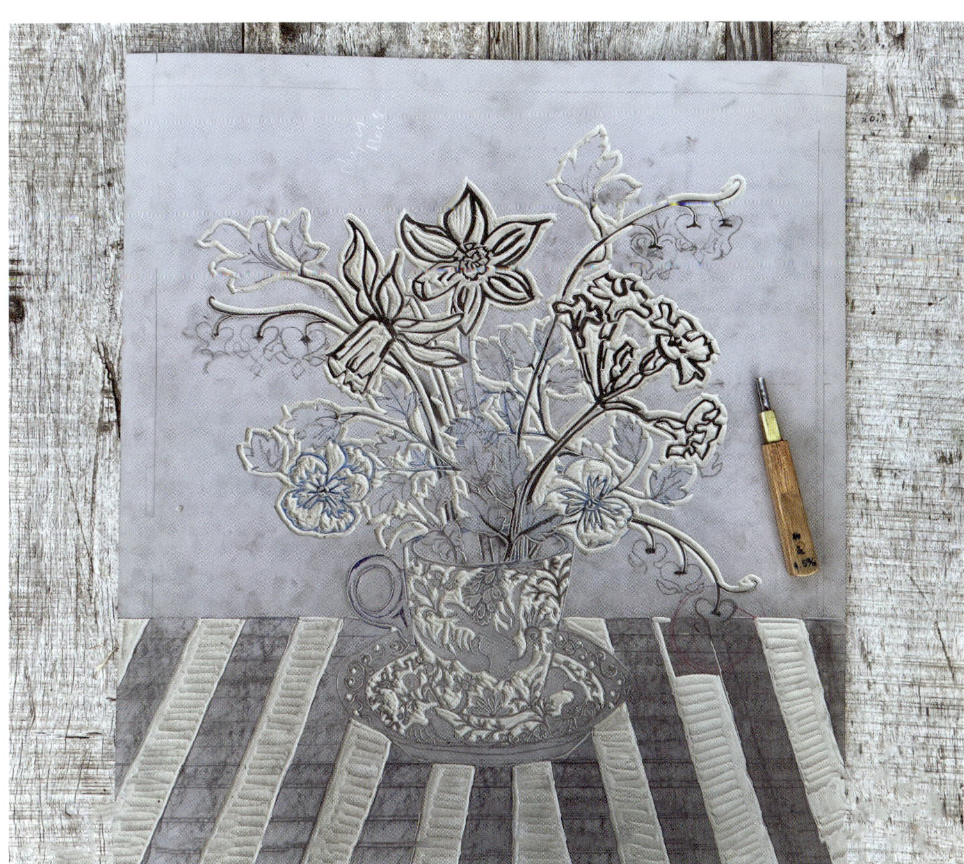

Block 2, having gone round the motifs once with the finest V-shaped tool and a second time with a U-shaped tool.

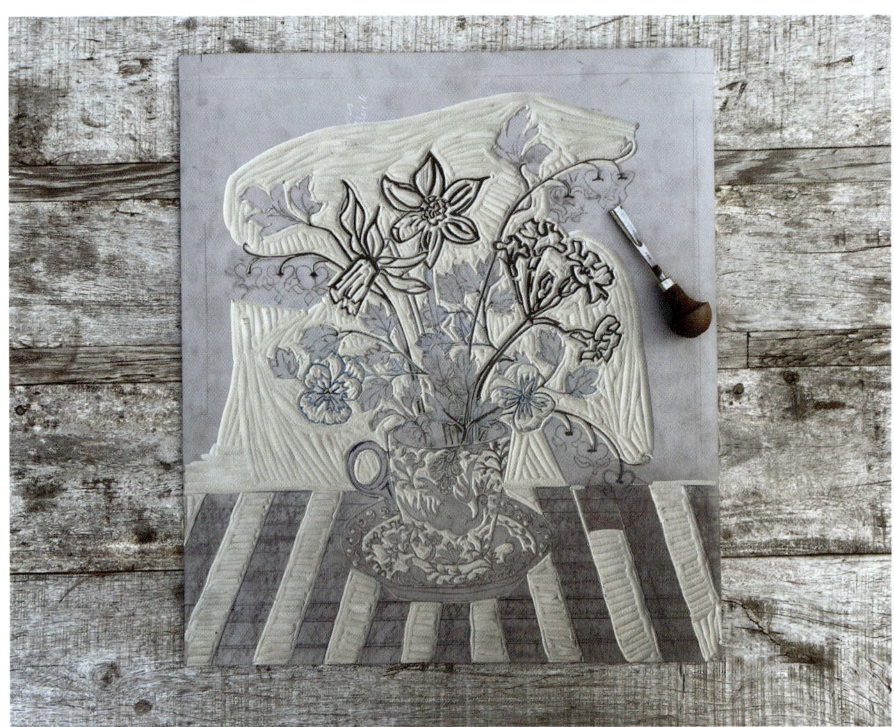

Block 2 with the background cut away. Notice that some of the excess lino is left in to save on unnecessary work. A large block like this will be inked using 5cm- (2in-) wide rollers. Gouge out the entire background all the way to the outer edges if the block is small.

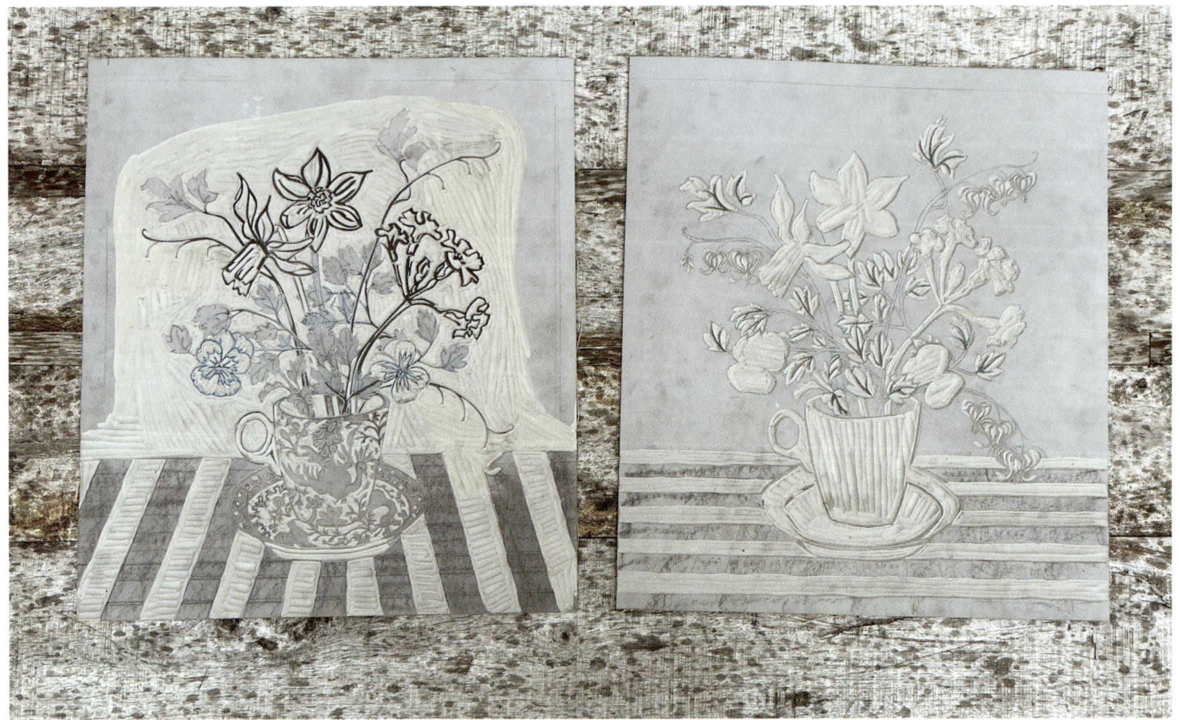

Block 2 (left) alongside Block 1 (right). Notice how the pendant flowers of the bleeding heart plant are cut from the background block but are absent from the shapes block. See also how I created the gingham tablecloth effect – Block 2 has vertical stripes, which will be overprinted with horizontal stripes on Block 1.

If you have large sheets of Japanese-made paper, you will need to cut them to the correct size. Otherwise, choose the appropriate size of paper for the print you are making (*see* Chapter 1 for advice on paper choice). It is good practice to allow a generous border all around your print of at least 5cm (2in). Ensure that your paper is cut accurately at right angles – a set square is useful for this.

Set up your printing area, separate to the area you will use to ink the blocks (alongside is fine, if space is limited). It is essential to keep this area clean, tidy and free of ink so as not to spoil the work.

Use thick, sturdy paper or card as a base/printing bed. This sheet must have at least one perfectly right-angled corner and be larger than the lino block. Stick this printing bed to the work surface with masking tape.

REGISTRATION

9. Now for the all-important registration. The method is simple and involves no special equipment. Take the block and place it face up, exactly corresponding to where it is to be printed on your sheet. If you plan a 5cm (2in) border, place the block exactly 5cm (2in) away from bottom-left corner and sides of the print bed. Use a ruler to mark this accurately. Taking a fine pen, draw around the block to accurately record the desired placement on the print bed. As your blocks are identical in size, they can each be placed within these lines.

This simple outline is a guide to placing the blocks. As long as you correctly place the lino within these guidelines and the paper lines up with the bottom corner of the base, you end up with a perfectly registered print. There are more complex ways that you can use to register your blocks, but I have found the simple method described above works perfectly well for my needs. You can buy special jigs or registration devices, but as these often require that the lino blocks be stuck to down to a piece of wooden board, I avoid them. Many printmakers do use these devices, though, so feel free to research and invest if that suits your needs. Other methods of registration involve taping interlocking tabs to your block and to the back of your paper.

With your paper ready and print bed set up with its registration marks, lay out the palette of inks. Don your apron and gloves – things are about to get messy!

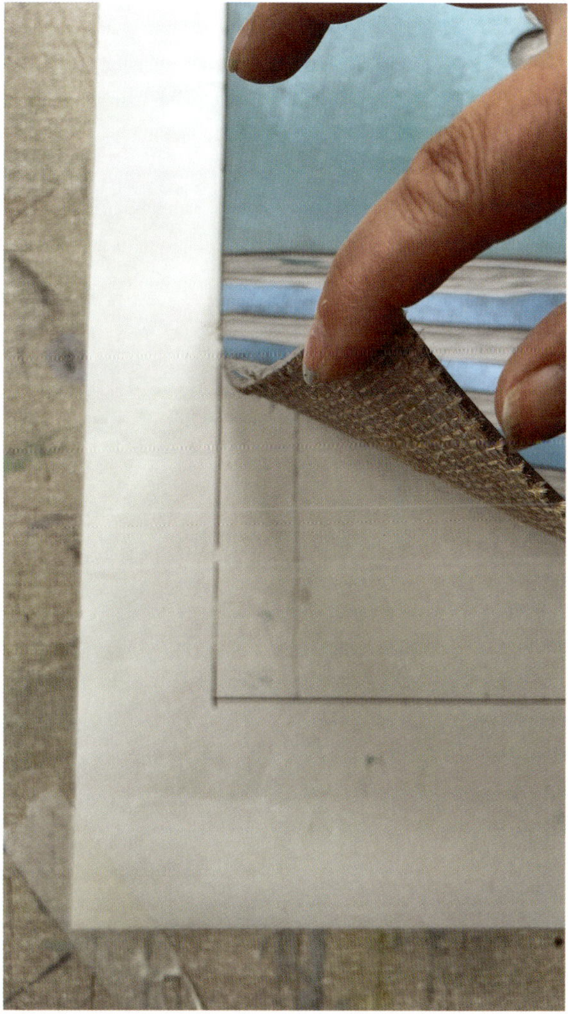

The bottom-left corner of Block 1, lifted to show the pen marks below, which indicate exactly with where it should be placed on the print bed. The pen lines correspond to the edge of the finished print, and are drawn at right angles to the edge of the print bed.

Set up the palette as described in Chapter 4. Mix enough of each colour for the whole printing session – judging this will come with experience. In general, it pays to lay out plenty of extender (tinting medium), opaque white and yellow ink. This must be balanced with a concern for not wasting expensive ink.

Use up to 40 per cent extender in mixes. If a colour is running low, instead of mixing it from scratch, try simply adding more extender to replenish it. The colour is weakened but something like a watercolour effect is achieved; the mix will be translucent. Adding white to a mix will make it more opaque as well as pastel.

INKING

10. Both blocks should be inked prior to printing, but Block 1 is printed first. Use a wide roller to apply a good layer of ink all over, moving the roller back and forth in all directions.

11. Use a separate roller for each colour and ink the block in the usual way, applying all the different colours. A note of caution, for a two-tone roller remember to pay attention to the direction of application (*see* Chapter 4). Keep to a back-and-forth

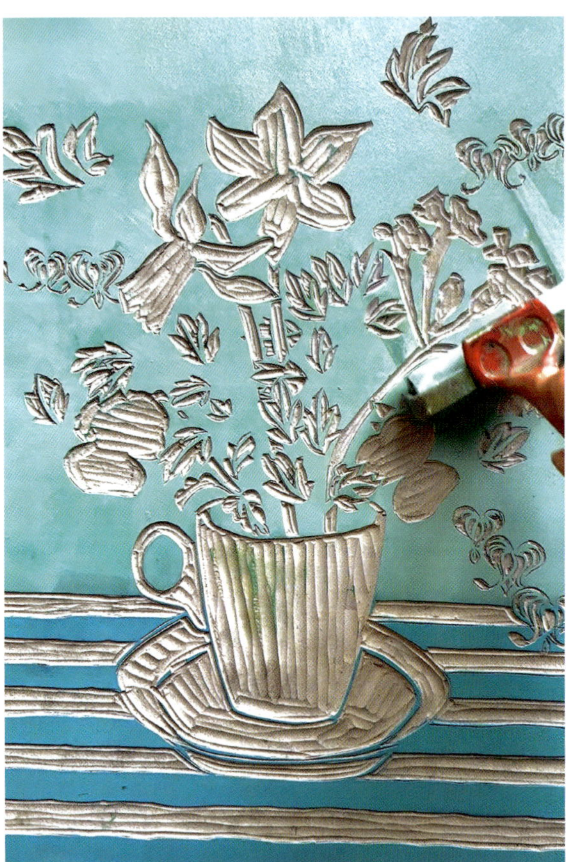

Block 1 is inked and printed first. For this print layer, I chose two colours, each inked with a separate roller. Select a 10cm- (4in-) wide roller for this to lay down the ink quickly with less effort.

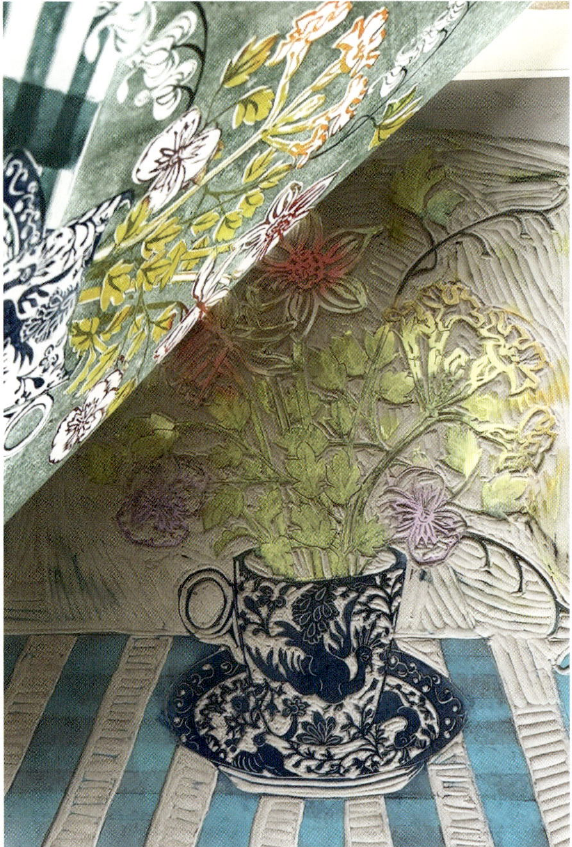

Block 2, ready to print. I mixed colour and prepared five separate rollers, one for each colour. Two-tone rollers are prepared: grey blending to pink for the daffodils and orange fading to yellow for the cowslip primrose.

motion in the same direction. (If you change direction you will lose the distinction between the two colours as the two tones, light and dark, will blend to a dull 'one-note' mid-tone colour and 'dirty' the roller for later use.)

Check all areas are well covered with ink, blending out any obvious harsh transitions from one colour to another by dabbing with a gloved finger. Finally, use a baby wipe to rub away any areas that have unwanted ink on them. Trim any stray hessian protruding from the edge of blocks – inky string will make a fuzzy mark on an otherwise clean border around your work.

12. Place Block 1 accurately within the guidelines on the print bed, first carefully pick up the printing paper, holding the bottom left-hand corner in your left hand and the upper right-hand corner in your right hand. Some papers have a right and a wrong side. You need to print onto the smooth side. (Textured papers are not suitable as the results look pale, mottled and badly executed.)

Line up the left-hand corner of the paper with the left-hand corner of the print bed. To do this accurately, pay attention to the corner – holding the paper between your index finger and third finger and using your thumb outstretched to line up the bottom edges. With this position held firmly, let the rest of the paper flop down to make contact with the block, using the right hand to guide it, if necessary. With a smaller print this is a simple matter and

KEEP YOUR HANDS CLEAN

Remove your gloves when handling clean printing paper to avoid inky finger marks on the edge of a perfect print. Hold your block from underneath, like a butler holding a tray, to keep your fingers as clean as possible. Use a wipe or apron to clean your hands as necessary.

CHECK THE EDGES

Pay attention to the edges of both the block and the shapes, as the roller can sometimes miss these, especially when the lino has been cut from a roll and will not lie perfectly flat. Time taken to check that the surface is well covered will pay off later.

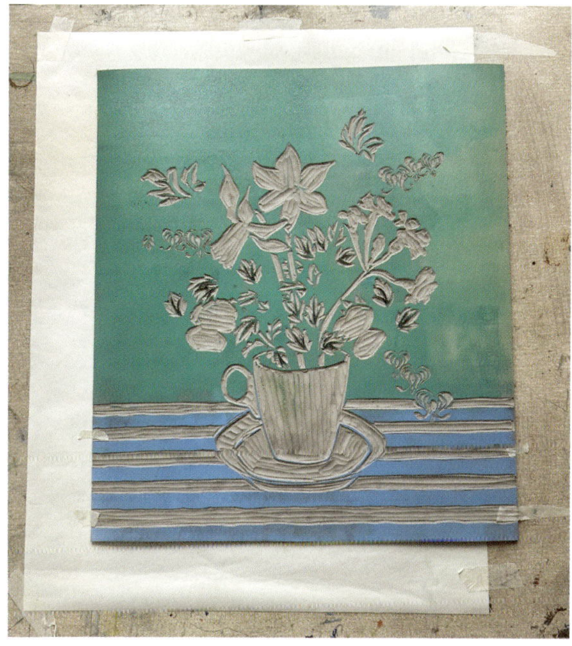

Block 1 in position on the print bed. Small strips of masking tape hold the block in place, preventing any movement during printing.

more a question of letting the paper go; large prints take a more coaxing.

13. With both hands now free, carefully smooth a hand across the back of the paper to adhere it to the sticky ink. Oil-based ink is tacky, so the paper should not move once positioned. Use the back of the baren or wooden spoon to rub firmly all over in a circular motion, using the heel of your palm in the bowl of the spoon. Stand up to print to use your bodyweight, being firm but careful not to move the paper out of position. If you have applied enough ink, this is rarely a problem.

Pay attention to the edges. To print these successfully, switch from using the heel of your palm to putting your fingers in the spoon and raising it slightly to really target these areas. Err on the side of caution; when I think I have rubbed all over well enough and I'm feeling a little weary, I take a breath and do 10 per cent more rubbing! Better to overdo it than to be disappointed. This is the last hurdle. The design will emerge through the back of the paper, which is helpful, making it obvious where to apply more pressure and where to leave off.

14. Pick up one corner of the paper and peel it back to reveal the first complete stage. Put your printed paper to one side for a moment, face up as it is sticky and wet.

15. Move on to the second and final print layer. Remove Block 1 from the print bed, holding it from the bottom like a tray as before. Replace it with Block 2, making sure the orientation and positioning are correct within your guidelines. Use masking tape to stick it to the print bed, if you wish.

Repeat the process as before, carefully aligning the paper, smoothing over the back of it with your hand so it adheres to the block and rubbing thoroughly to take a print. Apply pressure where necessary and leave off where there is a void. Employ the 10 per cent extra rule again, you are on the home straight – there are no second chances once the print is removed.

16. You have now made your first print – an artist's proof, no less. Congratulations – it's quite a momentous achievement. But no resting on your laurels; inspect your print, take stock and decide what you need to do next. Would you like to tweak the colours for your next print? Or is it perfect in your eyes and therefore you just want to repeat the process again and again to create an edition?

Try printing the same blocks with different-coloured inks. Creating a set of prints in different colours is known as a 'Varied Edition'. Label your prints accordingly using the abbreviation V.E. to denote this. One of the virtues of this method is that variations of colour are possible between prints. Thus, the same design will appear distinct from others within the edition (some to a greater degree of success than others). Start with small prints to learn without too much wasted effort.

In the next chapter, we will look at some extra techniques that you can use to add even more colour to your work. Of course, this is by no means necessary, but I am all for shortcuts and using watercolour by hand can be a quick and effective method to achieve beautiful and unusual results.

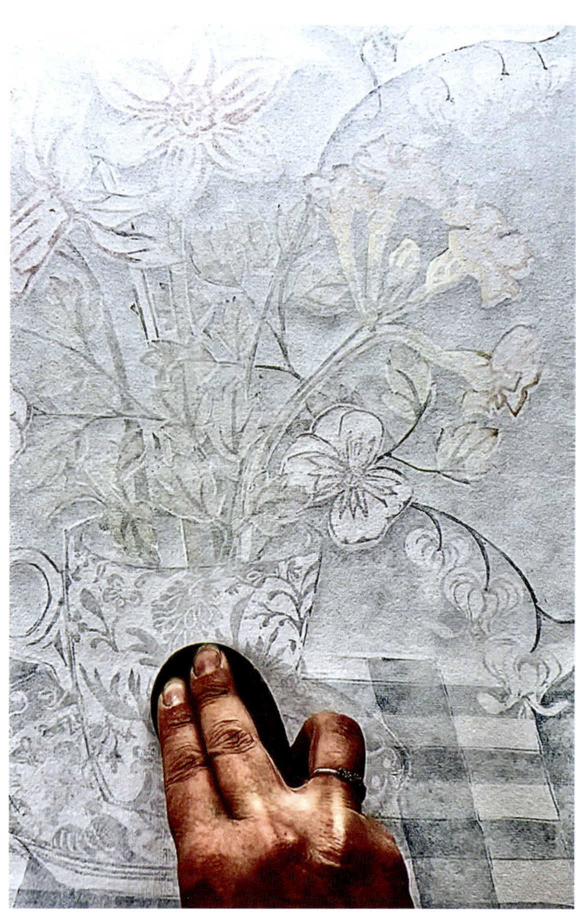

Taking the second print, lay the paper accurately on the block for a second time. Use a small wooden spoon or baren to rub all over the back of the paper. The design is visible through the paper – this helps us to know where to apply pressure in particular.

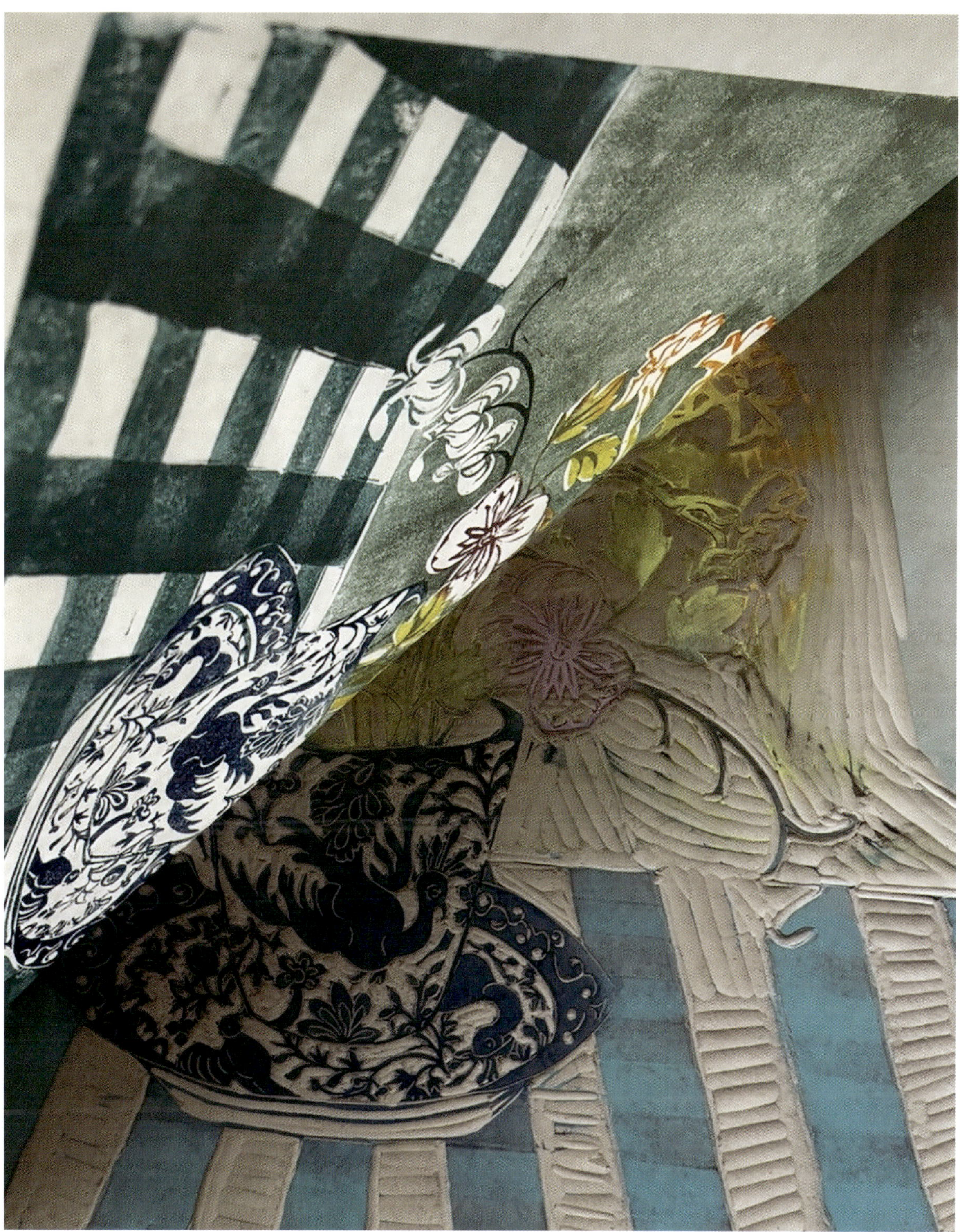

Removing the paper to reveal the finished print.

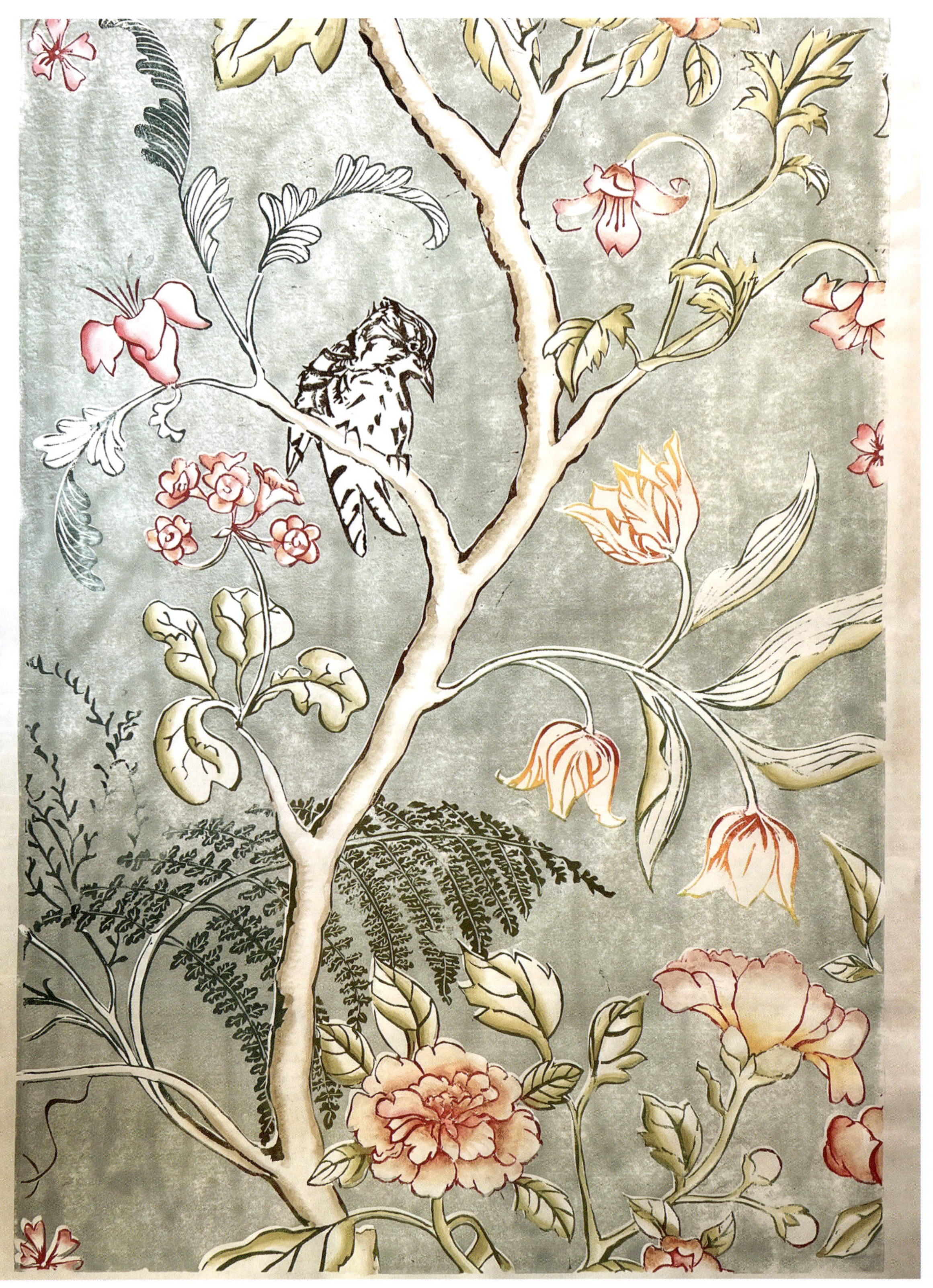

CHAPTER 6

ADDING WATERCOLOUR

Developing your practice keeps things fresh and exciting. Once you can make prints in a conventional way, why not try something different? You can invent new ways to add colour and use shortcuts that make your work unique. This chapter explores some of these additional techniques to try.

CREATING A LINE BLOCK PRINT FOR WATERCOLOUR PAINTING

Through experimentation, I started to add watercolour to my prints. Think of a print as a line drawing in a colouring book. The watercolour is an opportunity for colouring in, not in blocks of solid colour but with translucent washes that fade into the paper. The effect is surprisingly harmonious, considering that oil- and water-based media feature on the same piece of work.

If you have tried out some of the projects in this book, I encourage you to explore this technique. You can create a print from either a single block or from two blocks (consisting of a block for printing the background and another for the line drawing, as shown in Chapter 5) and then paint it.

You might wonder why to apply colour by hand when another block would suffice. The effect of tonal washes is unique and quick to achieve – there is no need to go to the trouble to cut and register a third block. A registration mishap late on in the process is a great disappointment and I never create more than two blocks for any one print as I find it too labour-intensive.

My inspiration came from hand-painted Chinese wallpapers and Japanese woodblock prints. I was inspired by the designs featuring huge peonies, exotic birds and wonderful cherry blossoms. I had learnt Japanese block printing using expensive hardwoods, such as cherry – the fine grain of the wood is suitable for printing fine lines. Lino is very tough, so using it to make such a 'line block' is a possibility. I knew from woodblock printing that watercolour could be used successfully on the same Japanese paper I use for linocuts, even though it is thin. After I made my prints I discovered that early Chinese wallpaper was in fact block printed, with some extra colour applied by hand. Made for the export market, it was cheaper to print it and add colour – the designs appearing to be unique and entirely hand painted.

Woodpecker and Peonies made from two blocks with watercolour added by hand.

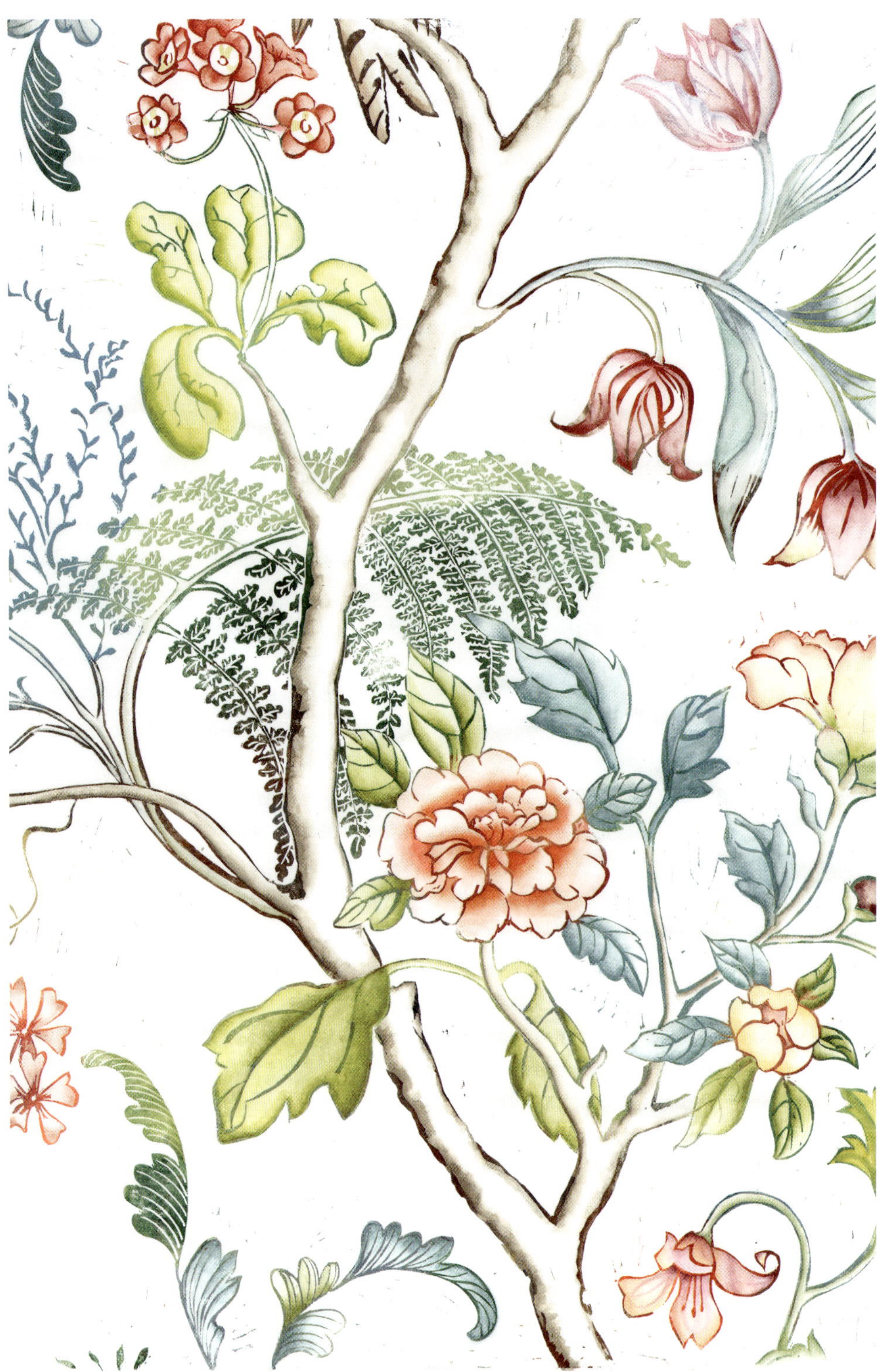

To understand this print, think of it in terms of a colouring book. It is made from one block that is inked up with many colours. The block itself is a 'line' block, i.e. cut to print the line drawing rather than any whole, filled-in shapes. Once these coloured lines are dry, they are painted with washes of watercolour.

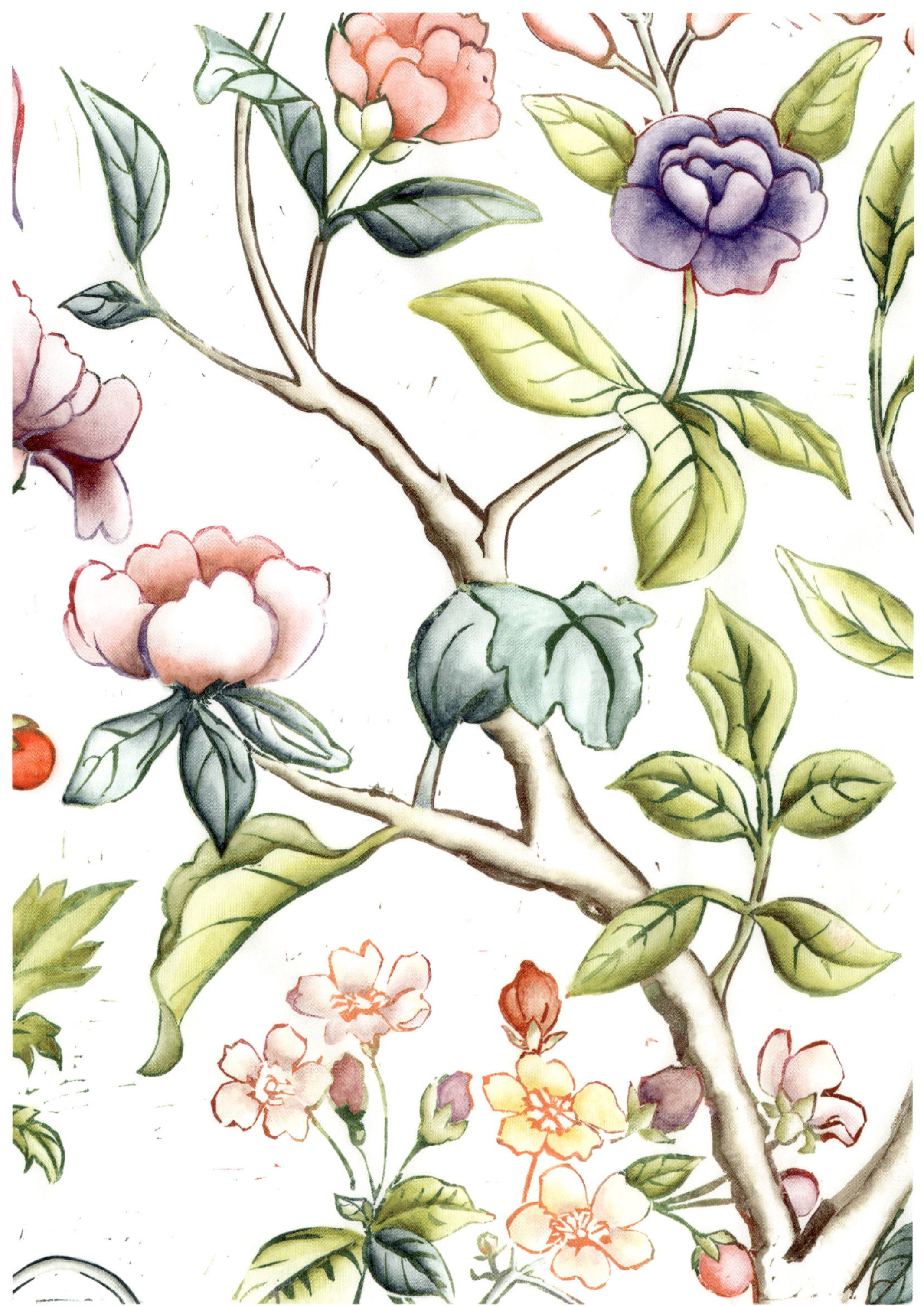

Japanese machine-made papers are a great surprise to work with if you've been used to thick watercolour paper. These Japanese papers are thin, yet tough enough to take print and watercolour well.

You Will Need

- **Papers** – Inexpensive Japanese machine-made papers with a mulberry silk-like quality, including: Awagami Hosho 80g, Awagami Masa, Awagami Silk and Inbe
- **Brushes** – Two good, medium-sized watercolour brushes, minimum size 6.

For this process to work, you must use the correct paper. A paper made for printing by hand that is also good for wet media is a must. Experiment with small packs of assorted Japanese papers available from printmakers suppliers (*see* Suppliers) as well as the recommendations above. A sable brush for watercolour is a wonderful, if expensive, tool. Alternatively, purchase good synthetic watercolour brushes of a similar size.

The two blocks for this print are identical in size and measure 65 × 90cm (26 × 35in). One block, for the background, is printed in grey-blue, while the second block, featuring the lines, is printed with multiple rollers – some prepared with two tones and others with single colours. There is plenty of gouged-out space between the areas in relief so it is possible to add many colours easily to such a large block.

To handprint something of this size, while possible, is nonetheless a real labour of love. This has been printed using my press. Hand printing a background of such a size would really work up a steam! Japanese paper comes in large sheets, but it was quite difficult to prevent it from creasing in the press. There is no reason a smaller print using this technique could not be created and pressed by hand.

Planning a Print to Paint with Watercolour

This method is most effective colouring certain botanical subjects. With large flower heads, each individual petal can be shaded, or the surface of leaves can easily and quickly be given soft tones.

For complex prints I make a plan, in pencil, of the areas that I intend to colour in with watercolour. With such a plan to guide me, I can be spontaneous with colour as I already know exactly where to place my brush. A proof, like a brass rubbing, taken from the block can be used to make a plan. Alternatively, keep a colour image of the botanical subjects alongside for reference while you paint your prints.

How to Prepare a Watercolour Palette

Take a small sheet of Japanese paper to practice on. The beauty of using this method quickly becomes apparent. Mix a few watery pools of the colours you want to use ready in your palette. If you've never worked with watercolour before, note that

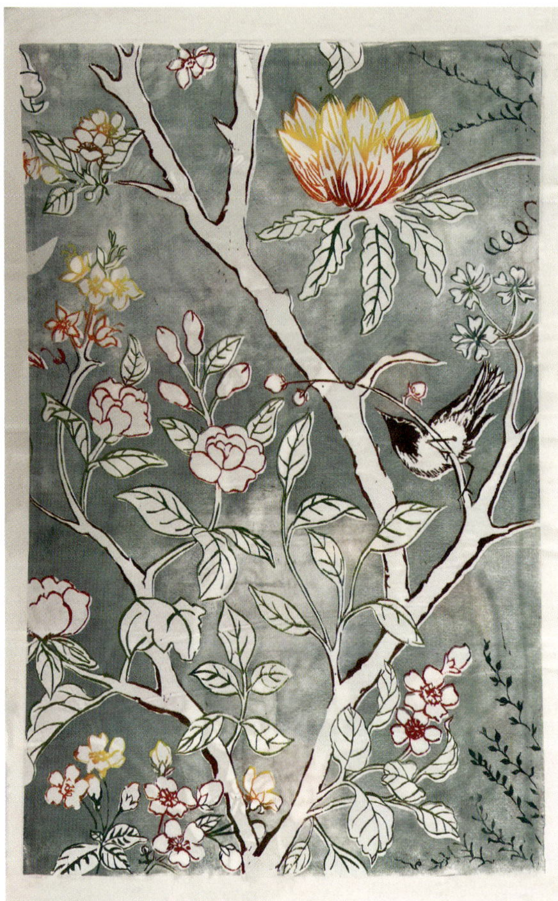

This print is made from two blocks only. This is how it looks before watercolour is applied. It certainly appears unfinished, and it is greatly enhanced by the final step of hand colouring.

you need to mix colours in the palette ready to load your brush with. To do this, start by charging your brush with plenty of water to release into a segment of your paint tray, making a well or pool of water to which you can add colour.

Watercolour is a translucent media, though a few specialist opaque colours are available. Adding white to mixes is not necessary. For a paler colour, add more water so the paper is seen through the wash. For a deeper colour, use more colour and less water, obscuring the paper below.

Load Your Brush with Colour and Apply

Start where you want the most intense colour and brush it on in one sweep, then take a second brush, loaded with clean water, and sweep along one side of the first stroke where you want it to fade out. The aim is to make the colour progressively paler and more translucent until it fades out completely. To achieve this, the second brush must be drier – damp but not overloaded with clean water. Have a piece of kitchen paper or rag on which to dab your brush

to remove some of the wetness. You risk cockling (wrinkling) the paper if it gets too sodden.

Choose plants and flowers with large areas of shading and colour that fades out. Study hand-painted eighteenth-century Chinese wallpaper for inspiration. Notice, for example, how the cherry leaves are depicted – where a leaf is partially folded we see the underside. Apply paint to create the tones there.

The technique of adding watercolour to a print can be a wonderful process for a printmaker as the chance to play with a fluid media brings with it welcome spontaneity. Having a rough plan on paper to show you where you want the colour is helpful. It speeds up the process, which is important if you have a lot of prints in the edition. A reference made from a proof like a brass rubbing is convenient as it provides a version of the print that is in the correct orientation. I use charcoal or a soft pencil for shading in the proof to produce a useful guide to follow when I am painting on the watercolour.

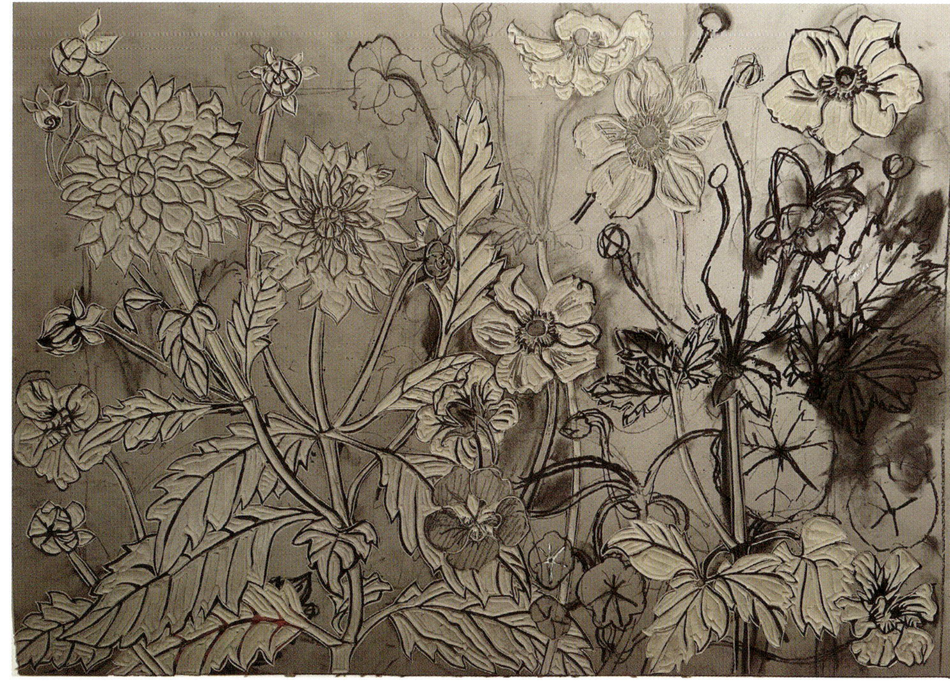

Here the cutting is nearly finished. Notice the charcoal drawn directly onto the block. Charcoal drawing produces lines thick enough to cut. They have the quality of calligraphy, which is further emphasised in the cutting of them.

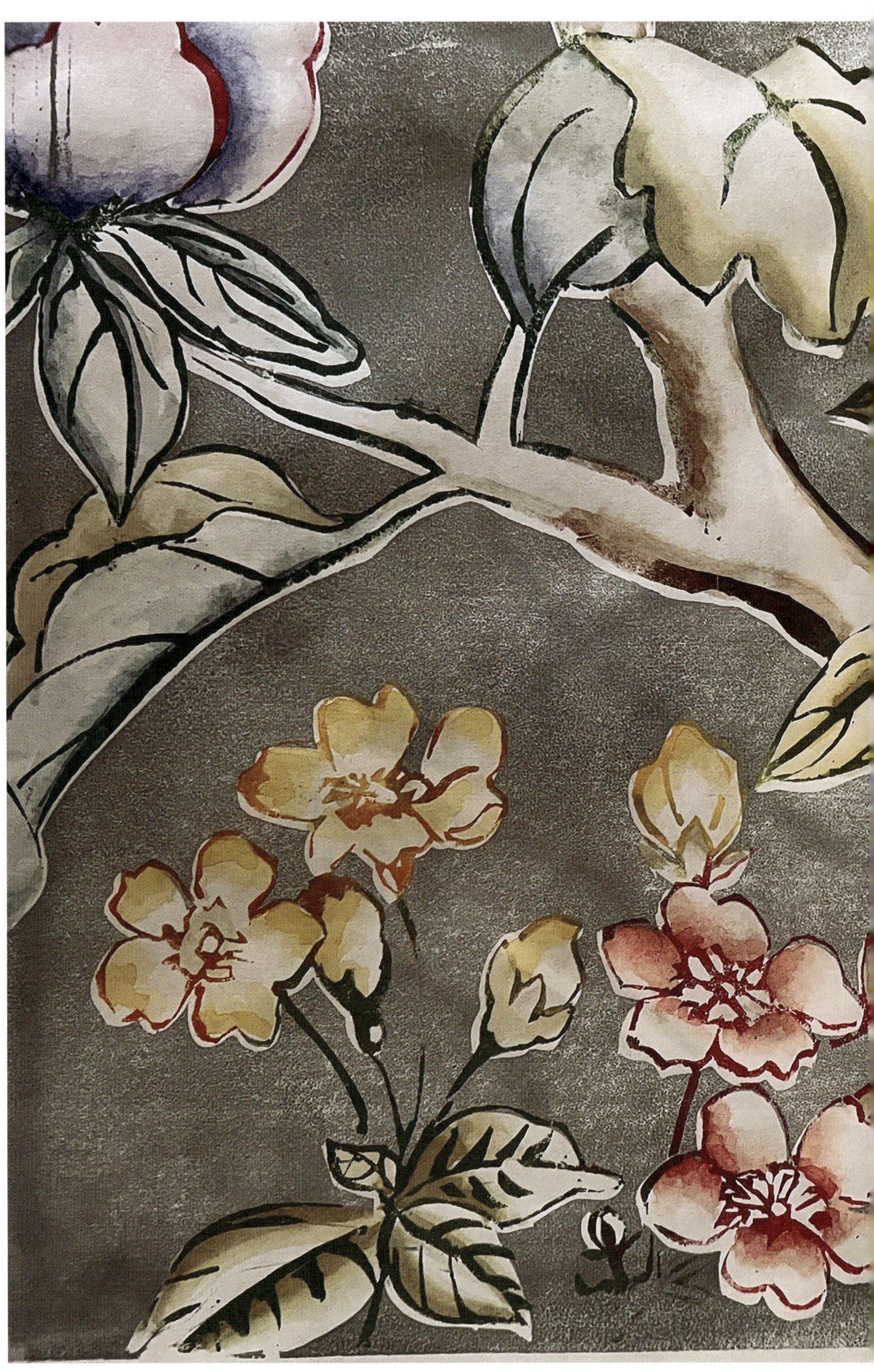

On this print, the emerging peony has been coloured blue, even though the printed outline is red. Refer to a plan made from a proof to apply the watercolour quickly, exactly where you need it. (*See* Chapter 5 for an example of proofing.)

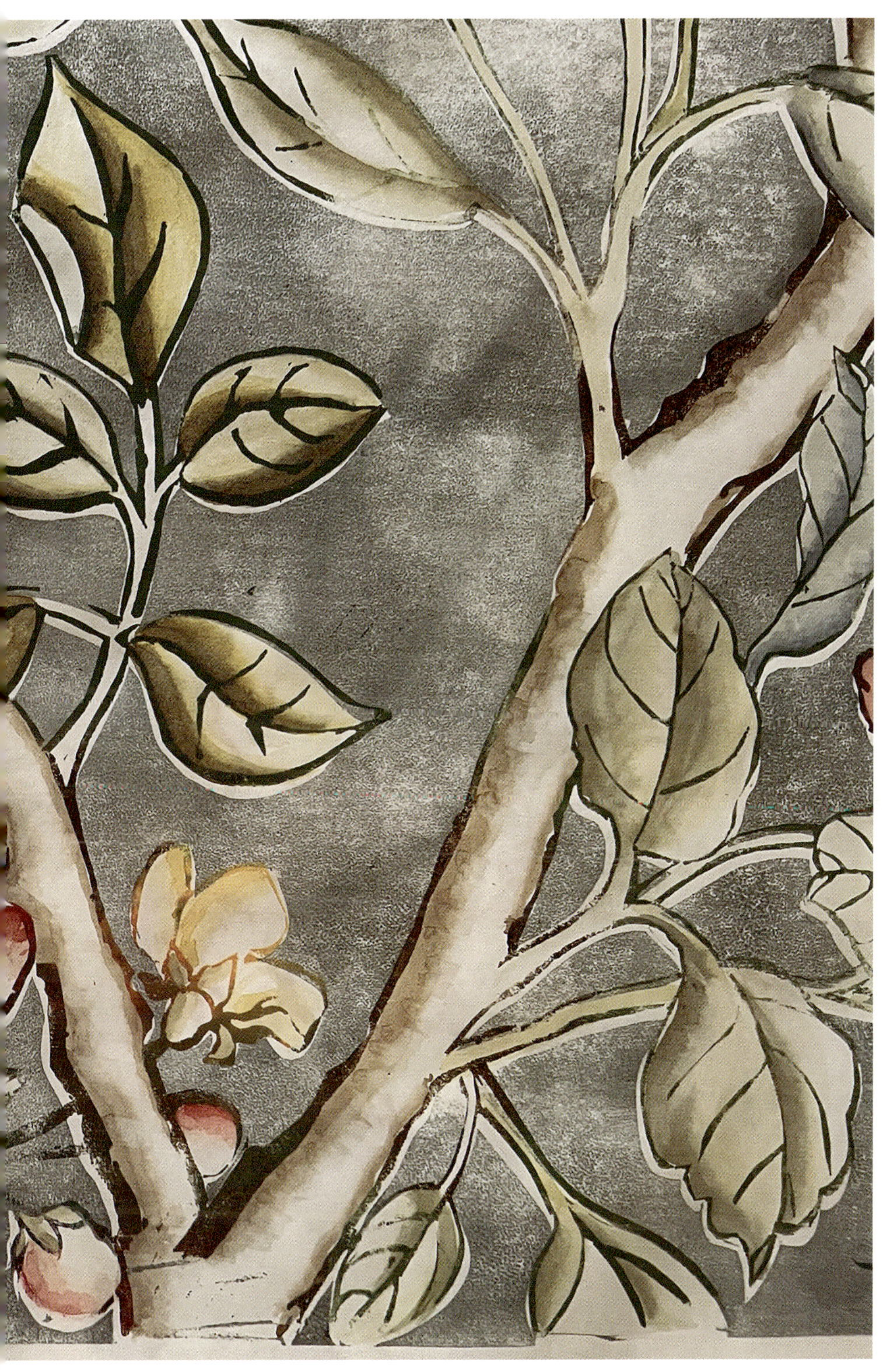

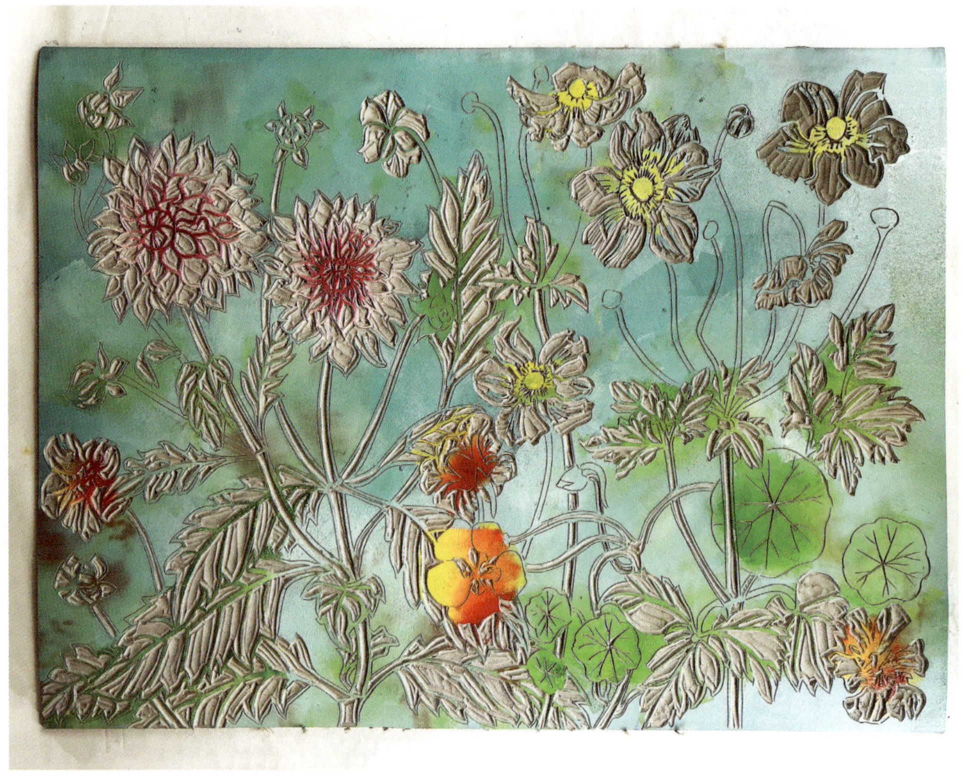

Apply the background ink layer using a wider 10cm (4in) roller in aqua blue, then use smaller 5cm (2in) rollers for the flower centres. For example, an ink roller prepared in plain yellow is used for the centre of the anemones. Dab on spots of ink to adjust the depth of colour in the centres to turn them from yellow to green or pink to crimson. Finally, blend the colours into the background with the larger blue roller to eliminate unwanted lines made by the edges of the coloured rollers.

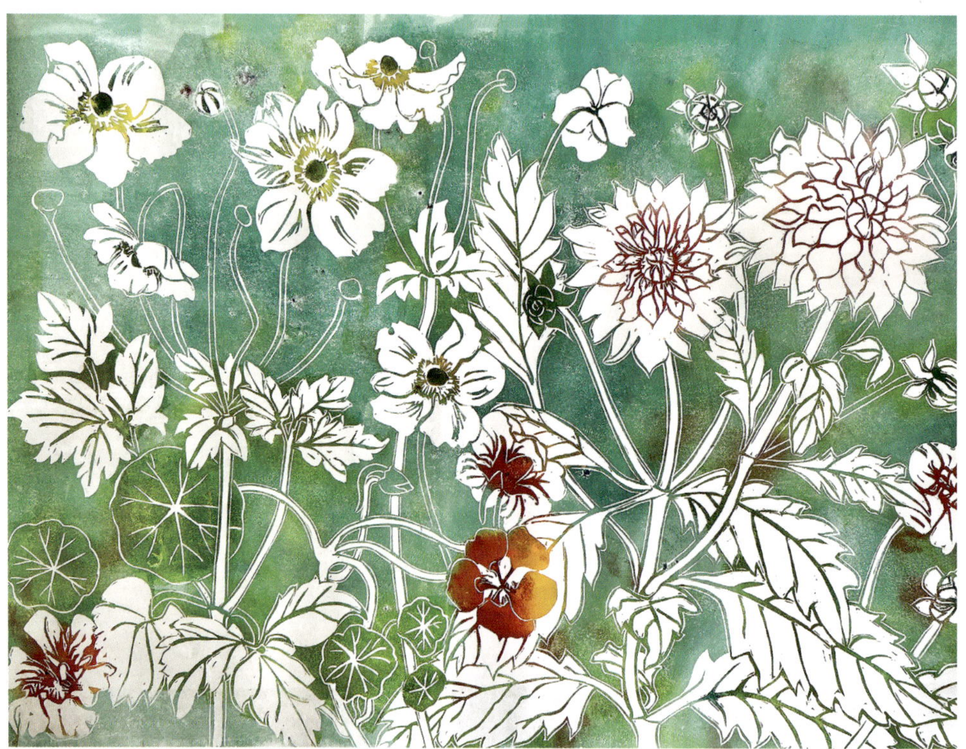

The dried print before its final treatment: hand applied watercolour. Notice the different areas around the print where the background is affected by the colours used. This process pushes the limits of what can be included on a single block and does require extra care and experience to ink it.

Demonstration: *Dahlias, Anemones and Nasturtium –*
Painting With Watercolour

The method I used to make this print was a shortcut for maximum 'colour payoff'. The idea came about from not wanting the extra work of making two blocks, and wondering if it would be possible to create a similar effect with only one.

This is a single-block print with a difference. In effect, it is a line drawing and a background combined into one. This makes it tricky to ink, so attempt this project when you have already become familiar with inking. The background has been left in rather than gouged away, so in that way it is different from the other single-block prints already described – something to experiment with as you expand your practice.

This technique is probably best limited to larger prints. I use 5cm- (2in-) wide ink rollers to apply colour to the inside of shapes, then blend those colours into the background. 'Spot' colours are also added by dabbing them on with a gloved index finger. Ideally, this design would be made easier to cut with an extra tool, a middle sized V, to remove lino from the tight corners inside shapes – of the dahlia flowers, for example.

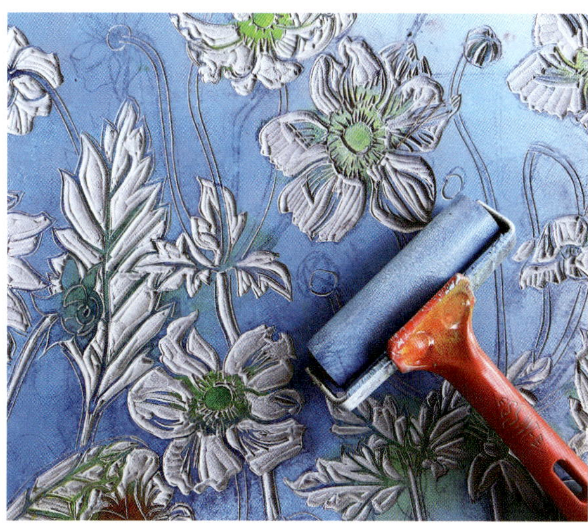

I applied blue background colour all over the block first in an even coating. Surprisingly, precision is not so important. I then applied ink to the centre of the flowers and leaves. Finally, the I used the blue roller again to blend any misplaced colour into the background.

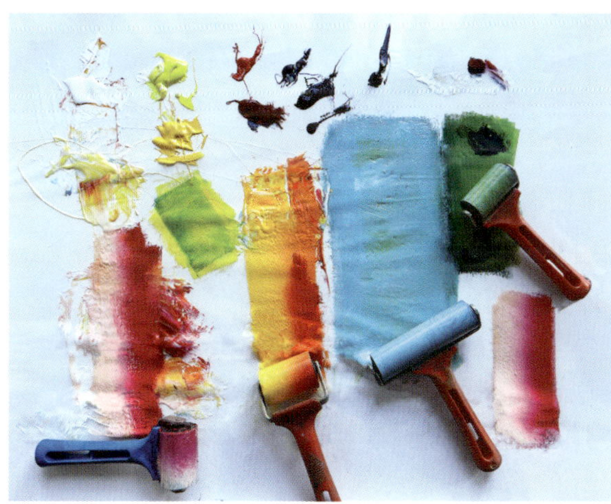

The ink palette used to print *Dahlias, Anemones and Nasturtium*. I used a 10cm- (4in-) wide roller for the background as there is more space to cover. The smaller rollers are better for getting into the awkward areas, such as the inside of leaves and flowers. When preparing a roller with two colours – pastel pink and crimson – the contrast between the colours needs to be exaggerated to be effective.

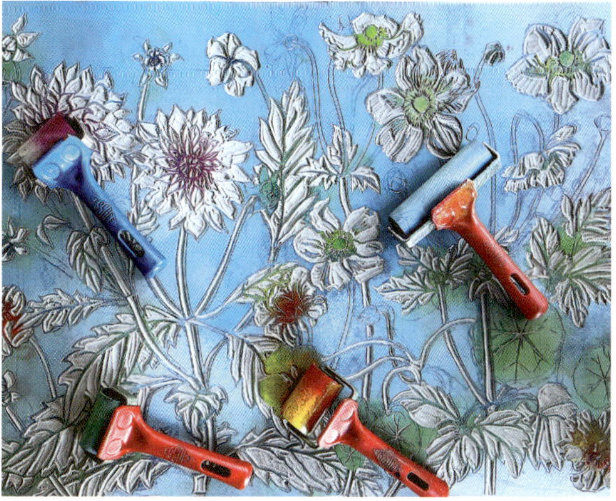

To illustrate, I have laid out the inking rollers in areas where they were used. The first ink roller covers nearly all of the block in blue. Then I use the coloured rollers as appropriate in the centre of leaves and flowers. The final step is to use a gloved finger to dab on extra colour in tiny areas, such as the centres of the Japanese anemones. Any harsh or obvious colour changes are blended in with fingers – no extra ink necessary.

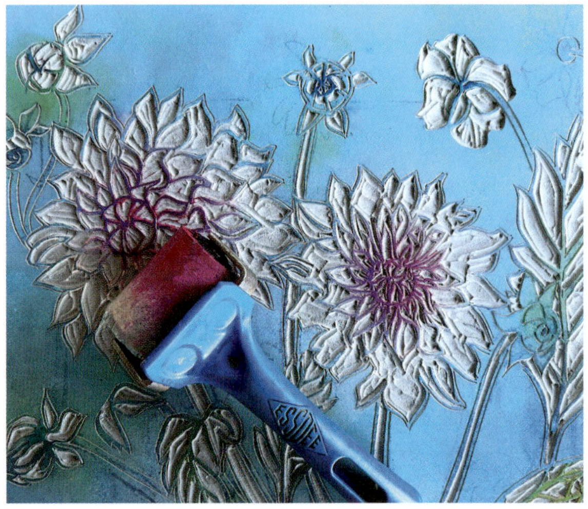

To apply deep crimson in the centre of the dahlia and light pink to the edge, I first used the roller in a back-and-forth motion on half of the flower. Then I swapped to my other hand to repeat the same action on the remaining half. The dark pink centre is maintained and light pink is applied to its outer petals.

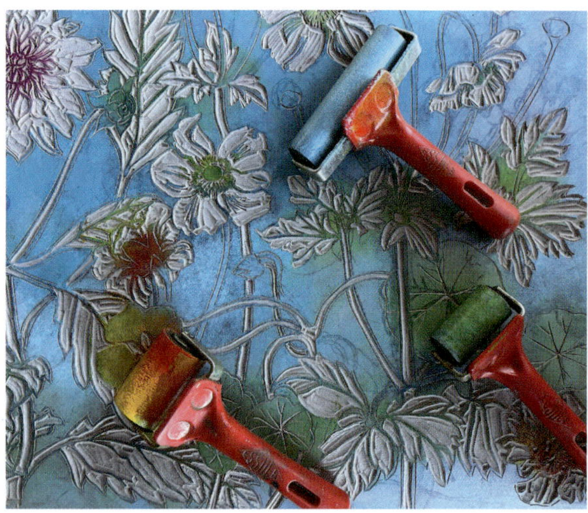

To make the centre of the anemone flower darker than the yellow stamens around it, I dabbed on dark ink with a finger. After applying the green to the leaf, I used the background roller with blue ink to even out the effect.

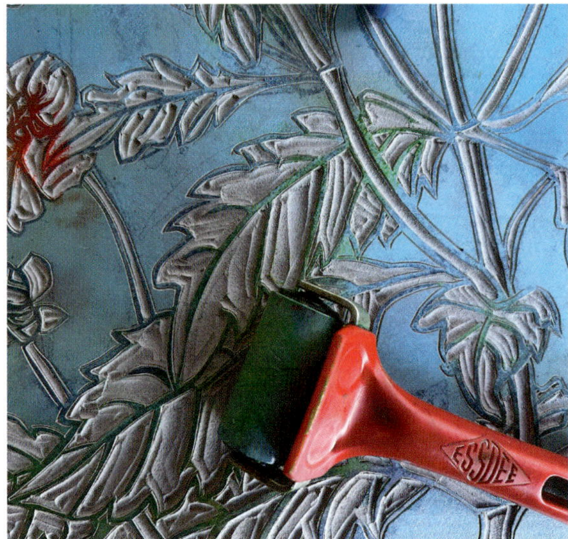

The centre of the dahlia bud on the left has been inked up with a finger to achieve the deepest tone. For speed, I dipped my finger into ink reserves already on the palette, undiluted for strongest pigment. A green ink roller is used for the veins of leaves as well as the nasturtium leaves in a different part of the block. The next step is to blend out with the wide blue background roller any areas where the green has been applied and is not wanted i.e. in the background.

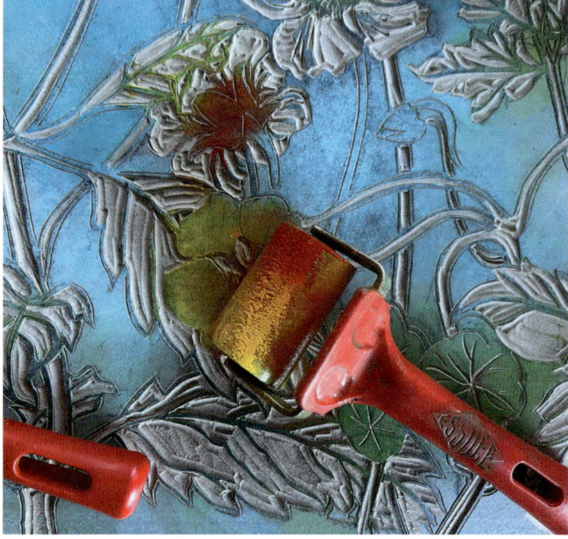

For this nasturtium flower, I used my finger to blend the ink into the background. I was careful not to apply the red onto the background itself, using a small square of paper as a masking device to help achieve this. I used my finger to dab until the yellow was blended in to the edge of the petal. The simple fine-cut lines of the block act as a barrier to separate the two colours – blue from yellow.

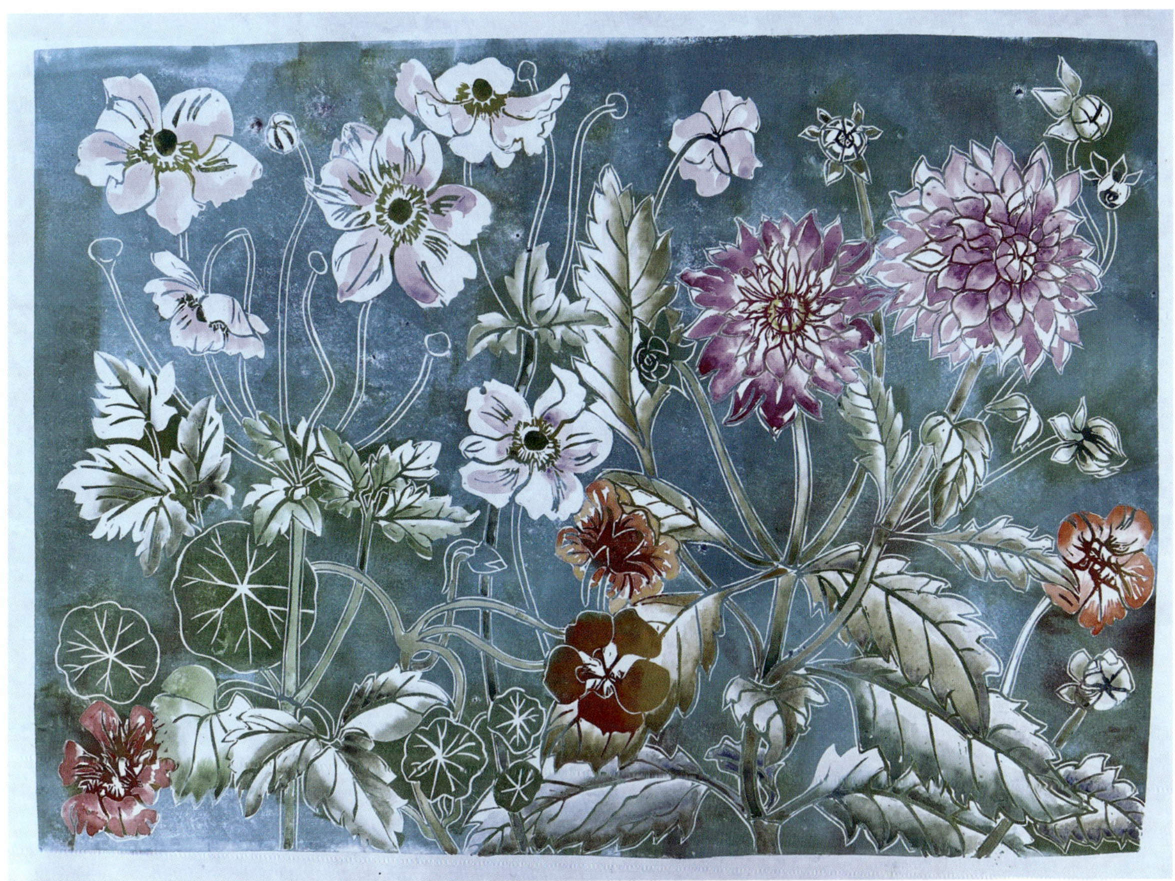

Anemones and Dahlias, the finished print with watercolour applied. Painting is not as tricky as it might look. Conveniently, the oil-based ink repels the water. A single sweep of the brush puts colour into the jagged edges of the leaves.

In detail, the following technique is used to ink it. First, blue-green ink is rolled over most of the block, all of the background area, then the insides of flowers and leaves are added in. This can only be achieved with oil-based inks as they can be blended on the block itself. To get into the awkward areas of internal shapes with ink, I used a small roller and chose relatively large subjects in the design itself. Anything small and fiddly against the background would be impossible to blend seamlessly. On this print, the dahlias are inked in two tones of pink and the nasturtiums in a tequila sunrise combination of yellow and red. Green is applied to the insides of leaves.

Notice on the finished print how the different inks have been blended into the background. It works, as the colours are quite close in hue – blue is next to green on the colour wheel. Even where red has been used for the nasturtiums, it also blends well. Dabbing on spots of colour with your fingers is effective and useful in a couple of scenarios. The whole centre of the anemone flowers are first inked up in yellow with a roller, then dark green is applied with fingers. This works because there is a gap between two areas in relief for the stamens. Any obvious straight ink lines made by the edge of the rollers would be a tell-tale sign. Use a small piece of paper as a masking device to avoid this, or blend away with a finger.

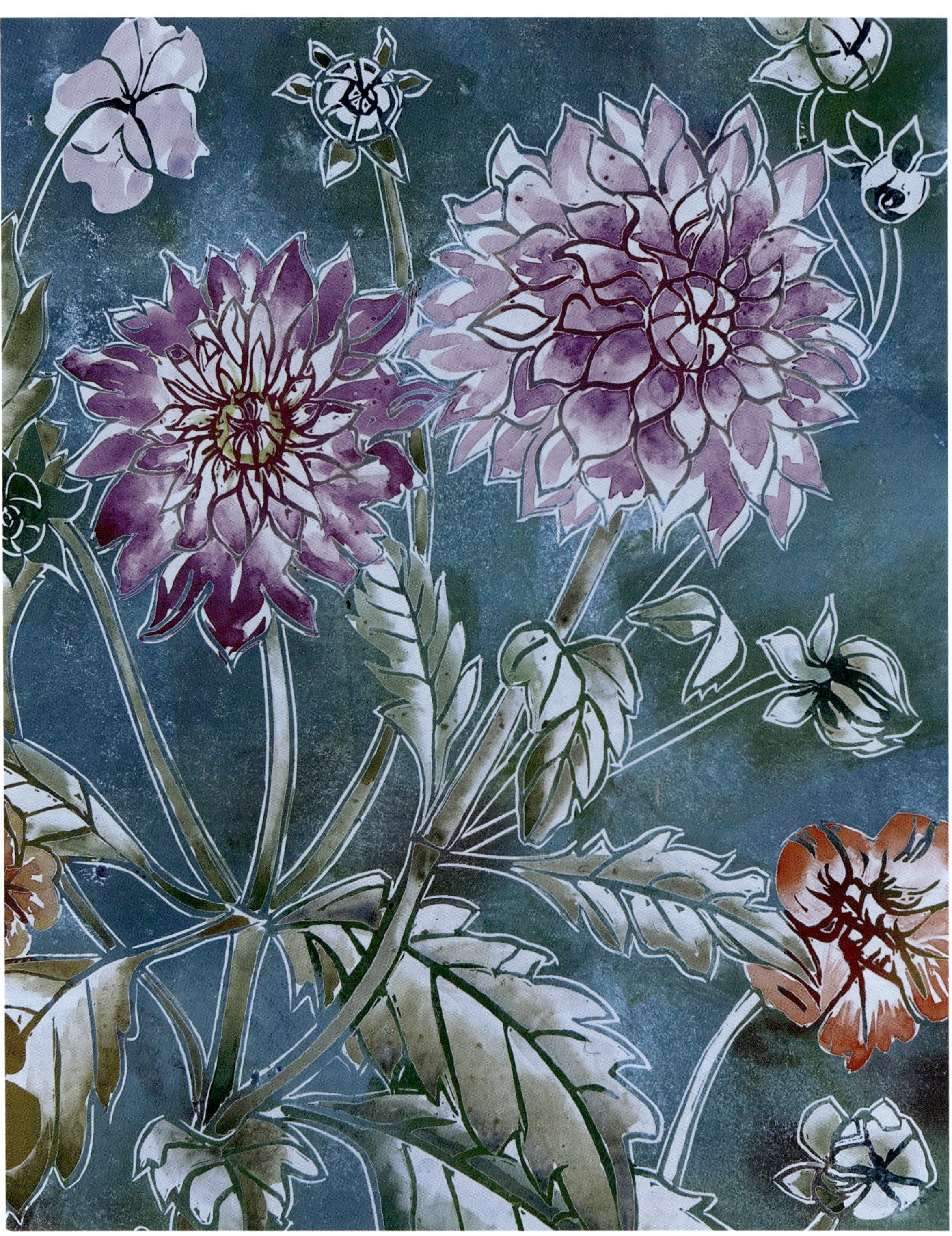

Like a colouring book of dreams. Apply the deepest colour to the edge of the shape and take a second brush with clean water to blend seamlessly into the paper.

THE INVERTED PRINT METHOD

Viola is another type of print made by adding watercolour. This is an example of a reverse or negative print made when the subject is cut out of a background, which is printed in a single flat colour. When the print is dry, the main subject is 'coloured in' with a brush and watercolour.

It can be tricky to achieve an even, flat black background such as this on a print. Leave out the extender from the ink mix and be sure to apply it to the block in a thick, even layer. When it comes to printing, apply pressure especially thoroughly to the details of your design as well as along the edges and into corners. If you have access to a printing press, heavyweight watercolour paper could be used instead of the thin Japanese papers. Experiment, but avoid very highly textured cold-pressed paper.

The message I hope to convey is that printmaking is a world of invention. Perfectionism is not helpful – we might think it motivates us, like a driving force, but ultimately it crushes our confidence because we don't enjoy ourselves and end up losing interest. Creativity feels closer to curiosity than to a search for perfection. It is a place where there's no right or wrong. When I let go of my expectations of how things should look, I tend to be more open to exploration. However, if you do feel unsatisfied, try putting your work away for a while, then look again at your print in a mirror – you might get a pleasant surprise!

I hope this chapter has given you plenty of scope to explore adding watercolour to your prints. For an even deeper dive into the potential of print, the next chapter brings us to a whole new world of pattern.

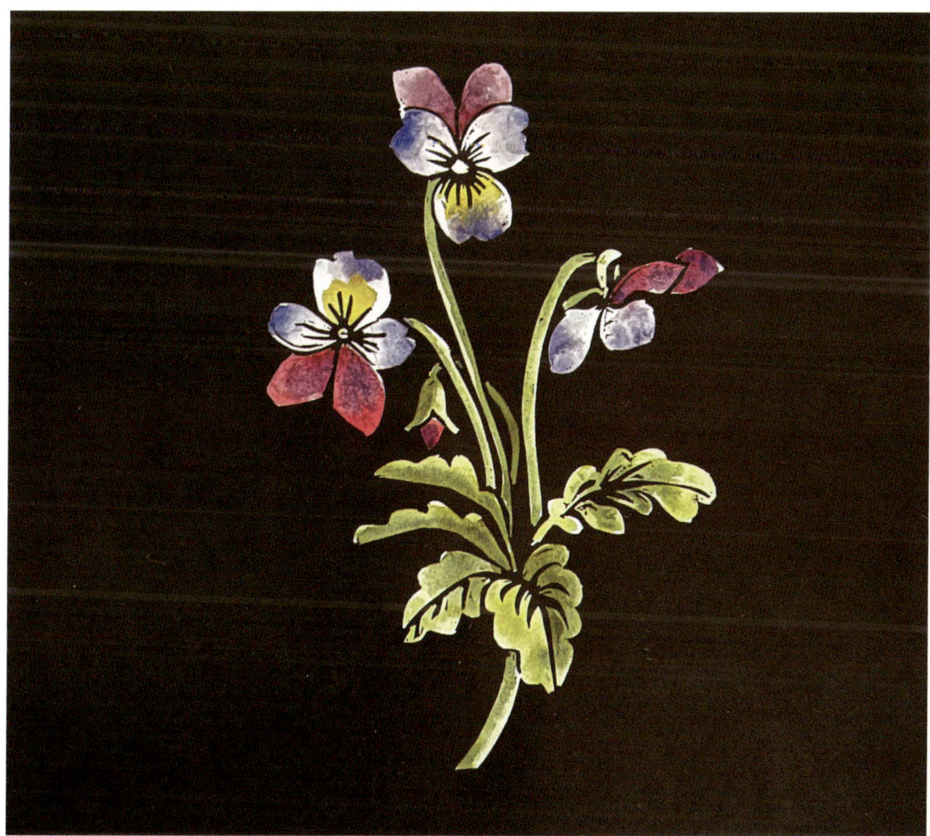

This 'inverted' print of Violas looks completely unfinished until the watercolour is added. As ever, it is essential that the correct paper is used. Japanese paper is thin, so great for hand printing, but it also takes wet media happily.

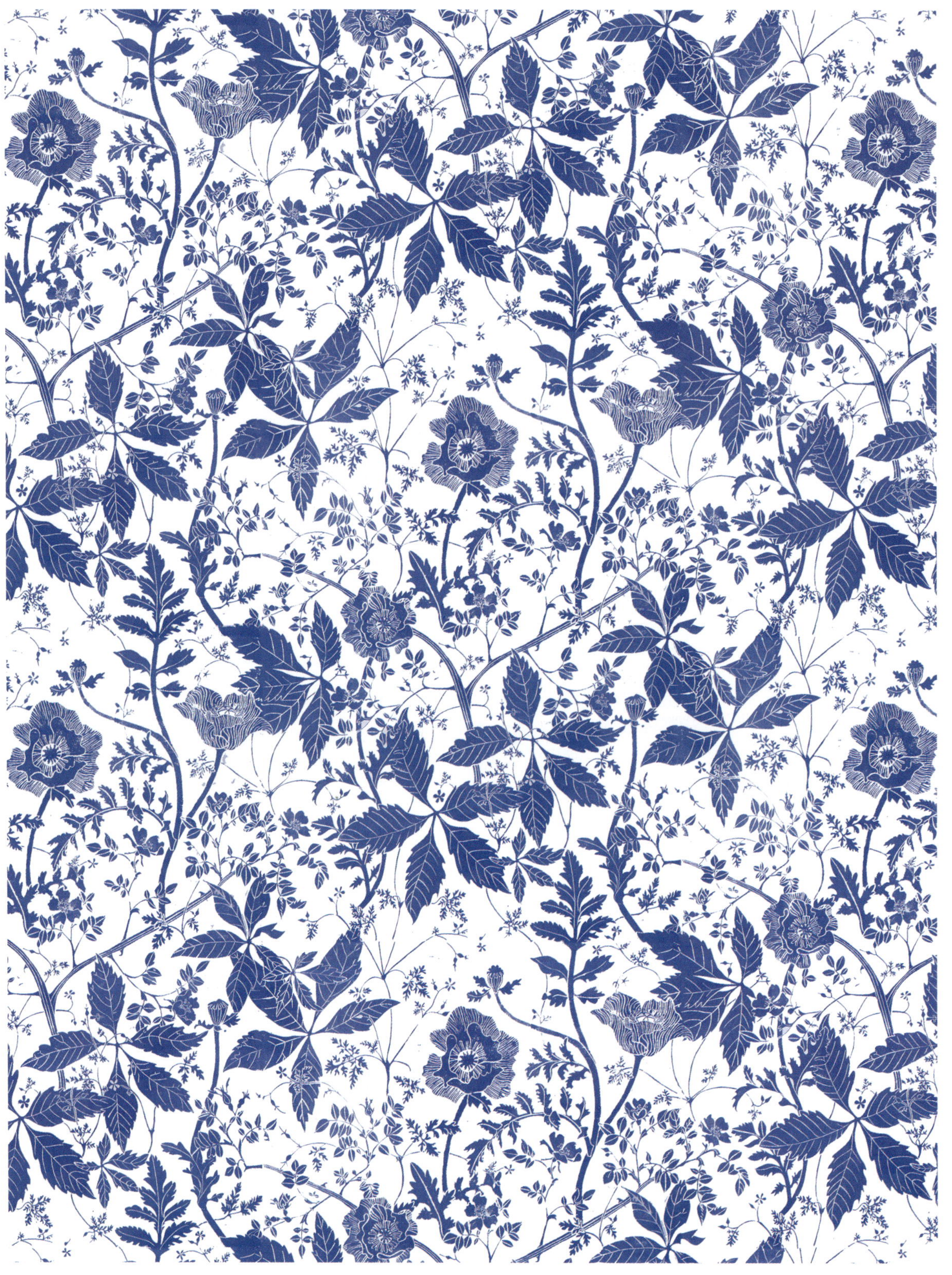

PRINTING BOTANICAL PATTERNS

This chapter is an introduction to pattern and surface design. It is a huge area of study and a wonderful challenge that, by learning to make lino prints, is open to you.

REPEATING PATTERNS

It is fascinating to see your design repeating. There are many types of repeat to explore; dot, brick, block, chequered, mirror, ogee and stripe, to name a few. An irregular, random pattern should look good, no matter where a frame is placed on it.

The *Poppy* wallpaper design given in the demonstration in this chapter has a half-drop repeat pattern with a diagonal rhythm. Large leaves criss-cross the surface, making diamond-shaped 'windows' for a poppy flower.

Hedgerow Tangle forms is an ogee pattern – two continuous curves narrowing and

Hedgerow Tangle: This image shows just one repeat block. The entire design is cut on one large block, approximately 50 × 90cm (20 × 35in), but it is in fact two repeats composed one on top of the other, in a near but not identical arrangement.

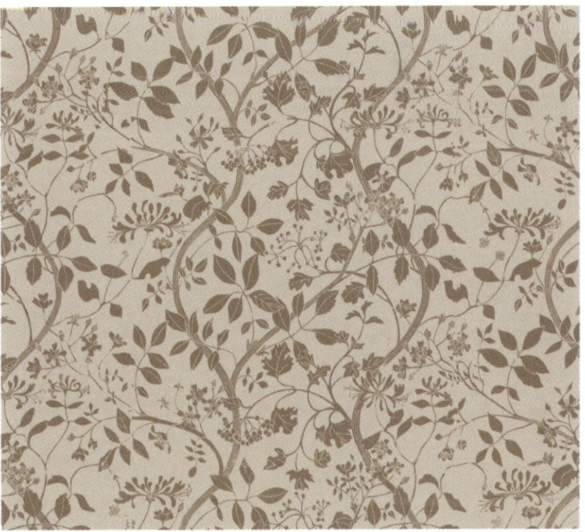

Hedgerow Tangle: the design repeats to form an ogee pattern.

A lot of the fun of designing repeats involves thinking about the rhythms they make. Consider how your motifs will repeat at the beginning of the design process when you plot a grid.

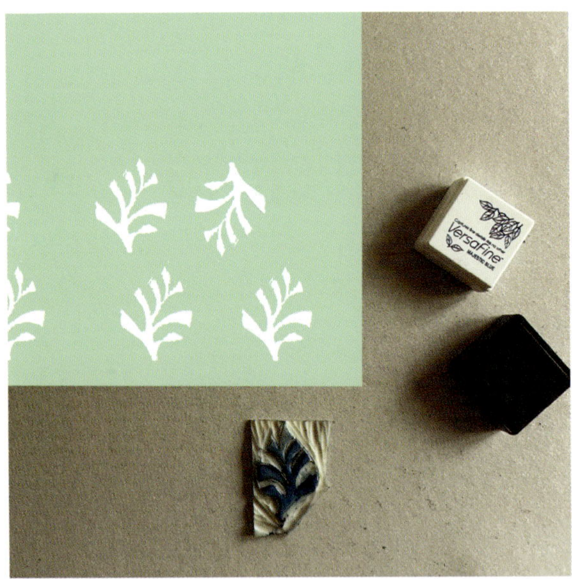
To make a simple stamp and experiment with different pattern layouts, try Japanese soft-cut vinyl and an ink pad.

widening – when it is repeated. The curves form perfect ovals, beautiful spaces to fill with your botanical designs.

Handprint or Digital?

Repeating patterns can be made from anything from a handheld stamp to a large piece of lino printed on a press, by hand or by standing (or jumping!) on the lino block. Take a photo or scan in a repeat print unit to create a digital file so you can upload your work to popular online digital printing services, such as Spoonflower (www.spoonflower.com).

Handprinting on Fabric

A lino block will print on fabric as well as paper. The oil-based inks recommended in this book also work well on fabric. Choose a fabric with a smooth

This is one repeat unit printed from a single large block of lino

Here the same unit is repeated to make the pattern *Winter Garden*.

Place a flat board on top of the lino before you stand on it to avoid pressing down on the gouged-out areas between the relief shapes.

texture – though I have had success with a medium coarse linen.

There are inks and dyes to experiment with, made especially for fabric printing. Remember, the viscosity will determine how suitable the ink will be. For using a roller onto lino, the ink will need to be relatively thick. Runny ink may fill up the fine details of a design. In this case, designing with simpler shapes may be a good approach.

If the block is small enough to be held in your hand, lay your fabric down first and stamp the block onto it. If the block is large, prepare a base with some give for it, such as a towel on the floor. Lay the fabric on top of that and then the lino, face down.

Inspiration From Pattern Makers

The large-scale repeats I create for wallpaper are printed with an etching press that I have adapted with a jig, but access to a press is not necessary to explore printing pattern.

The British designer Peggy Angus used simple household emulsion paint and handheld blocks made from lino, which she simply stamped onto the printing surface – both paper and fabric. The celebrated wallpaper artist, Marthe Armitage, began by standing on her lino blocks, which she laid out on the floor with the paper beneath. She now uses an offset lithographic press, which is extremely rare to come by today. The wallpaper-maker Hugh Dunford Wood uses household emulsion and jumps on his large lino blocks.

Design Considerations

My own work is of a large scale. Often one repeat unit measures the full width of a roll of wallpaper or cartridge paper, approximately 55cm (22in). I begin by drawing a grid. Each block on the grid represents one repeat block.

To make a design for digital reproduction, I plan it in multicolours. A design that will be printed by hand will be restricted to a single colour, so it requires careful planning. I choose subjects for their individual graphic beauty but also for how well they contrast with other parts of the design – light against dark, solid against airy. A print made from one colour relies on using unbroken areas of colour to give a sense of dark tones and compound, filigree or broken areas for light tones.

Exaggerate contrasts of size, mass and shape, such as putting a tangle of tiny leaves alongside a large, strong leaf form, or using spherical shapes with angular shapes, or composite shapes with simple flat forms. The aim is to contrast forms without upsetting harmony.

Scale and Function

The first job is to work out what scale you wish to work with. Consider the end use. How many whole repeats will fit across the width of a space? The width of lining paper or cartridge paper rolls for wallpaper vary at around 50cm (20in). To make a piece of decorated paper to use on a smaller scale, such as a bookbinding project, adjust the scale of the repeat unit and use paper with a grain that is multidirectional. If you intend to hand stamp, a repeat block should be small enough to be held comfortably. Perhaps you need to mount the lino on Perspex or wood by means of screws and glue.

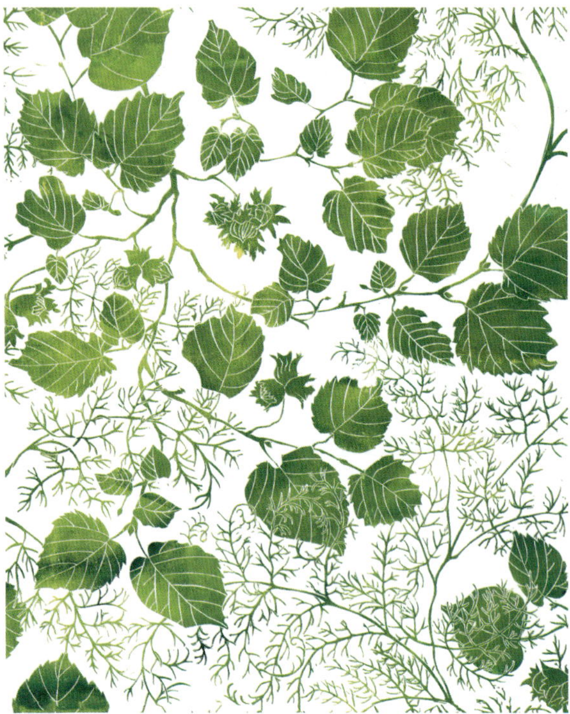

Printing a block by hand or with a manual press forces the printmaker to use just one colour, so all the interest needs to come from the forms themselves and how they interact. Creating a three-dimensional effect without relying on colour is part of the challenge.

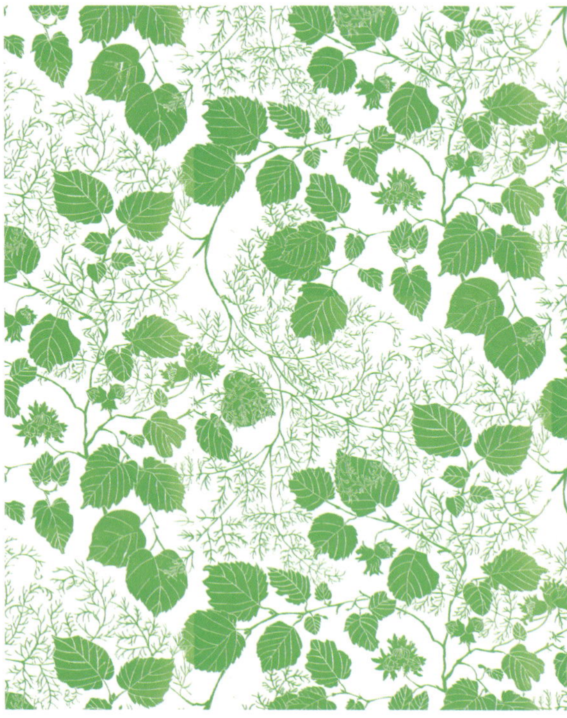

As with all the botanical prints in this book, arrange elements to convey a sense of depth, with motifs in front and behind. When designing pattern over a large scale, balance is important. A rhythm is created when the block gets repeated; the play of solid mass and lighter space is part of a pattern's success.

HOW TO CREATE A SEAMLESS REPEAT

Once you know the dimensions of your repeat block, draw up a grid on layout paper or in a sketchbook at a smaller scale to fit a few units comfortably. Work out the layout of your pattern. Each rectangle of the grid should correspond with the same ratio as your full-scale block, i.e. 5 × 4cm (2 × 1¾in) to represent 50 × 40cm (20 × 16in).

Have a selection of drawings and tracings at the ready. Fill your grid with simplified motifs. Draw in different colours, showing the main motifs in red, the secondary motifs in blue and the interlinking motifs in yellow.

Having made a line drawing of this arrangement, I turn the drawing in on itself. Next, the blank edges are repositioned so they join in the centre. With the spaces filled, the design will repeat continuously with uninterrupted or seamless edges; top, bottom and sides.

Notice how at this stage the plants are placed to fill the central area of the newsprint only, leaving the outer edges empty. Next, the four corners the drawing that meet in the centre are rearranged to become the outer corners of the design. This allows me to fill in the empty spaces easily as the gaps are now together in the centre. Draw to finish stems, extending them until they meet, twine and join, and half-drawn leaves are finished off. If a leaf is 'interrupted' by the paper's edge it is continued on the corresponding edge directly below to allow for repeat, top and bottom.

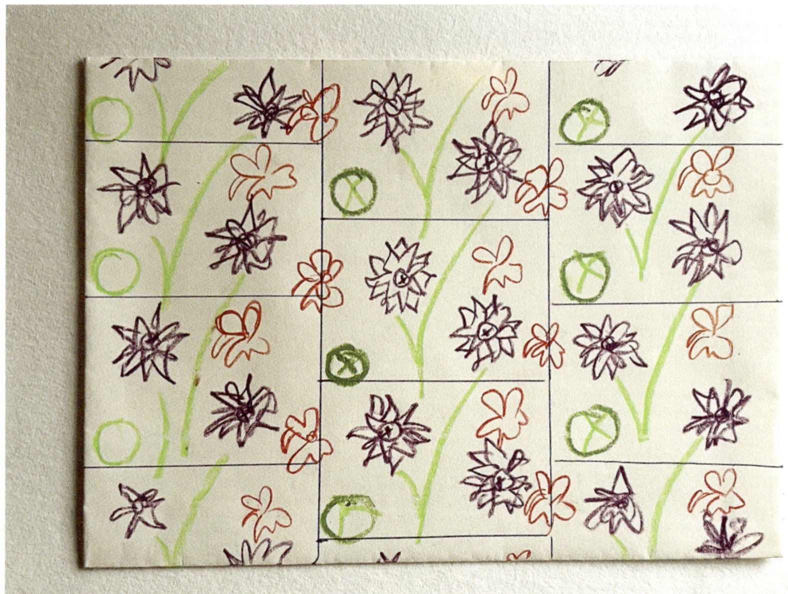

A grid to design a rough layout does not have to be a masterpiece. It is merely to understand how the design elements will relate to each other at the most basic level.

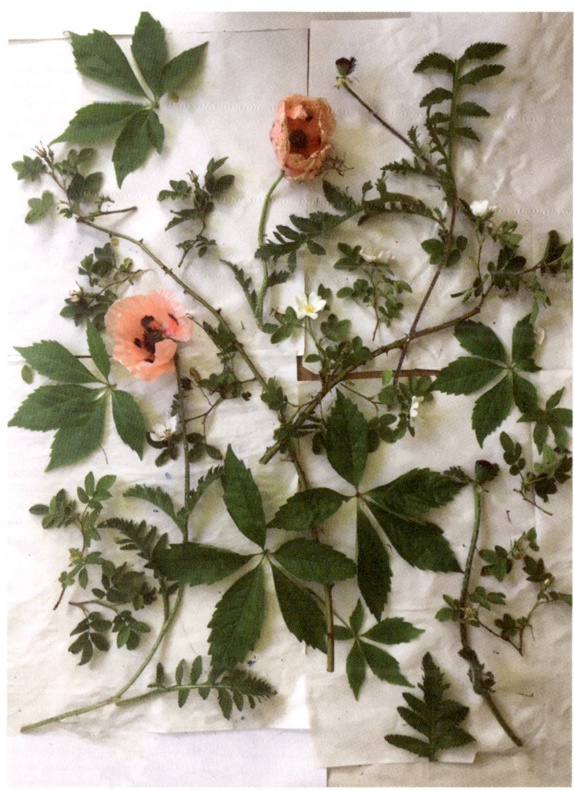

There are many ways to develop a drawing for your design. To create the seamless repeat *Poppy*, I laid out plants on my studio floor on four sheets of newsprint.

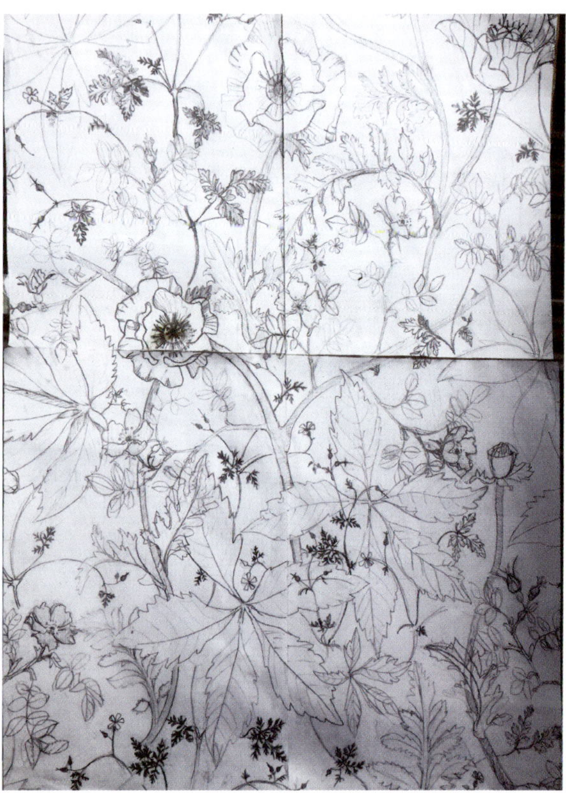

I then drew the same layout, in smaller scale, on four pieces of cartridge paper tacked together with masking tape.

Demonstration: *Poppy* – Creating a Seamless Repeat

1. Begin by taking a sheet of paper, the measurements of which correspond to a single unit of the grid layout plan. Draw your main subjects in their correct position according to the grid. Leave a space all around the edge of the paper, as these edges will become the all-important 'seams'. Do not take the design right up to and over the edge of the sheet (although it can go close to the edge).

In my example, I have included two purple dahlias and some surrounding details as well as a few nasturtiums, leaving space blank along top, bottom and sides. This is so I can fill them in later with the 'linking' elements to complete the design and make the edges of each unit seamless.

2. To work out how to link elements together, it is necessary to see the blank spaces that remain after it is repeated by half one drop. To do this, the block is repeated vertically, stacked one on top of the other. Then each column is staggered or 'dropped' halfway down, alongside its neighbour. Use a home printer or tracing paper to achieve this.

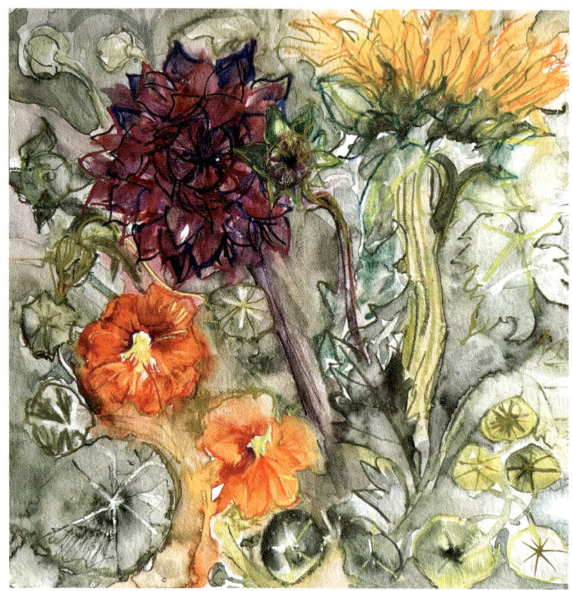

My original watercolour was the inspiration for the pattern.

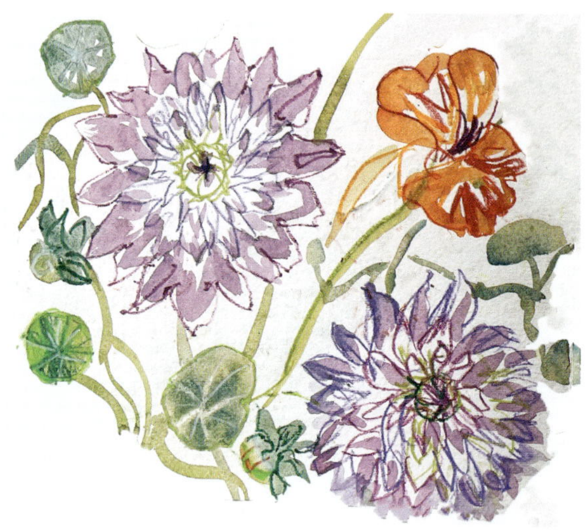

At this stage, include the main motifs of your design only rather than any 'infill' or linking elements. These elements must be confined to this sheet of paper and not go over the edges.

3. Cut out and number each sheet 1–4.

4. For a straight repeat, swap the top with the bottom on both sides. For a full drop repeat, swap over the diagonally opposite sides of the drawing, that is, swap top right with bottom left and top left with bottom right.

5. You can now fill in the remaining spaces with more design. To help you visualise how to fill in this remaining part, use the copies you made of your first motifs. Lay them down in their relative positions to get a better sense of your pattern and how the different elements relate to each other. You now have a larger area of pattern to be able to make decisions about how the elements will join together. Fill the space by drawing in your design.

6. With the design now complete, there is one more step to consider before you can copy it to your block of lino: where best to place the seams. In their current position, will the edges of your block be near invisible when you come to repeat it? The join where each repeat block meets its neighbour should be as discreet as possible.

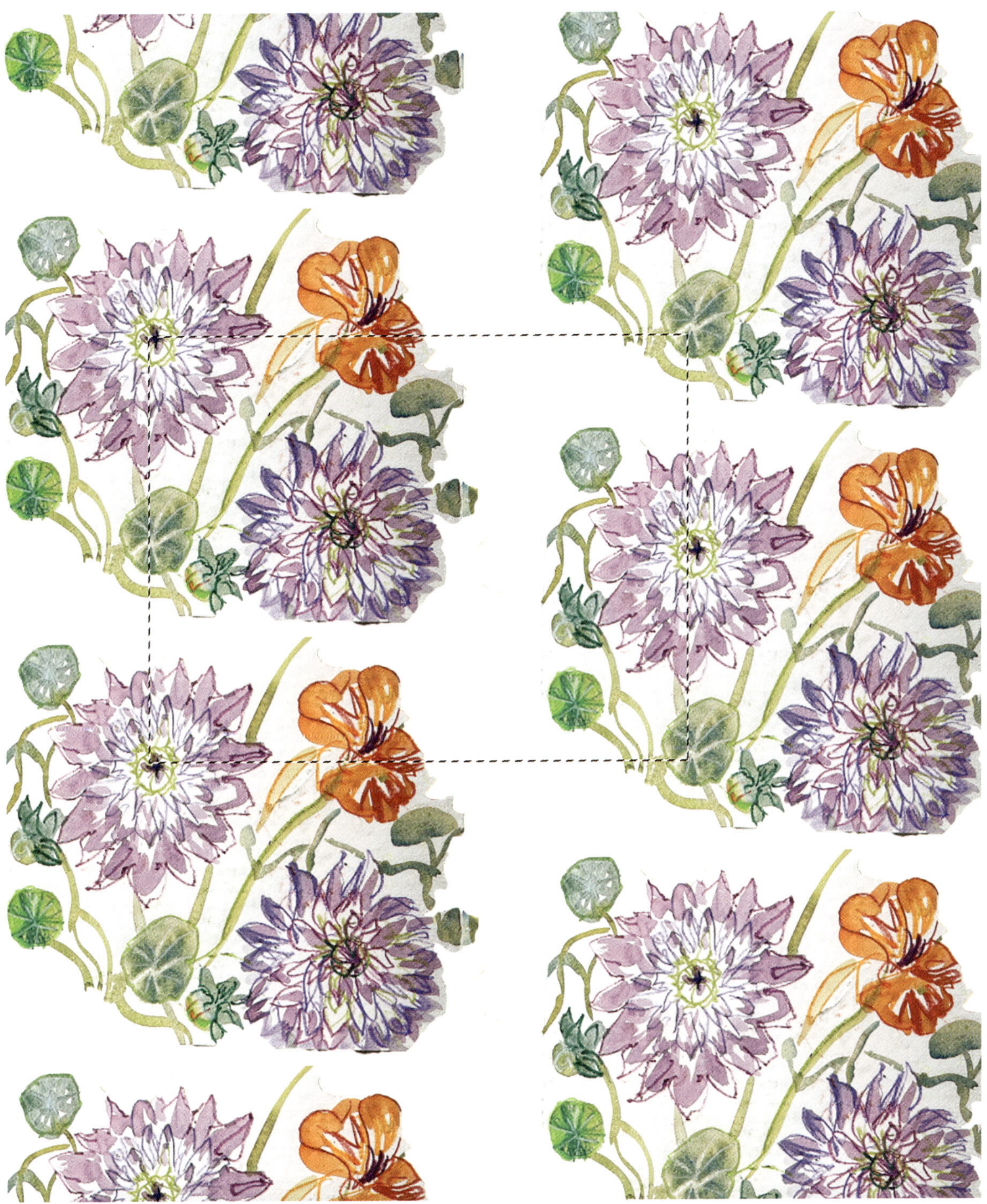

To repeat seamlessly, the blank spaces must be filled with the rest of the design. The design unit is half dropped as this creates a lovely diagonal rhythm.

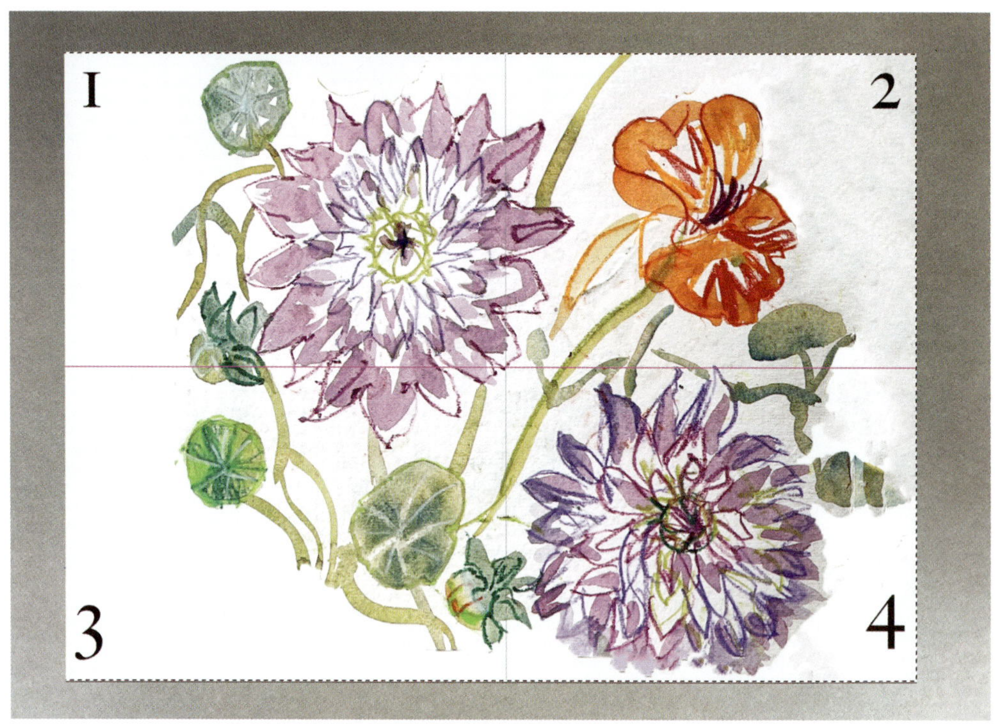

Cut out and number the sheets 1–4.

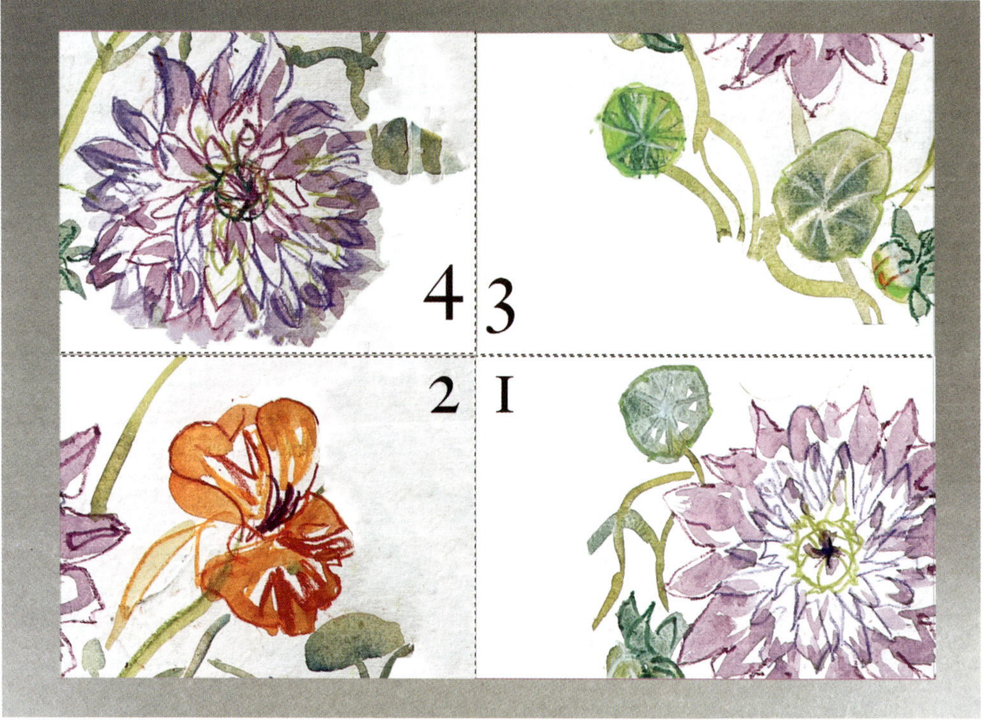

Turning the repeat unit (tile) in on itself. Now you can clearly see the spaces that need to be filled with design and how they relate to the whole. This arrangement makes a full drop repeat.

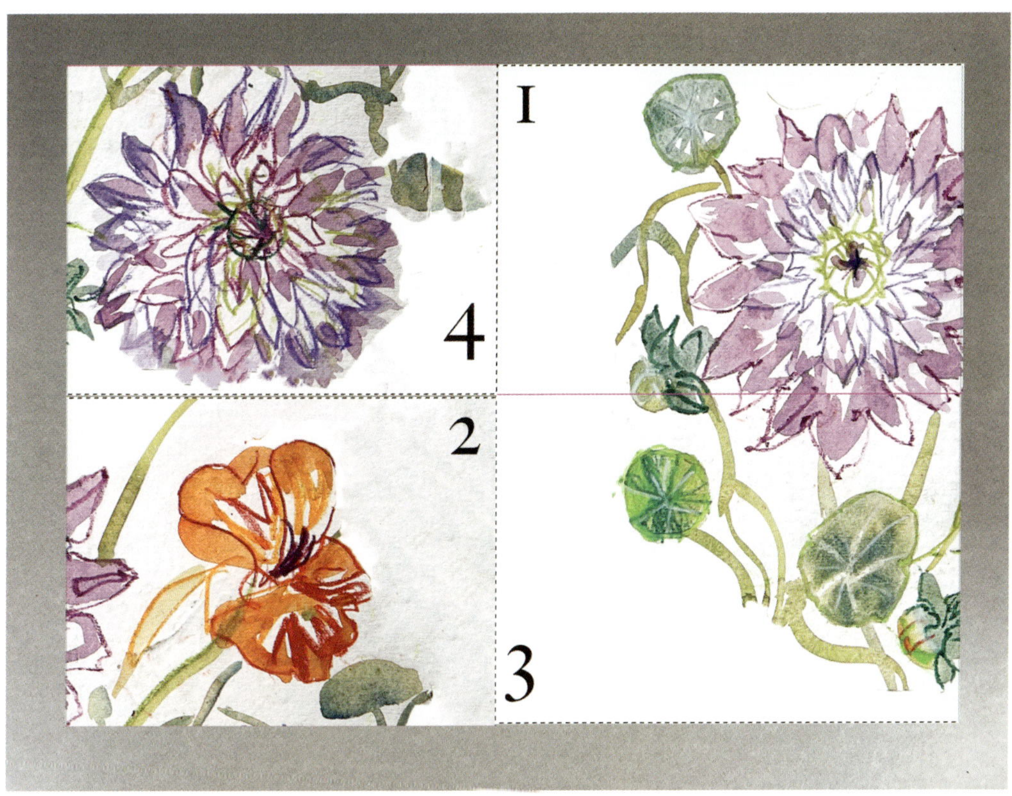

With this arrangement, the drop is only half the height of the tile, making a half-drop repeat pattern.

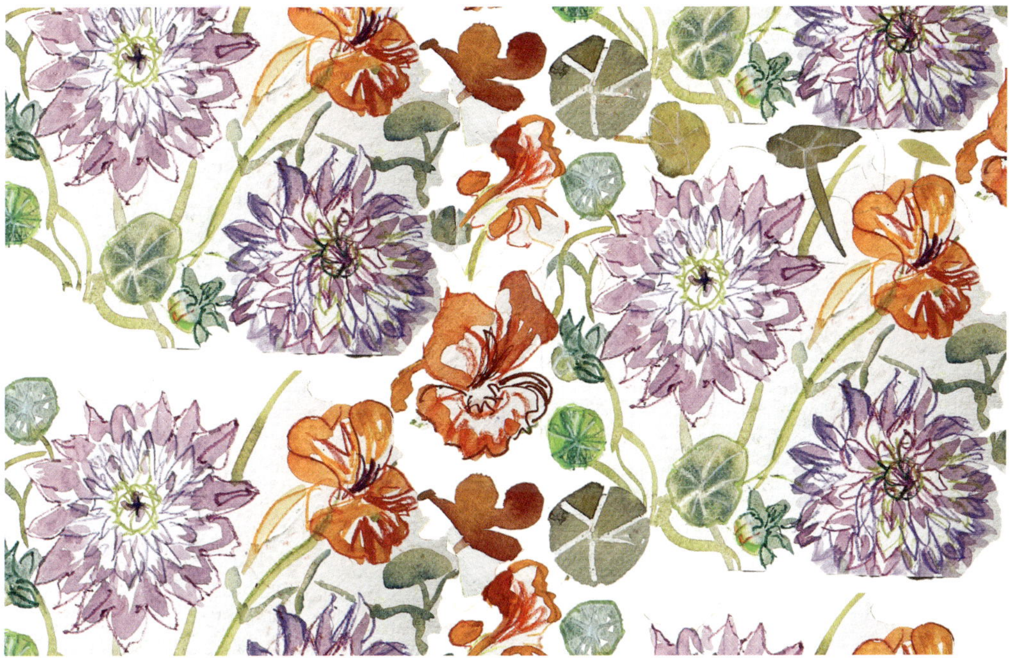

Lay copies in their relative positions to make it easier to fill in the blanks. Seeing a larger area of pattern helps to join elements together.

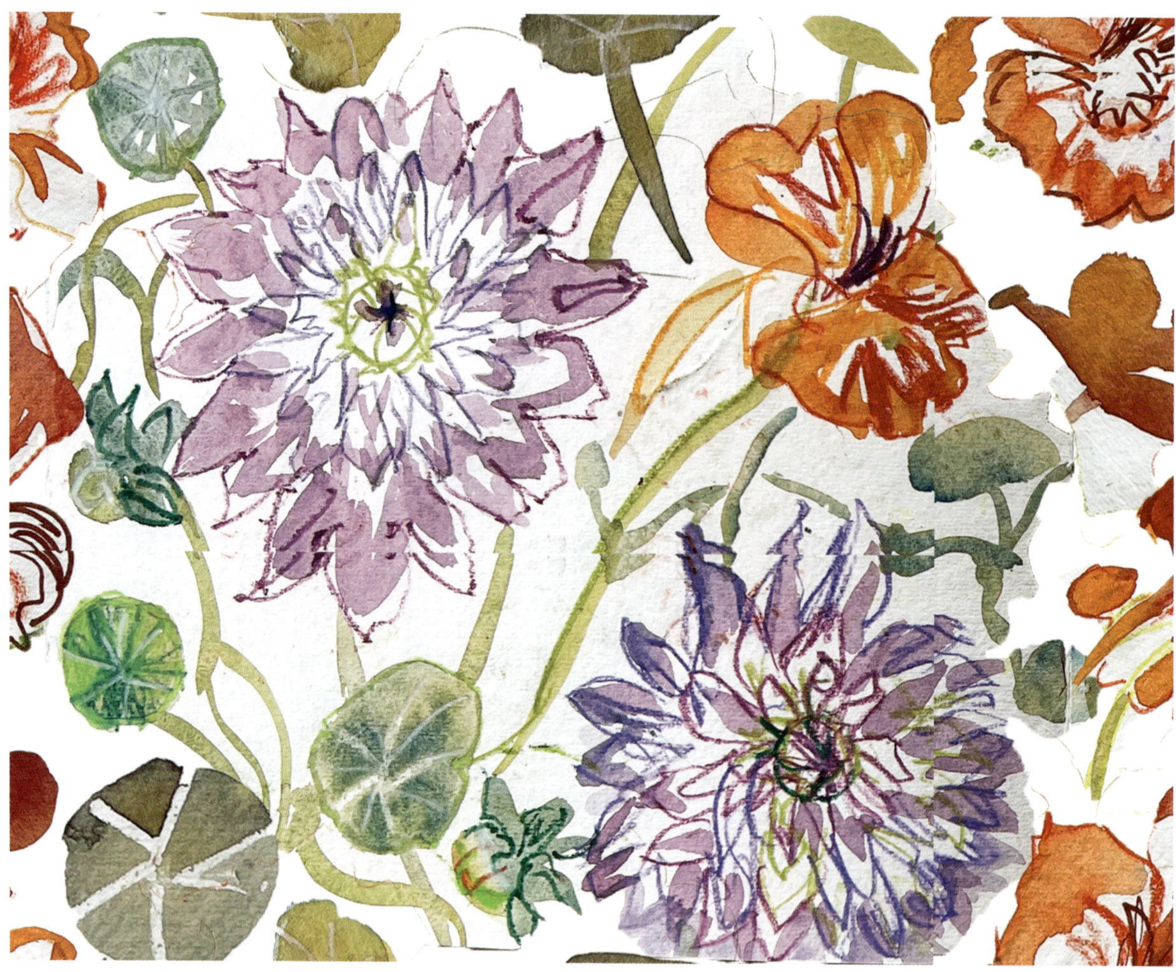

A single unit also known as a repeat block or 'tile'.

In practice, take the drawing, cut it into four pieces and rearrange them so that the 'new' inner seams become the outer edges. Stick them back together in this new configuration. This step can be skipped if you judge that the seams are not obvious. But if the seams cut straight through a beautiful flower that is a main feature, for example, then you will need to adjust them. A line that cuts through gouged-out empty space is a good place to start. The join line could be hidden, and least disruptive if disguised amongst a fussy part of the relief pattern too. Find a vertical and horizontal line that cuts through and interrupts most discreetly and use that.

7. The pattern is ready to either upload for digital printing or be made into a single tile of lino to print by hand, as follows. Copy the drawing to the block in the usual way. Cut a piece of lino that exactly fits your design on paper. Transfer your drawing, remembering to turn it over first and trace on the reverse if you wish to print it the same way round as you have drawn it.

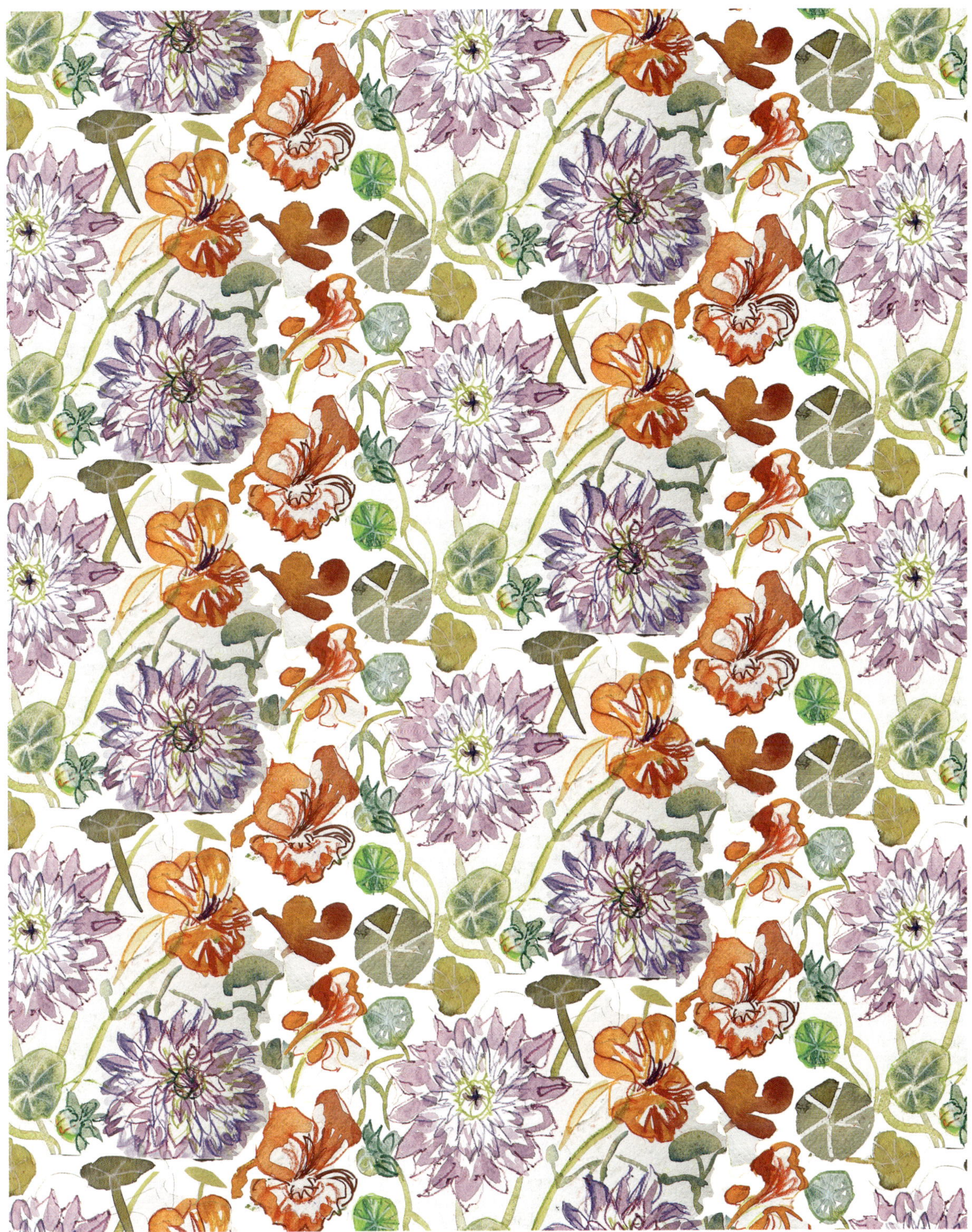

How the pattern would look when printed digitally.

INKING A BLOCK IN A SINGLE COLOUR

If your block is large, you may wish to purchase a wider roller than the 5cm (2in) one recommended for all the other prints in this book. When hand printing large pattern blocks for printing repeats, the convention of paper on top of lino below is reversed.

You have several options:

- Put your paper or fabric down first on an even surface such as the floor, a board or a table. If the block is very large and you need to stand on it to print it, make a sandwich of your block by placing a slim board on top.
- Apply pressure with a rolling pin or wide ink roller.

- Consider sticking the block to a piece of clear Perspex sheet so that you can easily see where to lay it down each time. Apply pressure, repeat and watch your pattern come to life.

There are many opportunities to have your designs digitally reproduced. Use Adobe Photoshop or other similar software apps to upload your designs and create digital files. Many online printing companies such as Spoonflower offer relatively inexpensive ways to digitally print designs onto a variety of textiles and products such as bags and tea towels.

As we reach the end of this book I hope you will feel that you have many tools to play with and an appreciation of the vast scope linoprint offers. Perhaps it's a form of madness, perhaps it's a labour of love; either way, I hope your forays into printmaking bring you much joy.

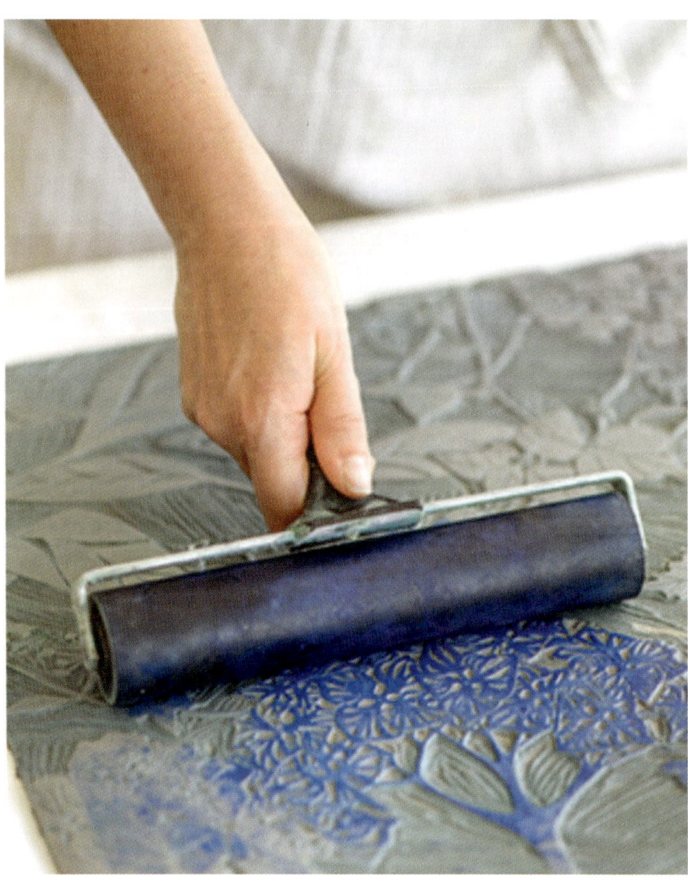

If your block is large, a wider roller is ideal. If you want to experiment with household emulsion, smooth foam rollers sold for eggshell and gloss paints are worth a try.

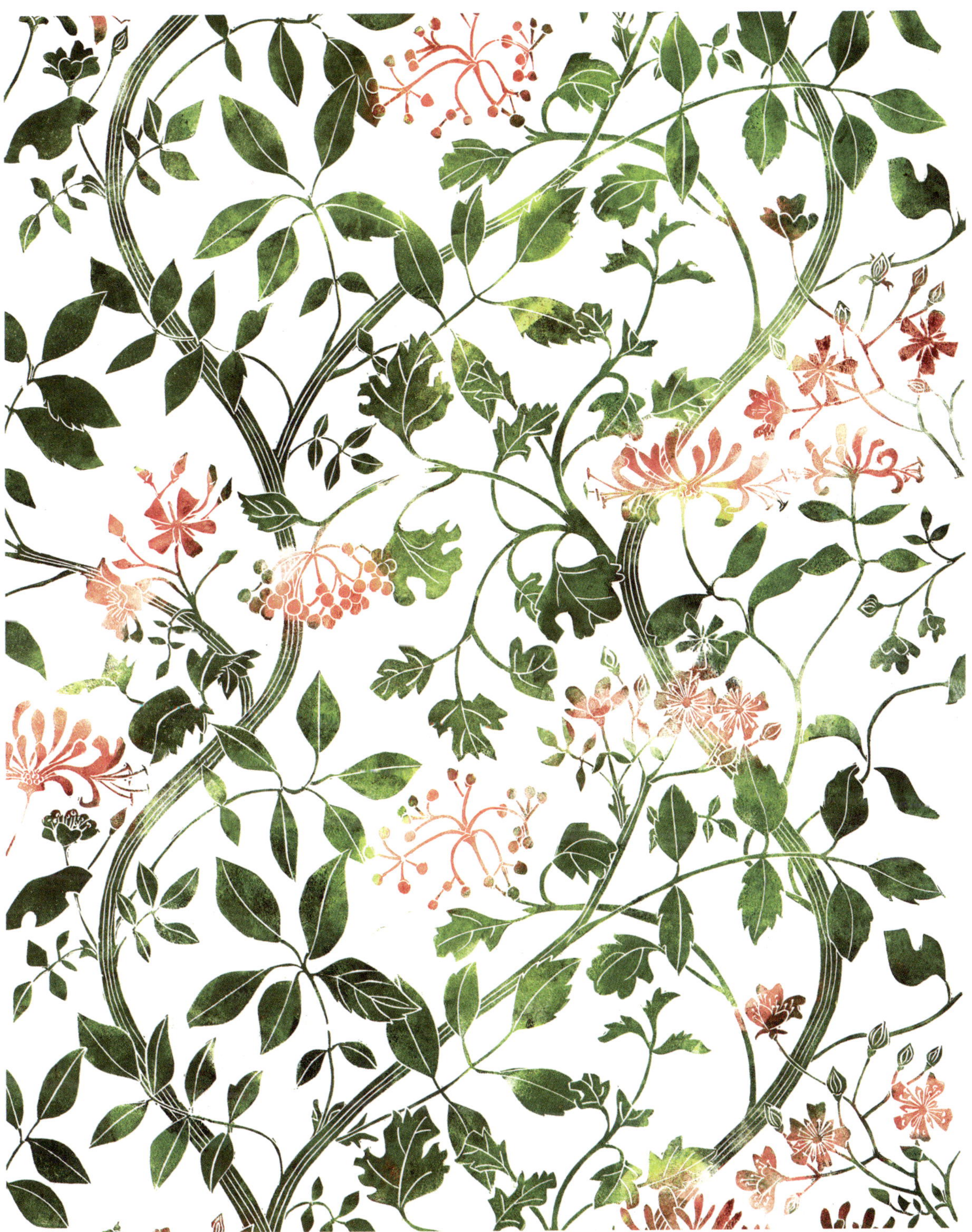

This *Hedgerow Tangle* is designed with two repeats that vary, but only slightly, one from the other – the placement is the same but small details are changes. This emphasises the handmade nature of it. The ogee pattern with its pleasing flow and the lack of uniformity rewards closer inspection.

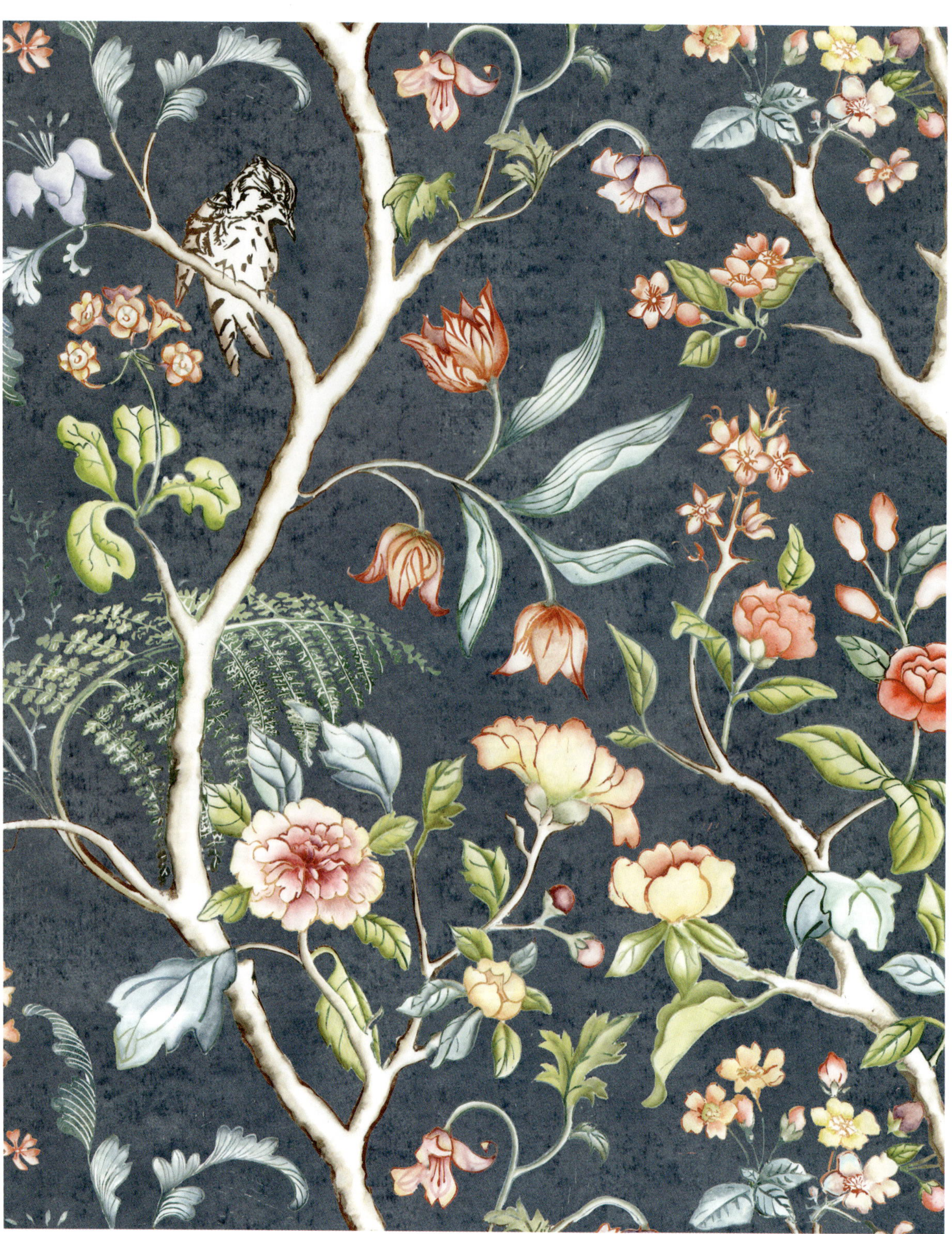

This design for wallpaper is huge in scale. It can be hand printed in a single colour manually on a press from two blocks overlaid: a line block and a background block – a lot of work. Digitally print your designs to make multicolours possible

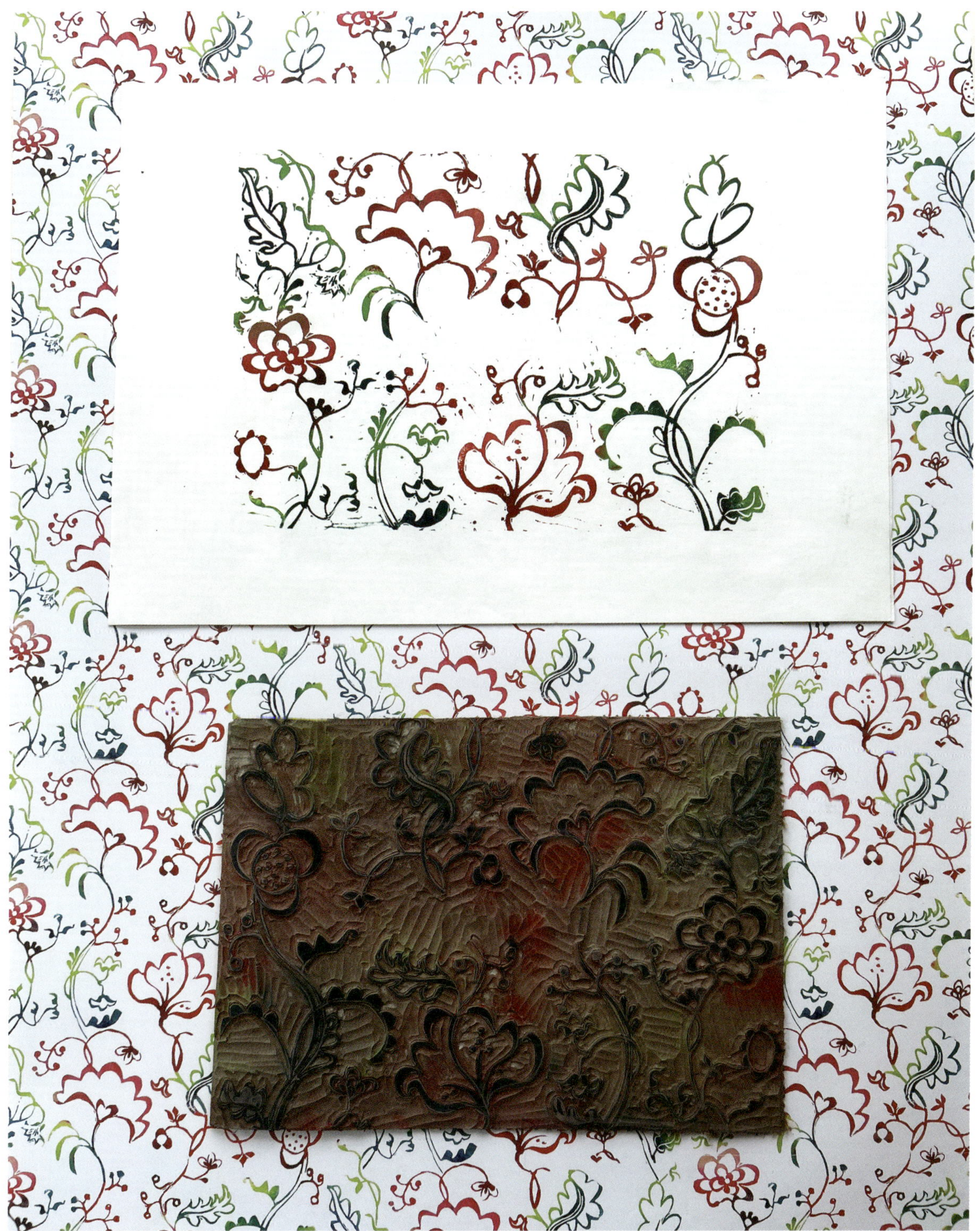

The inspiration for this pattern was a crewel work embroidered quilt from a historical collection in New England. From this starting point and using a stripe pattern, I developed a simple repeat block. The digitally printed pattern shown here was made by scanning in the handprinted repeat unit, also shown.

SUPPLIERS

Awagami Factory – *For Japanese Washi paper.*
https://awagami.com

Essdee – *Manufacturer of lino printing and Scraperboard products.*
www.essdee.co.uk

Handprinted – *Instructional videos accompany some of their printing products.*
https://handprinted.co.uk

Intaglio Printmaker – *Specialises in printmaking.*
https://intaglioprintmaker.com

Hawthorn Printmaker Supplies – *Specialises in the design, manufacture and supply of presses, rollers and inks.*
https://hawthornprintmaker.com

Jackson's Art Supplies – *Offers a vast range of art materials including printmaking.*
www.jacksonsart.com

Lawrence Art Supplies – *For art supplies and cutting tools. Also offers a tool-sharpening mail service.*
www.lawrence.co.uk

Pfeil – *Tools for woodworking, lino cutting, wood block printing and leatherwork.*
www.pfeiltools.com

INDEX

First published in 2024 by
The Crowood Press Ltd
Ramsbury, Marlborough
Wiltshire SN8 2HR

enquiries@crowood.com
www.crowood.com

British Library Cataloguing-in-Publication Data
A catalogue record for this book is available from the British Library.

ISBN 978 0 7198 4451 5

Cover design by Sergey Tsvetkov

Typeset by Envisage IT
Printed and bound in India by Parksons Graphics Pvt. Ltd.